Rot and Revival

Rot and Revival

*The History of Constitutional Law
in American Political Development*

Anthony Michael Kreis

UNIVERSITY OF CALIFORNIA PRESS

University of California Press
Oakland, California

© 2024 by Anthony Michael Kreis

Library of Congress Cataloging-in-Publication Data

Names: Kreis, Anthony Michael, 1986– author.
Title: Rot and revival : the history of constitutional law
   in American political development/Anthony Michael
   Kreis, University of California Press.
Description: Oakland, California : University of
   California Press, 2024. | Includes bibliographical
   references and index.
Identifiers: LCCN 2023048950 (print) | LCCN 2023048951
   (ebook) | ISBN 9780520394186 (hardback) | ISBN
   9780520394193 (paperback) | ISBN 9780520394209
   (ebook)
Subjects: LCSH: Constitutional history—United States. |
   Constitutional law—United States. | United States—
   Politics and government—History.
Classification: LCC KF4541 .K74 2024 (print) |
   LCC KF4541 (ebook) | DDC 342.7302/9—dc23/
   eng/20231018
LC record available at https://lccn.loc.gov/2023048950
LC ebook record available at https://lccn.loc.gov
   /2023048951

Manufactured in the United States of America

33 32 31 30 29 28 27 26 25 24
10 9 8 7 6 5 4 3 2 1

publication supported by a grant from
The Community Foundation for Greater New Haven
as part of the **Urban Haven Project**

Contents

Acknowledgments

This book would not have been possible without the incredible love and support given to me by my family, especially my sister, Amanda Bulik, and my grandparents, Harold and Barbara Conner and Richard and Linda Kreis. Often making homes away from home, I would not be where I am without the encouragement of my friends during this process, especially Barret Broussard, Kate Cassidy, Brandon Davis, Jessica Holbeck, Jonathan Keith, Andrew Moon, Nathan Rich, Laura Santangelo, and Evan Straub. Many scholars have generously given their time to help shape my work. I am particularly indebted to William Adler, Julia Azari, Mitch Berman, Evan Bernick, Meghan Boone, Josh Braver, Erin Fuse Brown, Jud Campbell, Josh Chafetz, Robert Chang, Brooke Coleman, Russ Covey, Katherine Mims Crocker, Clark Cunningham, Justin Driver, Catherine Baylin Duryea, Bill Edmundson, Blake Emerson, Michael Fix, Charlotte Garden, Desmond King, Hal Krent, Guha Krishnamurthi, Kevin Kruse, Sophia Lee, Paul Lombardo, Tim Lytton, John Travis Marshall, Darrell Miller, Merritt McAlister, Julian Mortenson, Luke Norris, Meg Penrose, Russell Powell, Heather Cox Richardson, Kermit Roosevelt, Chris Schmidt, Eric Segall, Miriam Seifter, Carolyn Shapiro, Andrew Siegel, Susan Smelcer, Chris Sprigman, Amy Steigerwalt, Lauren Sudeall, Karen Tani, Benjamin Waldman, Robinson Woodward-Burns, Quinn Yeargain, Julian Zelizer, and many others I am sure to have forgotten, for beneficial conversations, exchanges, and feedback that have improved the book. I am grateful to the law faculties at Chicago-Kent College of Law and Georgia State University College of Law for encouraging and supporting this project. I appreciate the contributions of participants at workshops and conferences at the University of Wisconsin School of Law, University of Oxford Pembroke College, University of Pennsylvania Carey School of Law, University of Notre Dame School of Law, Tulane University School of Law, University of Nebraska College of Law, Loyola University Chicago School of Law, Washington & Lee University School of Law, University of Richmond School of Law, Seattle University School of Law, Wake Forest University School of Law, and the Southeastern Association of Law Schools Annual Meeting from which I benefited while working on the book. I am also thankful for two excellent research assistants at Georgia State, Marquis Leary, Benjamin McMichael, and Emily Molinie. Finally, I want to thank my editor, Maura Roessner, whose enthusiasm and guidance was essential to bringing this project to fruition.

CHAPTER I

Judicial Review in the Puzzle of American Constitutionalism

The lionization of *Marbury v. Madison* as a triumph for the impartial rule of law sticks in the throat like a hair on a biscuit. In *Marbury*, the Supreme Court pronounced the power of judicial review—the authority to void laws inconsistent with the Constitution—and did so by striking down a statute that broadened the Court's jurisdiction. At first blush, it might seem that a decision in which the justices' purported fealty to the Constitution required them to act against their own self-interest would be a natural candidate to illustrate judicial independence and celebrate dispassionate legal reasoning. Yet when put in the historical context of 1803, uncritical praise for *Marbury* as an exemplar for apolitical constitutional decision-making is unjustified.

In his first month as chief justice of the United States, John Marshall continued in his prior role as Federalist John Adams's secretary of state. Holding two jobs proved too much. Marshall failed to execute one of his last responsibilities as secretary of state, to deliver a judicial commission to a newly minted justice of the peace, William Marbury. Marbury was a "midnight judge" installed by the Federalists to pack the courts with political allies before the transfer of power to President-elect Thomas Jefferson and the Democratic-Republicans who ousted the Federalist majority in the Election of 1800.[1] James Madison, Jefferson's new secretary of state, refused to deliver the commission.[2] Marbury applied to the Supreme Court directly for a writ of mandamus to command the commission's delivery. Marbury relied on the Judiciary Act of 1789 for the Court's authority to issue the writ.[3] After cobbling together a tortured reading of the law and the Constitution, the Federalist-controlled Supreme Court rejected Marbury's petition, asserting that the act unconstitutionally enlarged the Court's original jurisdiction.[4]

Undeniably, *Marbury* was crafty judicial maneuvering. The Court avoided colliding with a political tidal wave that threatened the Supreme Court's power. The justices forestalled dealing a blow to their co-partisan and hedged against the risk of issuing an order that the president, buoyed by another rout of the Federalists in the congressional elections of 1802 and 1803, might refuse to honor. And while *Marbury* is striking evidence of judicial acquiescence to emerging political orders, the decision tells only half the story. A few days after *Marbury*, the Supreme Court upheld the law repealing the Judiciary Act of 1801, one in a pair of court reform measures passed by the new Jeffersonian coalition in Congress that undid the Federalists' 1801 court-packing scheme.[5] The new Democratic-Republican majority ejected Federalist judges by abolishing the Federalists' recently created circuit courts, cancelled a Supreme Court term, reinstated Supreme Court justices' arduous traveling appellate-court duties known as "circuit riding," and restored the Supreme Court's full membership complement to six after Federalists shrunk it to five to preempt a Jefferson appointment.[6] The reality of 1803 upends the myth of *Marbury*. Far from avoiding politics, the Supreme Court capitulated to the new political order to preserve institutional capital. This moment in early American history challenges notions that politics and constitutional law are severable.

Was *Marbury* an extraordinary event of personalities or a prologue to American constitutional law as politics by another name? Are courts special institutions where logic prevails and precedent controls, or are courts institutions captured by politicians in robes? For years, constitutional law professors have waxed poetic about the virtues of the Supreme Court as a countermajoritarian institution that defends minority rights. Some scholars have spilled considerable ink impugning judicial review as too muscular or as deviating from democratic processes when the Court invalidates the majority's will. Regarding constitutional interpretation, some scholars argue that the Constitution has a discoverable, objective meaning driven by language, history, and tradition—often tightly controlled by the original authors' understanding of the text. Meanwhile, many other constitutional scholars reject interpretive schools that are shackled to dead hands, championing a constitution whose meaning evolves through time.

What is the institutional role of federal courts and the nature of constitutional law? This book argues that constitutional law is best understood through the diachronic lens of American Political Development (APD) and the concept of political time. This book uses the lens of American Political Development to better understand the relationship between dominant political coalitions, social movements, and the evolution of constitutional law. American constitutional law reflects the ideological commitments of dominant political regimes and intervening popular movements. In the long run, the Constitution is a vessel that holds a meaning that is only as virtuous as the enfranchised public is good.

Dominant regimes are formed by transformative presidencies, creating a set of governing principles that remake the political order for decades. In this sense, constitutional doctrine is a distillation of partisan politics. Moreover, just as political priorities dramatically change between the breakdown of a coalition and the emergence of a new order, constitutional principles are often sloughed off as ideological commitments change from one dominant regime to another. Unlike traditional legal scholarship analyzing American constitutional law, this book is not juricentric. Rather than approaching constitutional law in a manner that views courts as guardians of the Constitution and the central players in jurisprudential development, this work understands federal courts and the law they produce to be in dialogue with many other political actors.

This book examines how cyclical politics translated into constitutional jurisprudence through the time period between 1824 and 2022. While the book will provide a brief glimpse into the transition from the first party system that emerged between 1800 and 1828 and the rise of Jacksonianism, it primarily begins in the 1820s to capture the period when durable party structures began to emerge in the United States.[7]

Every election disrupts the status quo, but some elections manifest a sharp break from long-standing, prevailing norms and endow an incoming coalition with a mandate to refashion notions of legitimacy, rearrange institutional relationships, and establish a set of dominant ideological principles that shape the polity for years. The elections of 1800, 1828, 1860, 1932, and 1980 all represent order-shattering events that ushered in new, decades-long ideological regimes. These elections followed tumultuous events that large segments of the voting public perceived as national betrayals. The preexisting political order's inability to meet the exigencies of difficult periods in American history revealed that the regime was beyond repair. Political time is the measurement of these recurrent patterns.[8]

These periods between reconstruction and disjunction also align with trajectories in constitutional jurisprudence. Far from revealing a distinction between law and politics, a careful study of America's ideological regimes shows a tight relationship between the governing visions established by regime politics and the course of constitutional doctrine. However, the relationship between the two is more complex than what simply holding the mirror of opinion polls up to American constitutionalism might reveal. The judiciary does not merely reflect public sentiment or democratic demands at any given time. Instead, this book proffers that constitutional law is the byproduct of regime principles, institutional relationships, and the time-sensitive ordering of policy developments that produce new politics, causing the dominant regime to innovate and evolve. Federal courts, which are the products of the regimes that make them, are not institutions on a path separate from the rest of the nation's politics but have historically been and *should normatively be* governing partners that assist the regime in state building by articulating national values and disciplining outliers from the reigning order. The Supreme Court's function is to discipline others in service of the reigning political order. However, when the Court strays too far from the political mores of the moment and becomes a serious impediment to the regime's state-building ambitions, the Court will either capitulate or become a destabilizing force threatening the constitutional order.

CONSTITUTIONALISM AND AMERICAN POLITICAL DEVELOPMENT

American Political Development is the study of American politics through an exhaustive examination of political history. However, APD scholars do not seek to record history only to understand historical events and players. Instead, they want to explore history to identify patterns and processes of change. Instead of focusing on short-term, isolated questions about cause and effect, American Political Development inquiries tend to "trace[] institutional, ideological, and organizational patterns over long stretches of time" to avoid the biases that can emerge from studies of narrow, event-driven cause-and-effect relationships.[9] Studying law, politics, and society with a bias toward events that are related in close temporal proximity provides a mere snapshot of how the American state works.

Students of APD construct time differently from the way historians and constitutional scholars have traditionally tended to. Historians, for example, often identify moments that possess social, political, and cultural commonalities and organize periods like "the Era of Good Feelings," "the Gilded Age," or "the Progressive Era." Similarly, legal academics often refer to changes in constitutional doctrine according to or make thematic assessments of constitutional law fixed to a chief justice's tenure, like "the Warren Court" or "the Rehnquist Court." Such approaches to constitutional law are minimally helpful in answering questions about the Supreme Court and turns in constitutional jurisprudence like:

- How could the Waite Court, which gutted civil rights protections in the *Civil Rights Cases*,[10] rule in favor of Yick Wo's race discrimination claim three years later?[11]
- How could justices who championed the laissez-faire "Lochner era" strike down a law regulating bakery working conditions in *Lochner v. New York*,[12] then uphold both mandatory vaccination mandates in *Jacobson v. Massachusetts*[13] and milk dealer license requirements in *Lieberman v. Van de Carr*?[14]

The world of APD approaches time and periodization somewhat differently. More than just trying to unearth the historical record, APD focuses on the conditions that usher in significant shifts in politics, with an emphasis on institutions, structures, and regimes, and then seeks to understand how political development moves through time rather than homing in on how political events unfolded in relatively isolated, one-off timeframes. Thus, APD focuses less on "secular time" (i.e., the chronological passing of time) and emphasizes "political time." Political time measures ideological regimes between cyclical resets of the national zeitgeist's trajectory.

Another cornerstone of APD scholarship is a focus on path dependency and the idea that the ordering of events is consequential. History matters. The sequence and spillover of policy choices matter because "policies produce politics."[15] APD scholars aspire to identify critical junctures in institutional and policy maturation that can help explain why later developments occurred and to offer insights into why some potential roads of institutional and policy evolution were left untraveled.

The methods and lenses that constitute the core of ADP scholarship are ripe for application to the study of constitutional law and judicial institutions. While American Political Development richly covered ground in studying the presidency and the bureaucracy in the first two decades of its coming-of-age beginning in the mid-1980s, law and APD was a relatively less active subfield until the mid-2000s. Keith Whittington's *Political Foundations of Judicial Supremacy* from 2007 is inarguably the seminal book in the field exploring the American judiciary through national political development, and it taps into themes similar to those explored in this book. Whittington used a political regime framework to analyze how the courts and elected officials have worked to create and maintain judicial supremacy in the American system. In contrast, this book assesses political regimes' ideological commitments and critical decision points to explore the causal mechanisms between the ballot box, social movements, political party development, and constitutional jurisprudence. Similarly, Jack Balkin's 2020 book, *The Cycles of Constitutional Time*, also focuses on recurrent features in American politics to explain how the rise and fall of partisan coalitions, political polarization, and economic inequality contribute to constitutional dysfunction and shifting attitudes towards judicial review. Despite major works like Whittington's and Balkin's and despite American Political Development enjoying greater attention from political scientists in the past two decades, one scholar described Balkin's book as "one of the first major attempts to apply [APD] to the judiciary, particularly the Supreme Court."[16] This book continues to fill that gap.

American Political Development research, in its most general terms, differs from the work of traditional historians in a number of important ways. It attempts to identify patterns and causal mechanisms that account for outcomes in American history, to identify significant events in history and assess their longer-term significance, and to provide an understanding of how historical patterns reemerge while simultaneously acknowledging that contingent effects can create nuanced differences between pattern iterations. Through this kind of analysis, APD scholars can identify pathways of development that can help explain political outcomes and structural changes to American politics and constitutionalism through time. In this sense, there is a deep relationship between historians and APD researchers who value rich historical data and political scientists who value identifying cause-and-effect relationships. Unlike historians, APD work is acutely focused on the timing and context of structural changes through long periods of time. Differing from many political scientists, APD scholars do not emphasize generalizable relationships between variables. This book shares many of the same goals of historians and political scientists who study the Supreme Court insofar as it labors to synthesize bodies of literature from historians, political scientists, and legal academics in addition to unique primary sources. However, rather than considering the Court as an institution standing alone, this work considers the Supreme Court's institutional behavior and the development of constitutional doctrine vis-à-vis the presidency and the ordering of partisan regime-building.

Ultimately, law and APD can help reveal the role of courts in the wake of transformative events that produce durable shifts in governing authority. Law and APD can canvass the relationship between the judiciary's power and the coordinate branches. However, it can also tease out a better understanding of how courts participate in state building. And by focusing on history and institutions rather than the social and cultural dynamics of narrowly defined eras or individual members of the judiciary, law and APD scholarship can also help explain why cultural attitudes do not necessarily translate into constitutional change or how constitutional principles evolve in the wake of major economic challenges, political strife, social movements, and war—while also exploring how new, long-term governing principles emerge from these crises. For APD scholars, the ideas and values arising from national emergencies and national inflection points are of major consequence. These kinds of reformational ideas, which have multi-generational purchase power, can and should be treated as quasi-institutions unto themselves.

Because the Supreme Court's institutional capacity more readily positions it to pump the brakes on public policy than to accelerate it, the Court has been cast by some observers as operating in a legal arena disjointed from the political branches and without a role as an active part of state building. This is a mistake. The Court has been a critical partner alongside the coordinate branches and regime-allied stakeholders in state building. This institutional playmaking is lost in legal scholarship that too often attempts to draw a distinction between law and politics by relying on reductive definitions of the latter. Under any accurate description of politics, the courts are necessarily political. Politics is more than the lowbrow business of individual policy fights; politics also includes the crosswinds of structural and social forces at work. Politics is much more than partisanship; politics are the core ideological commitments and the Overton windows that have shaped American political thought for decades in ways that mirror prevailing regimes. This book's goal is to be neither deductive by assuming the existence of constitutional cycles nor an exercise of straight legal history that analyzes constitutional doctrine in secular time. Instead, this book aims to import American Political Development, with its dynamic understanding of politics in time, to shed light on the fact that Supreme Court is one of multiple important forces in shaping American political regimes.

POLITICAL AND CONSTITUTIONAL TIME

When legal academics bookend meaningful periods in judicial decision-making, the standard points of reference tend to be a collection of Supreme Court terms named after the presiding chief justice. While shorthand citations to the Warren Court or the Roberts Court might be a useful heuristic for identifying some jurisprudential themes, they obscure the decades-long continuity of ideological commitments in the American body politic. Instead, constitutional law develops in a distinct constitutional time, which is driven by the core tenets of the party systems that created them.

Ideological regimes begin with reconstructive moments and elections during which there are calls for fundamental changes to how American government operates and how public policy is thought of and advanced. Historically in American politics, these shifts coincide with the election of new, reconstructive presidents—Andrew Jackson, Abraham Lincoln, Franklin Roosevelt, Ronald Reagan—who fashioned American politics to reflect their ideological vision. Reconstructive leaders emerge when the preexisting party system is weak and disassembling, allowing them to repudiate the dominant coalition and redefine the fundamental principles of national government. Reconstructive presidential leaders take advantage of the preceding partisan regime, which collapses on the weight of its own success. These disjunctive coalitions are vulnerable because the terms and conditions for governing laid out years before to address earlier political crises become threadbare and cannot meet contemporary emergencies and dilemmas.

This is not to say that oppositional parties or crosscurrent political movements never find electoral or policy success. Instead, when they do, opposition parties and countervailing social movements interrupt rather than disrupt the partisan regime by avoiding direct conflict with the prevailing regime through the politics of triangulation.

These periods of ideological dominance and coalitional durability are reflected in constitutional law. As Robert Dahl wrote, regular turnover at the Supreme Court allows new political regimes to appoint judges that render decisions consistent with the ideological preferences of the political branches. Thus, "the policy views dominant on the Court are never for long out of line with the policy views dominant among law-making majorities."[17] Therefore, according to Dahl, "it would appear, on political grounds, somewhat unrealistic to suppose that a Court whose members are recruited in the fashion of Supreme Court Justices would long hold to norms of Right or Justice substantially at odds with the rest of the political elite."[18] One of Dahl's contemporaries, Robert McCloskey, offered additional evidence for Dahl's view. First published in 1960, McCloskey's *The American Supreme Court*, offered a treatment of Supreme Court jurisprudence showing how constitutional rules often reflected the mores of justices' times. This book taps into parallel themes but applies political science methods to identify the causal mechanisms and recurrent patterns in institutional development and American constitutionalism.

A regime theory of the Supreme Court and American constitutionalism contrasts with the concept of the "countermajoritarian difficulty" proffered by Alexander Bickel's 1962 book, *The Least Dangerous Branch*. In that highly influential work, Bickel suggested that judicial review was "deviant" with respect to democratic values because, when judges exercise judicial review, courts undo the majority's will as expressed through a representative legislature. But one law professor's "difficulty" was the virtue of others. Because Bickel was writing about a supposed countermajoritarian judicial disposition during the federal courts' jurisprudential crusade against Jim Crow and racial discrimination, the term, repurposed to represent the courts' role in protecting vulnerable minorities from the tyranny of the majority, became venerated in liberal legal circles. For decades, the legal academy took the proposition that courts acted as a countermajoritarian bulwark as received wisdom. As this book lays out, the constitutional displacement of segregation was made possible not by the majesty of judges acting out of principle and against popular will but by a constitutional order shaped by ideological commitments, majoritarian politics, and social movements.

More contemporary literature provides evidence of majoritarian constitutionalism like the regime thesis this book advances. Jeffery Rosen's historical analysis of the Court concludes that "the Supreme Court has followed the public's views about constitutional questions throughout its history."[19] Legal historian Michael Klarman surmised that the number of the Supreme Court's countermajoritarian "interventions can best be described as marginal."[20] Barry Friedman masterfully traces the way the public mood influences constitutional decision-making.[21] Other academics, like Gerald Rosenberg, have argued that courts are more apt to follow public opinion than act counter to it because courts lack the capacity to initiate social change.[22] Even if it is assumed that Dahl and his contemporaries were correct, slower turnover rates on the Supreme Court sometimes render the Court sluggish to reflect changing social and political moods. This trend notwithstanding, there is evidence that even without a steady turnover in Court membership, public opinion influences justices' opinions. Whether by membership turnover or shifting preferences mirroring broader societal change, judicial review often sanctions the policy positions taken by the dominant coalition.

The following chapters will identify and explore the partisan regimes in American politics, beginning with the fall of the first party system and the rise of Jacksonian politics with the election of Andrew Jackson in 1828. Each chapter considers the core principles articulated by reconstructive leadership that animated the national government during each regime. From there, the chapters unearth the relationship between the regimes' root philosophies and how that governing worldview underpins the constitutional jurisprudence of the era, thus drawing the connection between ordinary politics and a longer arc of constitutional development.

CHAPTER 2

Jacksonianism and the Constitution of White Prerogative

On July 4, 1854, the Massachusetts Anti-Slavery Society rallied outside Boston in Framingham, Massachusetts. In the unlikely scenario that the meeting was not designed purposefully to be an event to remember, it nevertheless had all the right ingredients. The star-studded Independence Day lineup featured some of America's most well-known abolitionists: William Lloyd Garrison, Stephen S. Foster, Sojourner Truth, Henry David Thoreau, Lucy Stone, and Wendell Phillips. The setup was brimming with blunt symbolism, capturing the nation's tense sectionalism and deepening political fissures.

An American flag was hung upside down over the stage, draped in black fabric. Two white flags with black bordering hovered in the background. One of the flags bore the name "Kansas," and the other was embroidered with "Nebraska," both of which were progressing toward statehood. The territorial Midwest was the epicenter of America's dispute over slavery expansionism thanks to the Kansas-Nebraska Act, which Congress had passed earlier in 1854. The act organized the two territories and provided that Kansas "shall be received into the Union with or without slavery, as their Constitution may prescribe at the time of their admission."[1] By leaving the decision over whether slavery would take root in Kansas to migratory patterns and local politics, the act ignited a powder keg in Kansas as proslavery and abolitionist settlers all flocked to the territory and fought violently to control the future state's fate.

Ensigns that read "Virginia" and "Redeem Massachusetts" were displayed. Festive ribbons decorated the Virginia flag, and somber bunting cradled the Massachusetts flag. The banners representing Virginia and Massachusetts conveyed a loud message: the American union was deeply unholy. More specifically, the flags signaled a condemnation of the Fugitive Slave Act of 1850.[2] The four-year-old law mandated federal government agents return those men, women, and children who escaped bondage in the South consistent with the fugitive slave clause in Article IV of the Constitution's guarantees. Just a few months earlier, that very federal law stirred passions in Boston because of Anthony Burns. Anthony Burns escaped enslavement in Virginia and sought refuge in Boston in early 1854. Burns's whereabouts were discovered through a letter he wrote to his brother, causing him to be located and captured by slave catchers in Boston. Despite public outcry during his rendition trial under the 1850 Fugitive Slave Act, the involuntary surrender of Anthony Burns back to Virginia was a fait accompli. Anthony Burns was back in chains only a month before the Framingham rally. Given the notoriety of the Burns tragedy and the intense backlash in Boston, it is unsurprising that plantation surveillance creep was top of mind for many attendees.

William Lloyd Garrison was the main act. He took the stage and, after reading from scripture, started burning documents. He clutched a copy of the Fugitive Slave Act. Garrison struck a match, ignited the paper, and threw it to the ground. Garrison shouted, "And let all the people say, 'Amen'!" The crowd responded, "Amen!" Next, Garrison torched a copy of federal judge Edward Loring's order to return Anthony Burns to Virginia. Like before, the crowd enthusiastically yelled, "Amen!" while the paper disintegrated. Garrison displayed a copy of the Constitution, which he proclaimed a "covenant with death; an agreement with hell," and then condemned: "perish all compromises with tyranny!" Garrison lit the Constitution aflame and pitched the smoldering paper. The charred embers were cheered on with a thunderous cry of "Amen!"

Whatever else might be said of the rally, it portended a dim future for the American constitutional order established during the Jacksonian Era. The "anti-elitist" political order that Democrats ushered in with the election of Andrew Jackson almost three decades before Garrison's constitutional indictment was untenable. The nation's leaders divided into one camp that clung to the Constitution's protection of property as a natural right, which necessarily entrenched slavery, and another camp that damned the Constitution as the Devil's work.

The Jacksonian constitutional order's ideological anchor was a localist, white supremacist populism, which provided the intellectual framework for the policy of popular sovereignty. This chapter shows how, over time, Jacksonian policy preferences (and popular sovereignty even more acutely) created new politics that destabilized the coalition in the 1850s as the nation expanded west. Throughout the Jacksonian period, the ideas that glued the Democratic Party coalition together informed the jurisprudence of the day as Jacksonians began to take the federal judiciary's helm. Constitutional doctrine reflected Jacksonian principles and reinforced the regime's power. And much like the public policy choices that eventually were the coalition's undoing, Jacksonian jurisprudence also played a critical role in destabilizing the Democratic Party and worsening the country's political polarization. Despite the Supreme Court stepping in to run offense for Democratic Party leaders as a way to resolve major national crises and release pressure on the Jacksonian regime, the Court had the opposite effect. It accelerated the nation's careening into civil war and constitutional reformation.

JACKSONIANISM AND THE COMMON MAN

For some time, there was a mythology about Andrew Jackson and the maturation of American democracy. Two famous anecdotes reflect this misplaced romanticism. The first story comes from Jackson's inauguration. After the president was sworn into office, he gesticulated to the crowd with a deep bow as a symbolic act of democratic fealty, and then onlookers left the Capitol's east portico. They walked down Pennsylvania Avenue to be received by the president. The White House, brimming at the seams with visitors, was a circus of spectators who enjoyed celebratory food and drink and destroyed furnishings and china while trying to meet the president. The second piece of misappropriated folklore involves a 1,400-pound cheese gifted to the president by New Yorker Thomas Meacham. After aging it a year, in February 1837, Jackson opened the White House to the public and divvied up the foul-smelling hunk of cheddar. These vignettes, bookends to Jackson's tenure as president, have been used to superficially depict Jacksonianism as a populist movement relatively untethered from a cohesive ideological governing vision, which ran no deeper than general discontent—thus the late nineteenth-century political scientist John W. Burgess described Jacksonians as "a mob of malcontents."[3]

In a sense, Jacksonian Democracy was neither Jacksonian nor democratic. Rather than instigating the drumbeat for the franchise's expansion, as the phrase might suggest, Andrew Jackson and the Democratic Party co-opted a preexisting movement to enlarge the American electorate and fused their populist ideological tenets with it. Jackson's election in 1828 came on the heels of nearly a decade and a half of American democratic expansion and rapid maturation. That pivotal election was the first one in which most white males cast ballots for president. This was made possible by liberalized voting laws in the aftermath of the War of 1812. States strove to expand the right to vote for all white men by eliminating property requirements. Connecticut, Massachusetts, and New York ended property requirements for voting in 1818, 1820, and 1821, respectively. Economic-based voting eligibility fell out of favor in the frontier. Except for Mississippi, which imposed a tax requirement for voting, no state admitted after 1815 required land ownership or a tax payment to cast a ballot. Critically, the lifting of economic-based limitations on the right to vote meant that express racial restrictions were necessary to exclude Black voters who might otherwise enjoy the liberal trajectory, which reinforced a racial hierarchy in favor of Jacksonians later on. Rogers Smith has recognized this interlocking effect: "[T]he pattern of enfranchising alien whites and disfranchising [sic] native free blacks and Indians was a symptom, but also a cause, of the racially articulated views of American identity."[4]

The trajectory of American politics' democratization cannot be understood without also understanding the effect of the Panic of 1819 on the public. The Panic of 1819 was the country's first economic depression caused by a flood of British manufactured goods into the American market, unscrupulous banking practices, wild speculation, and the overextension of credit. Americans, particularly in the West and South, came to see banking elites and the Eastern establishment as, in the words of Richard Hofstadter, "an alien power" that brought about a "cruel awakening for thousands who had hoped to become rich."[5] The expanding electorate, imbued with a greater populist spirit, recognized a relationship between individual welfare and participation in partisan politics. In response, states adopted homestead exemption laws, bankruptcy regulations, and anti–debtor prison laws. However, it was the cultural "breach [that] had opened between the party elites and ordinary" farmers and workers that laid the ground for Andrew Jackson and his Democrats.[6] Stephen Skowronek identified that this dynamic imperiled Jeffersonian Republicans because even though "the economic panic of 1819 had yielded to resurgent prosperity . . . the polity that emerged from [that] experience[] was quite different."[7]

A substantial plurality of this new, energized electorate, enthusiastic for the rough-around-the-edges Andrew Jackson, rallied around Old Hickory in the 1824 presidential election. Jackson lost the White House to John Quincy Adams because Jackson failed to secure a majority in the Electoral College, notwithstanding having won 41 percent of the national popular vote. Under the rules established by the Twelfth Amendment, the House of Representatives would choose the next president, with each state congressional delegation casting a single vote for one of the top three electoral-college vote-getters, Jackson, Adams, and Speaker of the House Henry Clay. Congressional backroom maneuvering between Adams and Clay handed the presidency to Adams. The swing of congressional delegation votes to Adams in Illinois and Maryland despite Jackson's popular vote wins in those states laid the path for Jackson's defeat. Clay brought Kentucky, Missouri, and Ohio (all states that Clay won and states in which Jackson came second in the popular vote) into the Adams column, clinching the win for Adams. As a reward for this politicking, Jackson alleged, without substantiation, that Adams handed the plum secretary of state appointment to Henry Clay. But Jackson's theory violated Occam's razor: there was no scurrilous and politically useful quid-pro-quo scandal; Clay simply disliked Jackson and his views.

The slow burn of anti-elite sentiment "hounded" Adams's administration from the get-go.[8] This act of deep democratic betrayal, deemed the "Corrupt Bargain," essentially kicked off the 1828 election that sent Jackson to the White House. Indeed, the election of 1828 was not about policy but rather about the 1824 house vote, out-of-touch bureaucrats, and nonproducing New Englanders who perpetuated what Harry Watson coined as tiny corrupt bargains.[9] This image resonated with many Americans who drew a connection between Adams and, as Daniel Walker Howe described them, "unpopular peddlers and storekeepers, notorious for cheating farm wives with wooden nutmegs."[10] Jackson described the 1828 contest as a "struggle between the virtue of the people and executive patronage;" but, he insisted, he held hope that a virtuous majority would drive the "demagogues who have attempted to retain power by the most corrupt means . . . into obscurity."[11]

Jackson emerged victorious in the election of 1828 by securing over 55 percent of the popular vote and two-thirds of the Electoral College in a contest that involved more mudslinging than serious politics. But while the 1828 campaign lacked overt policy debates, the Jacksonian age that sprung from it did not lack an ideological vision. The ideological paradigm was well suited for Jackson's burgeoning coalition, which had scattered interests but a united contempt for elites. The interactive effect of the common man's triumph and the evolutionary development of universal white male suffrage brought together a group of voters that included Southern slaveholders, urban workers, Catholics, immigrants, and western frontiersmen. An important commonality bound seemingly disparate groups to the racialized order of the period: "white farmers and workers as well as slaveholders [had] a sense of economic dependency on the maintenance of racial restrictions that seemed to make their lands, jobs, and wages more secure."[12]

Thrust into power amid the market revolution, Jackson's victory represented a vindication of producers over nonproducers and the incorruptible masses over the self-interested elite. Jackson's followers had a convergence of interests to keep the "elites" at bay. From their perspective, the old-guard governing class and predatory nonproducers threatened the vision of white supremacy and individual natural rights that lay at the heart of Jacksonianism. As John Gerring once noted of the Democratic Party in this period, "much of the party's programmatic consistency during this period is rightfully attributed to the forceful simplicity of a single perspective: antistatism."[13] Yet a greater complexity to the Jacksonian ideology is reflected in the era's politics, policy, and jurisprudence. The regime of Andrew Jackson hugged the idea of "popular sovereignty" tightly: a vision of white supremacy, localized decision-making, governmental noninterference, and imperial expansionism. The political impulses favoring antistatism, localism, and westward expansion, all wrapped up in white supremacy, are identifiable strands in American constitutional law during this period that reflected Jacksonian commitments. While antistatism and popular sovereignty glued the Jacksonian coalition together, it was increasingly indispensable after the Mexican-American War and led to the regime's violent undoing, especially as the Supreme Court constitutionalized popular sovereignty in *Dred Scott*.

Four early episodes in the Jackson presidency helped congeal Jacksonian ideology and stiffened adversaries into an oppositional political party, the Whigs, who not only envisioned a more active role for federal state building but opposed Jackson's use of executive power: the Second Bank of the United States charter, the Maysville Road veto, the Sunday post office battles, and Indian removal. These initial policy contests and the populist white supremacy that informed them are important ideological benchmarks that help explain Jacksonian constitutional development as it relates to the content of jurisprudence and how the courts used constitutional doctrine to empower the regime.

THE ANTEBELLUM POLITICS OF LOCALISM

In his first annual message to Congress in December 1829, Andrew Jackson advocated for internal improvement—investments in the nation's infrastructure—while at the same time signaling hostility to any legislative initiative that would require a robustly centralized endeavor. Jackson acknowledged that "appropriations for purposes of internal improvement" would be appropriate "when ever power over such subjects [i.e., infrastructure projects] may be exercised by the Central Government" and should be designed in a manner that would reconcile the "diversified interests of the States and strengthen the bonds which unite them." In a broader statement in support of local control over federal power, Jackson warned Congress to direct their attention only to projects truly national in character and to work "against all encroachments upon the legitimate sphere of state sovereignty."[14] In a later speech, Jackson recast his opposition to large-scale federal works projects and weaponized it against nonproducing elites. Jackson decried politicians who raised revenue "most oppressively on the agricultural and laboring classes of society" for projects that were outside "the range of the powers conferred upon Congress."[15]

Jackson put his view into action perhaps most famously in 1830. That year, Jackson vetoed a bill appropriating federal expenditures for the Maysville Road. The legislation would have permitted the federal government to buy 15,000 shares in the Maysville Road Company, which would then take that investment to build a road between Lexington, Kentucky, and Maysville, Kentucky, and connect to future roads to Ohio and Alabama. The construction, however, was entirely within Kentucky. Members of Congress who opposed the bill argued that the smallness of the project, if a legitimate object of federal investment, meant that no issue was too small to fall under the scope of national power, rendering the federal system meaningless. When he served as a member of the House from Tennessee, the fierce Jackson loyalist, James Polk, brushed off the argument that the road had any national value, telling his colleagues that if the road was as indispensable to the national interest as the supporters suggested, federalism was "but a rope of sand." Polk jabbed the road's supporters further, saying, "A little road, sixty miles long, in the interior of one of the States, important to bind us together in the Union! The idea is really amusing."[16]

Using this line of argument, Jackson described the Maysville Road Bill as local and outside the ambit of Congress's constitutional powers: To "disregard . . . [the] distinction [between national and local initiatives] would of necessity lead to the subversion of the federal system."[17] The veto had the added benefit of sticking a thumb in the eye of Kentuckian Henry Clay. Jackson's veto calcified the split between the Democrats' preference for decentralized programs and the Whigs' preference for centralized programs.

The Maysville Road veto reflected a blend of Jacksonians' opposition to the creeping authority of national regulatory power and opposition to the interests of well-to-do elites. That particular blend of Jacksonian concerns was not only reflected in the Maysville Road veto but also in Democrats' hostility toward social reformers. During this time, conservatives remained on tenterhooks watching the percolations of Evangelical social organizing, which had the potential to undermine the Jacksonian social project. Jacksonians' combined emphasis on local control and undercutting elites was key to frustrating social reform movements.

In 1832, Jackson altered American politics for decades and disrupted the constitutional order through the veto power, this time with a bill renewing the Second Bank of the United States charter. Though the institution did not regulate monetary policy or hold large reserves to act as a lender of last resort, the bank was the fiscal heart of the federal government, holding governmental funds, disbursing payments on behalf of the government, and issuing loans to members of the general public. During the Panic of 1819, bank president Langdon Cheves reduced the number of banknotes in circulation and the number of loans offered and demanded payment in specie on banknotes in the federal bank's possession from state-chartered banks, bankrupting those smaller entities. The bank also made a large number of foreclosures during the economic downturn. It was believed that the Second Bank had contributed to and exacerbated the financial hardships of the time, and public sentiment turned against it. Andrew Jackson capitalized on the opportunity in his broader effort to halt the growth of the federal government and attack out-of-touch nonproducing elites.

In 1832, four years before the charter's expiration, Congress passed legislation to extend the Second Bank's charter. As 1832 was an election year, supporters of the bank, including Jackson's main rival for reelection, Henry Clay, believed Jackson would be hard-pressed to not kill the renewal bill. Instead, Jackson bludgeoned bank supporters who represented the ideals of the first party regime, which, since 1800, had been dominated by Thomas Jefferson's Democratic-Republican Party. The party was controlled by republican nationalists who backed a limited but active federal government that invested in national infrastructure and institutions through centralized programming, known as the American System. With his veto pen, Jackson blocked the renewal bill, blasting the bank's undemocratic character and the benefits it bestowed on a few wealthy elites. This, he argued, laid the groundwork for "great evils" because of the inherent danger in any institution where there was a "concentration of power in the hands of a few men irresponsible to the people."[18] However, notwithstanding the Supreme Court upholding the constitutionality of the bank (and implicitly an entire swath of similar federal programs envisioned in the American System) in *McCulloch v. Maryland* just over a decade earlier, he did not veto the bill on policy grounds but on constitutional grounds. In contrast with the Marshall Court, which had in the years before Jackson's presidency reflected a "constitutional philosophy . . . supported by prominent elements of the dominant national Democratic-Republican coalition and by moderate Republican justices on both the federal and state bench" that backed internal improvement projects and creating national institutions, Jackson's veto message was a constitutional defense of the "common man," decentralization, and strict constitutional interpretation:[19]

It is to be regretted that the rich and powerful too often bend the acts of government to their selfish purposes. Distinctions in society will always exist under every just government. Equality of talents, of education, or of wealth can not be produced by human institutions. In the full enjoyment of the gifts of Heaven and the fruits of superior industry, economy, and virtue, every man is equally entitled to protection by law; but when the laws undertake to add to these natural and just advantages artificial distinctions, to grant titles, gratuities, and exclusive privileges, to make the rich richer and the potent more powerful, the humble members of society—the farmers, mechanics, and laborers—who have neither the time nor the means of securing like favors to themselves, have a right to complain of the injustice of their Government. There are no necessary evils in government. Its evils exist only in its abuses. If it would confine itself to equal protection, and, as Heaven does its rains, shower its favors alike on the high and the low, the rich and the poor, it would be an unqualified blessing. In the act before me there seems to be a wide and unnecessary departure from these just principles.

Nor is our Government to be maintained or our Union preserved by invasions of the rights and powers of the several States. In thus attempting to make our General Government strong we make it weak. Its true strength consists in leaving individuals and States as much as possible to themselves—in making itself felt, not in its power, but in its beneficence; not in its control, but in its protection; not in binding the States more closely to the center, but leaving each to move unobstructed in its proper orbit.[20]

Jackson's vetoes of the Maysville Road and the Second Bank charter renewal were more than a couple of one-off uses of the veto power in the ordinary course of policymaking. Instead, these were fundamental declarations of an ideological vision for the constitutional order. Jackson's actions were a proclamation that the Supreme Court did not have the ultimate word on constitutional interpretation and a declaration of the primary governing tenets of his namesake's regime. However, the Supreme Court that Jackson fashioned through the appointment of Chief Justice Roger Taney and Associate Justices John McLean, Henry Baldwin, James Moore Wayne, and Philip Barbour soon developed an economic constitutional doctrine around the contract clause and commerce clause that tracked their patron's vision. As early as 1829, the Supreme Court signaled a shift toward Jacksonian localism, but "Democrats desired to solidify a true Jacksonian majority" on the Court.[21] Two cases handed down in the final year of Jackson's term—under a Court remade entirely by the outgoing president—illustrate the Democrats' success as the Court worked to protect the power of states to operate in the commercial sphere, including the power to exclude.[22]

In *Charles River Bridge v. Warren Bridge*, the Taney Court ruled in favor of state power and against a theory of the contract clause that would entrench an economic advantage for one entity. In 1785, the Massachusetts legislature granted a charter to the Proprietors of the Charles River Bridge to allow the building of a bridge over the Charles River. The terms of the charter allowed the company to erect the span and collect tolls from travelers for forty years, after which the bridge would become the state's property. In 1792, the Commonwealth extended the charter to give the private entrepreneurs rights over the bridge for seventy years after its completion, after which the Commonwealth would assume ownership. In 1828, Massachusetts legislators provided a charter for a second bridge over the Charles. Under the terms of the Warren Bridge's charter, the investors could collect tolls until they recouped the costs of building but for no longer than six years. A toll-free bridge a stone's throw away from the first bridge, which was necessary to serve the growing population of Boston, would undercut the bridge's profitability.

In 1828, the Charles River Bridge stakeholders sued to enjoin the new bridge on the theory that Massachusetts impaired its implicit contractual obligations when it authorized the second bridge, thus violating the constitutional provision barring states from impairing contracts. Writing for a four-justice majority, Chief Justice Taney rejected the claim, reasoning that the terms of the charter should not be read to include implicit guarantees as the Charles River Bridge proprietors urged. Critically, for Taney, if the contract clause meant that once the state provided for a piece of infrastructure legislators were handcuffed, the nation would be "thrown back to the improvements of the last century, and obliged to stand still" out of a duty that smacked of "old feudal grants."[23] The *Charles River Bridge* decision marked Jacksonian jurisprudence's arrival, embracing state power, limited federal intervention, and the needs of the common man. The Taney Court saw no fault in the pecuniary interests of the few yielding to the interests of the public good.

The public good was also central to a key commerce-clause opinion handed down the same term as the Boston bridges decision, *Mayor of New York v. Miln*. In 1824, the New York legislature enacted a law requiring any passenger vessel coming from a foreign port or an out-of-state port to provide authorities with a written report detailing each passenger's name, age, and domiciliary. The law also empowered the New York City mayor to assess and collect security from the vessel master to insure against any passenger who relocated to New York and became a public charge. The law also empowered officials to remove noncitizens who required public financial assistance from the state and repatriate those who could not support themselves. The question before the Court was whether the New York law regulated commerce and, if so, whether the regulation of interstate and international commerce was the exclusive domain of the federal government.

The Taney Court upheld states' power to benefit Southern enslavers while also limiting federal power. At a time when the American enslavers, whose influence is commonly referred to as "slave power," was acutely sensitive about the authority to exclude people who might agitate social disruption and the ability of the federal government to undermine proslavery laws, it was essential for the powers that be to constitutionalize the Jacksonian ideal of strong but decentralized governmental authority.[24] As the advocate for New York argued to the Supreme Court, if the power to regulate, police, and remove persons was deemed commerce, either the federal government could supplant local law through federal legislation or, if the power to regulate persons was commerce and the power to legislate over interstate and international commerce was exclusive to Congress, then a multitude of state laws might be rendered constitutionally deficient:

[I]f the power to pass laws regulating the admission of passengers from Europe, falls under the power of regulating foreign commerce, that of regulating the arrival of passengers by land, falls under the power of regulating commerce between the states. If the one be exclusive, the other is exclusive; and all vagrant laws, all poor laws, and police regulations, become, at once, solely of federal jurisdiction. The laws of the southern states in relation to the intercourse and traffic with slaves, and to the introduction of colored persons into those states, also become the subjects of federal jurisdiction, and the state laws are abrogated.[25]

In *Miln*, the Court upheld New York's law on the premise that persons are "not the subject of commerce" in the way ordinary commercial transactions of goods constitute commerce.[26] As a result, New York's law was an exercise of the state's inherent police powers "to provide precautionary measures against the moral pestilence of paupers, vagabonds, and possibly convicts; as it is to guard against the physical pestilence, which may arise from unsound and infectious articles imported, or from a ship, the crew of which may be laboring under an infectious disease."[27] Fundamentally, New York exercised a core element of its sovereignty—the power to exclude—which could be wielded to suppress threats to the Jacksonian regime. If New York had the power to control freshly arrived Europeans, then South Carolina surely had the power to control the movement of free Blacks. The politics of exclusion and sectionalism, however, would eventually be the coalition's and, in turn, the nation's, Achilles' heel.

While New York legislators were preoccupied with the politics of exclusion and the teeming masses arriving from Europe, Jacksonians kept a watchful eye on Evangelical reform movements that sprung out of the Second Great Awakening's religious fervor, including abolitionism, Sabbatarianism, and temperance. For Jacksonian Democrats, these Whig Party–affiliated reformers constituted an acute menace.[28] Indeed, opposition to Christians seeking to bring the New Millennium—the one-thousand-year period after Christ's second coming when Christ would reign over Earth before the Final Judgment—to fruition was a vital glue for the Democratic coalition that could bind the interests of those favoring Indian removal, minority religious freedom, and slavery.

The United States Postal Service was the epicenter of two controversies highlighting the tension between Jacksonian politics and Evangelical zeal during the Jackson administration. One early religiously inspired social reform movement was Sabbatarianism. In the late 1820s, these Evangelicals organized in opposition to an 1825 federal law requiring federal postmasters to work for at least one hour on some Sundays. Anti-Sabbatarians, while not religious skeptics, "offered a separationist dissent," arguing that "Christianity was a private affair" and that, therefore, it was inappropriate to impose religious doctrine as a matter of public policy.[29] Jackson ally, Richard Mentor Johnson of Kentucky, issued a report as chair of the house committee overseeing the postal system that rejected calls to halt Sunday mail service. The report endorsed a strict separation of church and state, proclaiming, "[o]ur government is a civil, and not a religious institution."[30] Moreover, Johnson's report warned of the dangerous slippery slope federal lawmakers would go down should "it be conceded that they have a controlling power over the consciences of others."[31] For Congress to side with the Sabbatarians would be for legislators to establish a precedent so open-ended that it would be "impossible to define its bounds."[32]

Experience would caution some, like the Baptists and Methodists who had known oppression at the hands of more powerful religious interests, from countenancing the alignment of the latter with the federal government. So too with Catholic immigrants, an emerging Democratic Party constituency, who would wage their own battles against entrenched Protestant political power in the 1840s. For others in the Jacksonian fold, these reformers were emblematic of the same eastern establishment snobbery as the nonproducers and corrupt elite. In this vein, historian Bentram Wyatt-Brown noted that the anticlericalism peak was fueled "primarily [by] a lower class resentment of the success and the awesome innovations of educated, eastern middle-class churchgoers in building societies and founding newspapers to spread a puritanical conformity across the land."[33]

For Jacksonian Democrats, the danger posed by Sabbatarians paled compared to energized religious reformers clamoring for the destruction of slavery. Abolitionists' zeal to proselytize through the US mail in the summer of 1835 provoked Andrew Jackson's rage. That year, antislavery leaders settled on a plan to mail abolitionist literature unprompted to thousands of Southerners in the movement's first genuinely national attempt to spread their message. The mass mail campaign sparked riots in the South. It elicited a strong rebuke from the president, who defended enslavers from the campaign out of fear that the literature might incite a slave uprising. Jackson wrote to Postmaster General Amos Kendall that he "read with sorrow and regret that such men [as abolitionists] live in our happy country—I might have said monsters—as to be guilty of the attempt to stir up amongst the South the horrors of a servile war—Could they be reached, they ought to be made to atone for this wicked attempt."[34] Jackson instructed Kendall that postmasters should withhold the delivery of the abolitionist materials unless the addressee demanded it. Jackson knew that few Southerners would make such a demand and publicly align themselves with, as he described it, "villainy."

JACKSONIAN WHITE SUPREMACY AND THE WEST

Given that the impulse for Evangelical reform threatened the party's goals, it is little wonder that Jacksonian Democrats embraced disestablishment principles wherever they found religiously motivated calls for public policy. In 1830, Georgia Representative Wilson Lumpkin advocated for the forcible removal of Cherokee people from his state by railing against the fusion of religious advocacy and partisan affairs. Debasing religiously motivated opponents of the Indian Removal Bill as a bunch of "canting fanatics," Lumpkin offered the following proposition: "The religious people of this country are in the full enjoyment of religious liberty. It is all that the truly pious want. They want no 'Christian party in politics.'"[35] More than law, Jackson also rejected ceremonial gestures that might signal an endorsement of religion. In 1832, Jackson declined an invitation from the Dutch Reformed Church to proclaim a national day of prayer in the advent of a cholera outbreak. Jackson replied to the plea with a constitutional argument: "I could not do otherwise without transcending the limits prescribed by the constitution for the President; and without feeling that I might in some degree disturb the security which religion now enjoys in this country, in its complete separation from the political concerns of the general government."[36]

Beyond slavery, religious reformers further provoked the ire of Jackson and his acolytes because Evangelicals' idea of a benevolent empire threatened Indian removal: a policy of white dominion that was core to the principle of popular sovereignty. Jackson's zealous support for displacing Native people from their lands represented the period's embrace of westward expansion as key for a thriving white male egalitarian democracy. But the interference of proselytizing white Christians who had ventured into Indian-controlled territory to educate and convert through the establishment of federally funded schools was a thorn in Jackson's side. The impact of the missionaries' work to assist and indoctrinate Native communities was counterproductive from the Jacksonian point of view because "the more literate, prosperous, and politically organized" Native communities like the Cherokees of Georgia had become over time, the "more resolved they became to keep what remained of their land and improve it for their own benefit."[37] Representative Edward Everett of Massachusetts, who opposed the Jacksonian plan, connected the religiously motivated whites in Native lands with intensified resistance among Indigenous persons against abandoning Indian territory. Describing the Jacksonian narrative of the savage-yet-helpless Native population as a "distant tradition" and "poetical fancy," Everett rejoiced in the Americanization of Indigenous peoples helped along by Christian missionaries: "We are going, then, to take a population of Indians, of families, who live as we do in houses, work as we do in the field or the workshop, at the plough and the loom, who are governed as we are by laws, who send their children to school, and who attend themselves on the ministry of the Christian faith, to march them from their homes, and put them down in a remote unexplored desert."[38]

In 1830, Jackson addressed Congress to encourage aggressive federal policies to eject Native people from their lands. The tension between the preservation of Indigenous rights and the insatiable demand for white expansionism was at a fever pitch in Georgia and Alabama during the early years of Jackson's rise to power. Speaking to the demands of white Americans who wanted to assert jurisdiction over Indian lands, Jackson told Congress that it would be unthinkable that the government might "tolerate the erection of a confederate state within the territory of one of the members of this Union against her consent." Thus the federal government could not justifiably allow Native people to "establish a separate republic" within a state.[39] Jackson argued that westward settlement was crucial for white republican governance to thrive. To this end, Jackson spoke of dispossession as a moral imperative in 1830: "What good man would prefer a country covered with forests and ranged by a few thousand savages to our extensive republic, studded with cities, towns, and prosperous farms, embellished with all the improvements which art can devise or industry execute, occupied by more than 12,000,000 happy people, and filled with all the blessings of liberty, civilization, and religion?"[40]

The inherent right of white male dominion over Native people was at the heart of Jacksonian thought, echoing beyond the halls of power of the capital city. Capturing this essence, in 1835, the Tennessee Supreme Court depicted the colonization of the Americas as a noble pursuit that required some negotiation with Indigenous communities but necessitated brute force:

Thus surrounded by savages destroying each other, for mere pastime, with the fierceness of wild beasts, a colony was attempted in their midst on the coast of Carolina, and, after a struggle of about three-fourths of a century, was fairly crowned with success. This great effort to build up a civilized community was accomplished partly by compacts with the Indians, partly by laws passed for their government, but mainly by the sword. The tribes found inland have passed under the dominion, and melted away under the influence and superior powers, mental and moral, of the white man, as did the savages of Europe, Asia, and Africa pass under the dominion of the Romans, and as will him of Australasia, Africa, and the Rocky Mountains be compelled to submit to the stroke of fate sooner or later—to accept a master or perish. It is the destiny of man. Ignorance and division cannot stand before science and combination, nor can the civilized community exist by the side of a savage foe.[41]

This ideological impulse animated support for Jackson's Indian Removal Act in 1830, which empowered the president to negotiate treaties with tribal leadership to cede their land to white Americans in exchange for lands west of the Mississippi. And because white man's democracy (and the clamoring for lands, especially after 1829 when gold was discovered in Cherokee territory in Georgia) was an interest superior to tribal sovereignty, negotiated treaties with tribal leaders did not require even a whiff of democratic legitimacy from the federal government. This was famously the case with the Cherokees of Georgia, who, against their wishes, had their lands negotiated out from under them by a representative and were subsequently forced out of their lands at the end of a bayonet during the Trail of Tears. The aggressive claims made by disciples of Jacksonianism that white dominion compelled taking over tribal lands and expanding state jurisdiction over those lands ran counter to the doctrine of discovery, as the Court held in *Worcester v. Georgia*.

In *Worcester*, the Supreme Court, led by John Marshall, invalidated a Georgia law that extended the reach of state law into the Cherokee Nation. Christian missionary Samuel Worcester lived on Cherokee lands but refused to apply for the license Georgia law mandated of white persons entering Cherokee territory. License applicants were required to take an oath swearing allegiance to the State of Georgia and pledging to be governed by Georgia law. Refusing to submit to the state's mandate, Georgia prosecuted and convicted Worcester. The Supreme Court held that the doctrine of discovery did not permit Georgia's unilateral usurpation of tribal sovereignty. As Maggie Blackhawk has described, the doctrine "meant that the United States had inherited the artifacts of colonialism by inheriting domain over Native lands. But the doctrine solely provided the United States with the ability to exclude other European sovereigns from purchasing Native lands."[42] The Court's decision was met with derision best reflected in President Jackson's thinly sourced but famously attributed quip, "Well, John Marshall has made his decision, now let him enforce it."[43] No matter the truth of the Jackson quote, the fact remains that, as Keith Whittington has observed, "Jackson's hostility to the Marshall Court was often intense, and when the Court became an obstacle to his own political goals, he was prepared to ignore it." Still, Jackson was less enthusiastic about institutionally gutting the power of federal courts because they could prove useful for advancing his goals.[44]

The Marshall Court's softer approach toward the constitutional status of tribal sovereignty yielded to Jacksonian racial jurisprudence. In *United States v. Rogers,* the Supreme Court upheld an indictment against William Rogers for the murder of Jacob Nicholson on tribal lands. Though both men were white, each was adopted into the tribe by the Cherokee Nation. Thus, Rogers claimed that the federal government did not have jurisdiction over him because his alleged crime involved two people with tribal status. Writing for the Court, Chief Justice Taney rejected the idea that a white man had no continued obligations to the United States despite his place in a tribal community. Bethany Berger describes *Rogers* as "signal[ing] a shift in federal Indian law and policy, heralding a move from viewing Indian tribes as sovereign governments to viewing them as collections of individuals bound together by ethnicity."[45] Taney's opinion was unmistakably an endorsement of white supremacy and crafted a legal mechanism to ensure the federal government could maintain control over Indian lands. A person's obligations and responsibilities to their own race subordinated all other interests. The chief justice expounded:

> The native tribes who were found on this continent at the time of its discovery have never been acknowledged or treated as independent nations by the European governments, nor regarded as the owners of the territories they respectively occupied. On the contrary, the whole continent was divided and parcelled out, and granted by the governments of Europe as if it had been vacant and unoccupied land, and the Indians continually held to be, and treated as, subject to their dominion and control.
>
> It would be useless at this day to inquire whether the principle thus adopted is just or not; or to speak of the manner in which the power claimed was in many instances exercised. It is due to the United States, however, to say, that while they have maintained the doctrines upon this subject which

had been previously established by other nations, and insisted upon the same powers and dominion within their territory, yet, from the very moment the general government came into existence to this time, it has exercised its power over this unfortunate race in the spirit of humanity and justice, and has endeavoured by every means in its power to enlighten their minds and increase their comforts, and to save them if possible from the consequences of their own vices. But had it been otherwise, and were the right and the propriety of exercising this power now open to question, yet it is a question for the law making and political department of the government, and not for the judicial. It is our duty to expound and execute the law as we find it, and we think it too firmly and clearly established to admit of dispute, that the Indian tribes residing within the territorial limits of the United States are subject to their authority, and where the country occupied by them is not within the limits of one of the States, Congress may by law punish any offense committed there, no matter whether the offender be a white man or an Indian.[46]

Westward expansion did not stop with the Indian Removal Act during the Jacksonian era. It continued apace into the 1840s with the annexation of Texas, a diplomatic resolution to the Oregon boundary dispute, and a military victory over Mexico in the Mexican-American War. Expansion under the mantra of Manifest Destiny was a key theme in the 1844 Democratic Party platform. Even the oppositional Whigs warmed to territorial expansion after stumbling over the question in their 1844 electoral defeat by distinguishing themselves as favoring expansion by negotiation rather than by violent force. During this decade, the federal government made the United States an intercontinental power, taking over a swath of territory that would include Texas, New Mexico, Arizona, California, Oregon, Washington, and Idaho, in addition to land that would round out the boundaries of Montana, Colorado, Kansas, and Oklahoma. The successful clamoring for an imperial expansion of white man's democracy was as much an achievement for the Democratic Party as it would be its undoing—another example of policy producing new politics.

Ralph Waldo Emerson predicted presciently that the "United States will conquer Mexico, but it will be as the man swallows the arsenic, which brings him down in turn. Mexico will poison us."[47] It did not take long for Emerson's fears to become realized. One sign of the new political stage created by territorial expansionism was the coagulation of antislavery politics. What had started as a religious movement rooted in the Second Great Awakening was then operationalized into organized political action, most notably with the founding of the Free Soil Party in 1848, which demanded "no more Slave States and no more Slave Territory." The party's platform decried the stranglehold of the slave power, proclaiming, "Let the soil of our extensive domains be kept free for the hardy pioneers of our own land, and the oppressed and banished of other lands, seeking homes of comfort and fields of enterprise in the new world."[48] The pangs of westward expansion gave birth to a political creed and party-building exercises that fed into what would later become the Republican Party.

The Mexican-American War ended with the Treaty of Guadalupe Hidalgo's ratification in 1848. New decisions about the reach of slavery arose because the treaty provided that Mexico cede the land that now makes up the American Southwest to the United States. An earlier law, the Compromise of 1820, permitted the admission of Missouri and Maine as offsetting slave and free states, respectively, and banned slavery west of the Mississippi and north of Missouri's southern border in the Louisiana Territory. A second grand compromise would be necessary for the land newly acquired from Mexico, but the matter had exigency because the discovery of gold in California in 1848 prompted a flood of settlers to the West Coast. But to admit California as a free state consistent with the geographical principle laid down in 1820 meant upending the political balance in the United States Senate, which had an equal number of slave and free states. The political crisis was an opportunity for Southerners like Senator John Calhoun to saber rattle. Famously, Calhoun threatened disunion:

> If you, who represent the stronger portion, cannot agree to settle [regional disagreements] on the broad principle of justice and duty, say so; and let the States we both represent agree to separate and part in peace. If you are unwilling we should part in peace, tell us so, and we shall know what to do, when you reduce the question to submission or resistance. If you remain silent, you will compel us to infer by your acts what you intend. In that case, California will become the test question. If you admit her, under all the difficulties that oppose her admission, you compel us to infer that you intend to exclude us from the whole of the acquired territory, with the intention of destroying irretrievably the equilibrium between the two sections. We would be blind not to perceive, in that case, that your real objects are power and aggrandizement, and infatuated not to act accordingly.[49]

Senator Henry Clay of Kentucky and Senator Daniel Webster of Massachusetts brokered the Compromise of 1850. The deal consisted of five laws: California was admitted as a free state; the slave trade was abolished in Washington, DC; the Utah Territory and the New Mexico Territory were established; and the Fugitive Slave Act, which required that slaves be returned to their enslavers no matter what jurisdiction they fled to and imposed an obligation on the federal government to capture and return runaway slaves, was enacted. To Emerson's point, the Compromise of 1850 aroused abolitionists who ardently opposed the Fugitive Slave Act and spurred the Free Soil Party, a forerunner to the Republican Party, which while not an abolitionist movement per se, emerged in opposition to the expansion of slavery into western territories.

Territorial expansion also meant the government had to expand—including the federal judiciary. While the nation's ideological trajectory was shaped by the move westward, the government structurally required new courts and more judges during the Jacksonian years, entrenching Jacksonian and slaveholding interests in the federal judiciary. As Justin Crowe has explained:

> [N]ew states required new circuits, that new circuits required new justices, and, that those new justices were—as a result of the norm of geographically representative appointments—expected to come from one of the new states in the new circuit meant that the composition of the Court was inextricably tied to the politics of regionalism and statehood admission. Which territories were admitted to the Union when and how they—together with existing states—were organized once included in the circuit system suggested who could be appointed to the Court and, in turn, what type of body the Court was likely to be.[50]

In addition to structural retooling within the federal government, the success of white expansionism demanded a new political pivot. Popular sovereignty—the principle that local democratic processes should resolve these major questions—was front and center. The idea, of course, was not a terribly new innovation as it was consistent with longstanding Jacksonian principles that embraced democratization and a small federal government footprint. Indeed, Andrew Jackson's Farewell Address contended more than a decade before the 1850 compromise that local democracy was essential for the United States' long-term survival, insisting that the American people should "[n]ever for a moment believe that the great body of the citizens of any State or States can deliberately intend to do wrong" and that a continued aim of government should be to "maintain unimpaired and in full vigor the rights and sovereignty of the States and to confine the action of the General Government strictly to the sphere of its appropriate duties."[51] Popular sovereignty was also central to the 1848 Democratic Party platform. They resolved:

> That Congress has no power under the Constitution to interfere with or control the domestic institutions of the several States, and that such States are the sole and proper judges of everything appertaining to their own affairs, not prohibited by the Constitution; that all efforts of the Abolitionists or

others made to induce Congress to interfere with questions of slavery, or to take incipient steps in relation thereto, are calculated to lead to the most alarming and dangerous consequences; and that all such efforts have an inevitable tendency to diminish the happiness of the people, and endanger the stability and permanence of the Union, and ought not to be countenanced by any friend to our political institutions.[52]

Though the Democratic Party lost the 1848 presidential contest to Zachary Taylor and the Whigs, it wrested control of Congress from the Whigs. With the malleable Millard Fillmore occupying the White House after Taylor's death and control of the Senate and the House firmly in hand, the Democratic Party's governing philosophy carried the day. Eschewing the old strategy that sought to manufacture a balance of political power between states or regions of enslavers and states or regions opposed to slave power, the voting public would choose whether their states would recognize or disfavor enslavement. The Compromise of 1850 was another notch in the Jacksonians' belt, but the victory was more self-immolation than long-term success. The coalition would soon fall victim to its own accomplishments as the political trajectory of the 1850s proved too fraught for the nation to avoid civil war—and Chief Justice Taney's Supreme Court took center stage.

Continent-wide expansion opened up new possibilities for commercial development, but reaping the economic benefits of America's untapped natural resources required settlement, infrastructure, and territorial organization. Democratic Illinois representative Stephen Douglas, who wanted Chicago to be the eastern terminus for the western railroad, pushed for territorial organization. But maintaining the Missouri Compromise's prohibition of slavery north of the 36°30' latitude line was unpalatable to Stephens' co-partisans. The compromise predated the Jacksonian period and was inconsistent with the principle of popular sovereignty. The 1854 legislation championed by Douglas organized Kansas and Nebraska into territories provided that Kansas "shall be received into the Union with or without slavery, as their Constitution may prescribe at the time of their admission," and repealed the Missouri Compromise line.[53]

THE CONSTITUTION OF WHITE PREROGATIVE AND THE TANEY COURT

The Taney Court's jurisprudence mirrored and strengthened the Jacksonian state as a blend of antiemancipatory white nationalism and a preference for fixed local control. In addition to the *Rogers* decision in 1846 that hyperracialized the law governing Indian tribal sovereignty, four other defining cases rounded out the racial meaning of citizenship and the power of the state: *Prigg v. Pennsylvania, Jones v. Van Zandt, Strader v. Graham,* and *Dred Scott v. Sandford.*

In *Prigg v. Pennsylvania,* the Court endorsed the precept that private violence against Black persons fell within a zone of constitutional protection.[54] The question in *Prigg* centered around the Fugitive Slave Act of 1793, which empowered federal and state judges to adjudicate claims of runaway slaves. In 1832, Margaret Morgan, born enslaved in Maryland, left the state and relocated to Pennsylvania with her free Black husband, Jerry. Evidence indicated that Margaret's enslaver released her from bondage. However, upon his death, the successor to the estate demanded that Margaret and her children (one of whom was born in the free state of Pennsylvania) return to Maryland as fugitive slaves. Edward Prigg was hired to hunt and return Margaret Morgan from York County, Pennsylvania. Prigg went to the local justice of the peace to secure a warrant to remove Morgan and her children. Despite having commanded the local constable to seize the family, the local magistrate refused further cooperation. No warrant was issued. Prigg nevertheless seized Morgan and her children and absconded with them to Maryland. Because he failed to secure proper authorization from a Pennsylvania officer before bringing the Morgans back to Maryland, Edward Prigg was subsequently charged and convicted of violating Pennsylvania law for kidnapping Margaret Morgan and her children with the intent of returning them to slavery.

The Taney Court blessed the slavecatcher's lawlessness in *Prigg.* The Court held that under the United States Constitution, enslavers had an inherent claim to self-help—a right to hunt down runaways and bring them back. Congress had an implied power to enact a fugitive slave law to give the fugitive slave clause teeth. According to the Court: states could not impose additional legal requirements that impeded the federal law on slave hunting; seized persons were entitled to no due process rights; and the procedural rights provided under federal law to ensure the identity of captured Black persons were not required if the hunters availed themselves of their common-law right of recapture by self-help. Crucially, the opinion written by Justice Joseph Story gestured to the idea that the federal government could not commandeer state judges to enforce federal law but would require the assent of the state legislature. Story wrote, "As to the authority so conferred upon state magistrates, while a difference of opinion has existed, and may exist still, on the point, in different states, whether state magistrates are bound to act under it, none is entertained by this court, that state magistrates may, if they choose, exercise that authority, unless prohibited by state legislation."[55]

The Court's ruling in *Prigg* is among the worst in the Court's history. The Taney Court endorsed private violence against Black people as a matter of constitutional right as a clear reflection of Jacksonian political thought. Even though the Court recognized a federal power to protect slave-owning interests, the decision was undoubtedly antistatist. Enslavers could do the dirty work of retrieving human property through the common law right of recaptation, eschewing the need for the state altogether. The *Prigg* decision further yoked the meaning of citizenship to whiteness. Snatching Black persons on behalf of planters in the South—no matter whether they were free or enslaved since the hunted had no due process guarantees whatsoever—was a constitutionally protected right of violence, which all states were obligated to respect after *Prigg*. Violence against whites disrupted the peace, so states could punish it; violence against Blacks was a legitimate business. Furthermore, the Court's indication that the federal government could empower but not command state and local officials to enforce national laws, an anticommandeering doctrine of sorts, was consistent with Jacksonian demands that local control was vital to the republic's success, in part, to curb the impact of social reformers.

In *Jones v. Van Zadnt*, the Court reaffirmed that unrestrained private violence was a de facto norm accepted by the constitutional order because the presumptions that might typically accompany the privileges of citizenship did not apply to Black persons no matter where they were in the United States.[56] In that 1847 decision, the Supreme Court ruled on the scope of section four of the Fugitive Slave Act, which provided civil penalties against persons who knowingly harbored or concealed escaped slaves to prevent their capture. Van Zadnt picked up slaves in his wagon in Ohio, a few miles from Kentucky where Jones held them in bondage. The Court held that Van Zandt was strictly liable under the Fugitive Slave Act of 1793's civil action provision to Jones. The jury did not have to find that Van Zandt had actual notice that the people he assisted were on the run from their enslavers. Rather it was sufficient that "[t]here was a clandestine reception of the slaves, and without lawful authority, and a concealment of them in a covered wagon, and carrying them onward and away, so as to deprive the owner of their custody."[57] Just as in *Prigg*, citizenship and the protection of the law was an entitlement closely intertwined with whiteness. Even in a free state like Ohio, Black persons were not afforded the de facto presumption of free citizenship that white Americans enjoyed. The Jacksonian Supreme Court rendered decisions that drew Black persons outside the body politic and the law's protection before the infamous Dred Scott decision. Between *Prigg* and *Van Zandt*, the Taney Court articulated that nonwhites in the United States were subject to the whims of their white neighbors' moral values or lack thereof and that those white Americans who extended the hand of friendship to Black men and women did so at the risk of financial pain.

The jurisprudential trajectory of *Prigg* and *Van Zandt* naturally brought the Court to the peak of Jacksonian constitutionalism in *Dred Scott v. Sandford*. Dred Scott was born into slavery in Virginia and eventually moved to Missouri, where he was sold to an army surgeon, Dr. John Emerson. Emerson took Scott to an army fort in Illinois, a free state, and later to a military outpost, Fort Snelling, Wisconsin Territory, in what would later be the State of Minnesota. Through the Missouri Compromise legislation in 1820, Congress banned slavery in the area Emerson brought Dred Scott.

In the first lawsuit Scott brought, captioned *Scott v. Emerson*, the Missouri Supreme Court addressed whether Dred Scott was a slave under state law. As the high court noted in Scott's case, "Persons have been frequently here adjudged to be entitled to their freedom on the ground that their masters held them in slavery in territories or States in which the institution was prohibited."[58] Given the extensive period in which Emerson intentionally held Dred Scott in Illinois and Wisconsin Territory, Scott had a strong claim to freedom under Missouri law.[59] However, the Missouri Supreme Court ruled that Dred Scott remained a slave, noting that Dr. Emerson did not remove Dred Scott from Missouri on his own volition. Dred Scott could not claim that his enslaver willingly brought him to free territory because, in the view of the Missouri justices, the army doctor "was ordered by superior authority to posts where his slave was detained in servitude, and in obedience to that authority he repaired to them with his servant, as he very naturally supposed he had a right to do."[60] The majority opined that the outcome was not only justified because of the underlying facts but also because the law needed to act as a counterweight to abolitionists:

Since then not only individuals but States have been possessed with a dark and fell spirit in relation to slavery, whose gratification is sought in the pursuit of measures, whose inevitable consequences must be the overthrow and destruction of our government. Under such circumstances it does not behoove the State of Missouri to show the least countenance to any measure which might gratify this spirit. She is willing to assume her full responsibility for the existence of slavery within her limits, nor does she seek to share or divide it with others. Although we may, for our own sakes, regret that the avarice and hard-heartedness of the progenitors of those who are now so sensitive on the subject, ever introduced the institution among us, yet we will not go to them to learn law, morality or religion on the subject.[61]

It was that perilous moment of sectional distress in which the Supreme Court stepped in to settle the next round of litigation brought by Dred Scott. This time, Scott brought his case for freedom in federal court on the jurisdictional grounds that ownership of Scott had been transferred to a New Yorker, John Sanford. Because Sanford claimed to be a citizen of Missouri, the federal court presumptively had the power to hear his new claim in the first instance because of the Constitution's conferral of jurisdiction to federal courts in lawsuits between citizens of different states.

In a decision by Chief Justice Taney, the Supreme Court declined to assert jurisdiction over Dred Scott's lawsuit because Scott was neither a citizen of Missouri nor a citizen of the United States because, as a Black person, the Constitution excluded him from the national political community. Thus, Scott could not litigate in federal court. Taney, speaking for a 7–2 majority, reasoned that, because at the time of the founding Black persons were subjugated and treated as an inferior group, they could never be citizens of the United States entitled to bring claims in courts:

> They had for more than a century before been regarded as beings of an inferior order, and altogether unfit to associate with the white race, either in social or political relations; and so far inferior, that they had no rights which the white man was bound to respect; and that the negro might justly and lawfully be reduced to slavery for his benefit. He was bought and sold, and treated as an ordinary article of merchandise and traffic, whenever a profit could be made by it. This opinion was at that time fixed and universal in the civilized portion of the white race. It was regarded as an axiom in morals as well as in politics, which no one thought of disputing, or supposed to be open to dispute; and men in every grade and position in society daily and habitually acted upon it in their private pursuits, as well as in matters of public concern, without doubting for a moment the correctness of this opinion.[62]

Taney's opinion was sweeping, going well beyond the threshold question about jurisdiction—a question that could have resolved the litigation alone. There was an overhanging question concerning whether Dr. Emerson freed Dred Scott when Scott was brought into Wisconsin Territory given that federal law banned slavery. After all, Dr. Emerson's assignment to Fort Snelling was north of Missouri's southern border, the geographic line established by the Missouri Compromise, where slavery was prohibited. The Supreme Court determined that such a result amounted to a Fifth Amendment violation by depriving persons like Dr. Emerson of their property rights.[63] Without federal law impeding, the remaining issue was what state law governed the status of slaves. On this point, the Court held that Dred Scott's claims to freedom were a matter of Missouri law and that his transient presence in a free state was of no matter. Citing an earlier case to a similar effect from six years earlier, *Strader v. Graham*, the Supreme Court reinforced the principle that because Scott was held as property in Missouri, state law was dispositive of his status as a slave.[64] A fixed localism—the law of an enslaver's permanent residence—was the third nail in the coffin against claims brought by people of color in courts contesting their status as enslaved persons.

The *Dred Scott* decision was the culmination of Jacksonian philosophy in constitutional jurisprudence—but the decision is also an example of how the causal direction of a regime's undoing can originate in jurisprudence and radiate outward. Indeed, *Dred Scott* undermined the very coalition that brought it into being. The Taney Court protected a vision of whiteness as an essential feature of American participatory democracy, an antistatist impulse manifest in its interpretation of the Fifth Amendment's property rights, and a constitutional regime that emphasized the primacy of local control and localized popular decision-making. Though the Taney Court's pro-enslavement constitutional jurisprudence peaked in 1857, the ideological underpinnings of the latter can be traced back to major political statements unrelated to slavery that were core to Jacksonian identity, like the Maysville Road veto or Sunday post office deliveries, and that complemented overtly racist political commitments like Indian removal and racialized voting requirements that supported nearly three decades of dominant Jacksonian thought.

Between the full-throated embrace of popular sovereignty and proslavery expansionism, Jacksonian Democrats in the 1850s continued to pour gasoline on the political fire of a fractured, sectionally divided country. Popular sovereignty ignited a bloody battle over slavery in Kansas with violence breaking out between proslavery and antislavery forces in the struggle to secure the future state's position in the union.

Democrats nevertheless remained unapologetic in their defense of white nationalist popular sovereignty and continued to advocate for Jacksonian ideas even after the unrest in Kansas and rising tensions across the United States in response to the Supreme Court's brutal ruling against Dred Scott.

In an 1857 speech, Frederick Douglass explained that he did not think proslavery politicians got what they hoped to wrestle out of the *Dred Scott* decision—namely, a permanent settlement on slavery in America or a cooling of the abolitionist movement. On the contrary, Douglass accurately predicted that the American public might find itself fraying rapidly because the Court could not settle a matter that was intrinsically a moral question over which there was no compromise possible:

> I have no fear that the National Conscience will be put to sleep by such an open, glaring, and scandalous tissue of lies as the decision is, and has been, over and over, shown to be. The Supreme Court of the United States is not the only power in this world. It is very great, but the Supreme Court of the Almighty is greater. Judge Taney can do many things, but he cannot perform impossibilities. He cannot bale out the ocean, annihilate this firm old earth, or pluck the silvery star of liberty from our Northern sky. He may decide, and decide again; but he cannot reverse the decision of the Most High. He cannot change the essential nature of things—making evil good, and good, evil.[65]

The popular press echoed the idea that the Taney Court did more to accelerate sectionalism and deepen political division, sometimes using *Dred Scott* to attack the legitimacy of the Court. Rather than settle the matter of slavery, a column from the *New York Evening Post*, reprinted in the *Chicago Tribune*, proclaimed that the Taney Court ushered in a "new federal constitution" that would only fan the passion of abolitionist fervor. The Court's decision would "blow [antislavery feelings] into a stronger and more formidable flame." Far from constitutional fidelity, the correspondent accused the "five slaveholding judges on the bench" of national betrayal for "alter[ing] our constitution for us" by "espous[ing] the doctrines lately invented by the southern politicians" and "seek[ing] to engraft them upon our code of constitutional law."[66]

The *New York Tribune* attacked the legitimacy of the Supreme Court, writing that "[a] more preposterous suggestion cannot be made than that their opinions, where Slavery is concerned, are entitled to respect or should receive any consideration among the people of the Free States. These men are, from position, by social relation, by political connection, irretrievably committed to the support of every demand of the oligarchs ... They are High Priests of Slavery."[67] The *New York Tribune* had already pilloried the integrity of the Supreme Court, damning those in the *Dred Scott* majority who "dragged their robes in the kennels of slave-breeding politics." While urging readers to fight the rulings of "despotic courts," the paper recognized in real time the imminent danger of a decision like *Dred Scott*, which rallied supporters who attacked its opponents as traitors and galvanized opponents who saw the decision's supporters as an existential threat to liberty and human rights.[68] The *Tribune* acknowledged the tinderbox Democrats had created and the substantial risk of social agitation and dangerous polarization threatening the union in Taney's wake.

The pages of oppositional newspapers were replete with charges that the Supreme Court had essentially become a mouthpiece of the Democratic Party. And these castigations made by the political press for the Court's slavery jurisprudence were well founded. In addition to other long-standing Jacksonian era prerogatives like opposition to a national bank, support for local infrastructure investments, religious liberalism especially for Catholics, and limited federal revenue intake, the 1856 Democratic Party platform launched a vigorous defense of slavery, local power, and popular sovereignty. The heirs of Jackson's party declared that Congress lacked any constitutional authority "to interfere with or control the domestic institutions" of states and that the "efforts of the abolitionists ... to induce Congress to interfere with questions of slavery, or to take incipient steps in relation thereto, are calculated to lead to the most alarming and dangerous consequences."[69] For Democrats, the principle of popular sovereignty as embodied in the Kansas-Nebraska Act was the answer to the nation's ills. In contrast, the Republican Party was founded in 1854 in direct response to Congress's handling of the Kansas Territory. Republicans accused Democrats of hoping to "embroil the States and incite to treason and armed resistance to law in the Territories; and whose avowed purposes, if consummated, must end in civil war and disunion."[70] In a campaign biography of James Buchanan that could have substituted any number of passages in Taney's *Dred Scott* opinion, Democrats articulated a Jacksonian vision for white man's democracy in plainly racial terms:

> All good and reasonable men must therefore be convinced that the peace, prosperity, and safety of twenty millions of the happiest, freest, and most advanced white men, with their noble structure of republican government, cemented by the blood, the sufferings, and treasures of their ancestors, should not be sacrificed—nay, not even jeopardized for the supposed inter-

ests of three millions of the African race, who, whatever may be their present condition, are certainly better off than any other three million of their own race of which we have any knowledge.[71]

The Supreme Court did little to settle the political tension caused by slavery; instead it contributed to the nation's unraveling. Democrats, like Illinois's senator Stephen Douglas who emerged as a national figure in the Democratic Party in the 1850s, continued to press for popular sovereignty and the democratic value of white supremacy. In his seventh debate with Abraham Lincoln in the contest for the United States Senate seat in 1858, Douglas confidently proclaimed, "Let each State stand firmly by that great Constitutional right, let each State mind its own business and let its neighbors alone, and there will be no trouble on this question."[72] In an earlier speech, Douglas also reaffirmed the undercurrent of the Dred Scott decision, telling spectators that the United States government "was made on the white basis, by white men, for the benefit of white men and their posterity forever, and should be administered by white men and none others."[73]

White Democrats praised *Dred Scott* as a matter of faithful constitutional interpretation. Republicans in state legislatures worked to blunt the decision's impact and pilloried the justices as blithering partisans. New Hampshire, Vermont, New York, and Ohio state legislatures all adopted resolutions affirming state citizenship regardless of race or color. In an advisory opinion, the Maine Supreme Judicial Court proffered that Maine law "does not discriminate between the different races of people which constitute the inhabitants of our state; but that the term, 'citizens of the United States,' as used in that instrument, applies as well to free colored persons of African descent as to persons descended from white ancestors."[74]

Pennsylvania state senators introduced a resolution calling the Supreme Court "little less than the willing tool of Pro-Slavery politicians" and the decision in Dred Scott "a more monstrous perversion of truth and right than any to be found in the records of any nation calling itself free and enlightened."[75] A Pennsylvania legislative committee studying *Dred Scott* blasted the justices for being "open, bold, dictatorial, and tyrannical" and introduced a refined resolution deeming the Court's decision to nationalize slavery notwithstanding a lack of jurisdiction "obiter dicta, coram non judice, and inoperative as law."[76]

A joint legislative committee drafted a resolution condemning the Court's majority as the representatives of a "sectional and aggressive party" who had "lost the confidence of the people" of New York.[77] An Ohio house committee offered a resolution imploring Ohio's congressional delegation to pursue institutional rearrangement by rebalancing the Court—perhaps by expanding the full complement beyond nine members—and to "use their best endeavors to obtain such modification of existing laws as will secure to the Free States their just representation."[78]

The Supreme Court's decision in *Dred Scott* alone did not mark the death knell of the Jacksonian regime. To the contrary, Chief Justice Taney helped Democratic Party politicians rally into a cohesive force in defense of the Supreme Court, the Constitution as interpreted by Democrats, and Jacksonian principles. Moreover, in some state elections in the North, Democrats made inroads, taking back seats in state elections in the autumn of 1857, previously lost to oppositional parties. The Court did, however, hyperpolarize the antebellum body politic and provided another layer of motivation for opponents of the Jacksonian regime to marshal their forces under a more unified Republican banner by stirring fears of a slave power conspiracy. It was the interaction of Dred Scott's intense polarization effect and the Democratic Party's self-immolation over Kansas statehood that strained the national state that Jacksonian Democrats made.

As the Supreme Court's treatment of chattel slavery embroiled the nation, blood continued to spill on the Kansas plains over the state's future and the status of slavery. Because of this unrest and President James Buchanan's bungling of Kansas's admission, the Democratic Party's cohesiveness evaporated. After a territorial election ripe with fraud perpetrated by anti–free state Missourians that gave a proslavery faction control of the territorial legislature, two warring constitutional conventions were held in the state. The first of these was held in Topeka in late 1855 by free-staters who rejected the legitimacy of the territorial government. The document produced by this group banned slavery from Kansas but limited suffrage to only white men and "every civilized male Indian who has adopted the habits of the white man."[79] Congress rejected the Topeka Constitution.

In 1857, a second constitutional convention was held, authorized by the proslavery territorial legislature. This convention, held in Lecompton, Kansas, presented a constitution for a popular referendum that would either recognize Kansas as a slave state or as a quasi–slave state and permit the continued recognition of property rights over slaves already in the state—an entirely unenforceable provision that would allow slavery to gain a foothold in Kansas. Because it was an election without a choice, antislavery voters refused to participate in the referendum and the slave state constitution passed by a margin of 6,226 to 569. The free-state legislature organized a vote on whether either Lecompton proposal should be adopted or rejected. In that poll, 10,000 voters rejected both versions of the constitution, and under 200 would have approved either version of the Lecompton constitution.

Notwithstanding evidence of widespread opposition to the Lecompton constitution among Kansas settlers and the questionable legitimacy of the territorial legislature that approved the meeting that drafted it, President Buchanan urged Congress to admit Kansas into the union and accept it. Hoping to resolve the Kansas question and bring another slave state into the Democratic Party fold, Buchanan betrayed the principle of popular sovereignty that justified the entire Kansas-Nebraska enterprise in the first place. However, rather than acknowledge the problems that plagued the legitimacy of the Lecompton constitution's ratification, Buchanan attacked free-staters as being in "almost open rebellion" against the territorial government and accused their ratification-vote boycott as motivated by a desire to "adhere to their revolutionary organization" and the proposed Topeka Constitution.[80] Buchanan told Congress that the opponents of the Lecompton constitution lost the right to claim Kansas' admission violated democratic norms because they forfeited their voice:

> The sacred principle of popular sovereignty has been invoked in favor of the enemies of law and order in Kansas. But in what manner is popular sovereignty to be exercised in this country if not through the instrumentality of established law? In certain small republics of ancient times the people did assemble in primary meetings, passed laws, and directed public affairs. In our country this is manifestly impossible. Popular sovereignty can be exercised here only through the ballot box; and if the people will refuse to exercise it in this manner, as they have done in Kansas at the election of delegates, it is not for them to complain that their rights have been violated.[81]

Northern Democrats in the House, including Stephen Douglas, balked at the president's urging while the Senate agreed to admit Kansas. Northern Democrats joined Republicans to block statehood under the Lecompton framework by a vote of 120–112. Eventually, a compromise bill offered by Democrat William Hayden English from Indiana passed. It promised immediate statehood for Kansas if voters ratified the Lecompton constitution in a clean vote. Kansans overwhelmingly rejected the proposal, with 1,926 votes in favor of a pro-enslavement constitution and 11,812 votes against.

Buchanan's eagerness to quickly dispense with the Kansas question and cement political power for the Democratic Party backfired, exposing sectional intraparty divisions in a moment of a rapidly destabilizing political landscape. As historian William Freehling explains, "Where Buchanan considered Popular Sovereignty a treasured weapon to keep the slavery controversy out of Congress, Douglas considered local self government itself the treasure. Where Buchanan, a narrowly practical lawyer, demanded that the letter of a legal process be legitimate, Douglas, a charismatic seer, insisted that the spirit of democracy be sustained. Where Buchanan had to have his southern support, Douglas had to have his northern constituents."[82]

The fissure opened in 1858 failed to heal. In the lead-up to the 1860 presidential election, Democrats split into Northern and Southern factions, nominating Stephen Douglas and John Breckenridge, respectively. Conservative Southern Whigs who opposed secession but rejected hard-line approaches to the question of slavery formed a fourth party, the Constitutional Union Party, which siphoned off electoral college votes from the Upper South. Meanwhile, forces opposed to the Jacksonian regime successfully won a majority of Electoral College votes, sending Republican Abraham Lincoln to the White House despite his winning only 40 percent of the popular vote.

For slave-state leaders, the writing was on the wall: their power was waning. For his part, Buchanan attempted to dissuade Southerners from talk of secession after Lincoln's election and encouraged a return to popular sovereignty. In his annual message to Congress in December 1860, he ironically implored the North to leave Southern slaveholders alone by likening Southern states to foreign nations. Buchanan said that "the people of the North are not more responsible and have no more right to interfere than with similar institutions in Russia or in Brazil."[83] Buchanan also proposed allaying Southern fears and shoring up his party's crumbling coalition by constitutionalizing popular sovereignty— a particularly rich idea given his decision to press a thumb on the scale in favor of a proslavery Kansan minority—with an amendment imposing a federal "duty of protecting" slavery in all territory governed by the United States "until they shall be admitted as States into the Union, with or without slavery, as their constitutions may prescribe."[84] Buchanan's pleas fell on deaf ears. A few weeks later, South Carolina seceded.

The *Dred Scott* decision and the Kansas-Nebraska Act were the Jacksonian regime's pinnacle legal achievements—the ultimate materialization of the regime's ideological commitments crystallized into constitutional and statutory law. Yet these achievements were also at the center of the regime's undoing. Nothing but an order-shattering series of events striking at the heart of the Slave Power in favor of constitutional reformation would allow the nation to remain whole.

CHAPTER 3

Civil War, Constitutional Reformation, and Free Labor

Abraham Lincoln's inauguration came on the heels of a collapsing three-decades-old Jacksonian political order. That political order, grounded in principles of strict constitutional construction, laissez-faire economics, and constrained federal power, was waning. James Buchanan's presidency acutely imperiled Jacksonianism's sustainability. His tenure was marred by gross maladministration and endless crisis. Even Buchanan's inaugural speech was remarkably injudicious, describing slavery's territorial expansion as "happily, a matter of but little practical importance."[1] The sweeping ruling from the Supreme Court two days later in *Dred Scott*—which Buchanan lobbied members of the Court for behind the scenes—dumped fuel on the fire of antislavery politics. Happy or unimportant it was not.

The definitive ruling that Black Americans possessed "no rights which any white man was bound to respect" and the invalidation of the Missouri Compromise[2] was intended to bring finality to the question of slavery and keep the divisive question from fracturing Congress. However, the Court's Jacksonian jurisprudence only deepened national divisions and antagonized dissenters within the Democratic Party. Buchanan's political fecklessness plunged the nation into more chaos and division over the course of his presidency. He fumbled Kansas's admission to the union and the bloody turmoil between abolitionists and proslavery forces. An economic downturn and widespread corruption again revealed the administration's ineptitude.

Abraham Lincoln's election offered the potential for a new era in the American body politic. The nation's first Republican president, Lincoln, secured power after a campaign that balanced radicalism and pragmatism. Lincoln had a vision to transform what he described as a "rotten democracy," not by slavery's abolition but by preventing "the spread and nationalization of slavery."[3] Lincoln's position was calibrated to reflect his party's baseline sentiments; however, it was well out of step with the dominant Jacksonian political ideology. The Republican Party's opposition to the antebellum party system was more broad-based than the politics of antislavery, however.

Republicans framed their anti-Jacksonian politics as opposition to rule by the "slave power" oligarchy and the rigged labor system of slavery that supported it. In contrast to the Democrats, the Republicans stood for free labor—the idea that every person can improve their station in life through their labor and the protection of private property, which would enhance productivity and yield spillover benefits to society. Monopolistic grips on property or power threatened free labor principles and the ability of Americans to avail themselves of the nation's natural bounty. Part and parcel of this ideology was the viewpoint that slavery enriched the ruling few at the expense of poor whites. This interest-convergence argument for improving white economic prosperity through the cessation of slavery's spread found support in the party's western base, diverging from the party's more radical wing in New England.

Republican victories in the election of 1860 and Southerners' rejection of the prevailing governing coalition invited an opportunity for the transformation of the American political order. The ability of Lincoln and the Republicans to mold the nation's political likeness in their image was aided by Confederate states' secession. Without Southern Democrats to stand athwart the making of a new political order, Lincoln and his congressional co-partisans had a relatively free hand to remake the republic. They championed a robust national government that would advance the principles of free labor and preserve the union. In time, this new regime would oversee a military victory that freed millions of enslaved persons. But beyond bringing rebel Southerners to heel, the Republican wartime agenda would trigger a new business class that shaped American political thinking for decades. As John Hope Franklin explains, "the bitter struggle that ended in emancipation had spawned in the North an industrial plutocracy that was seeking to keep a stranglehold on government in order to maintain its intrenched position."[4]

The federal government ballooned under Republican control. In 1862, Congress enacted the Legal Tender Act to finance the Union's military campaign with paper currency that lacked the backing of gold or silver.[5] Congress democratized government-held property by parceling out land to individuals willing to work the plots and by allotting land for institutions that would provide education in agriculture and mechanics in the Homestead Act of 1862 and the Morrill Act of 1862, respectively.[6] To further expand the national footprint westward and promote industrious free labor, the Republican Congress created the Department of Agriculture.[7] Lincoln also signed into law the Pacific Railway Act, which chartered a new railroad corporation and authorized land grants and subsidies for the construction of a transcontinental railroad.[8] The federal government forged a national banking system in 1863 with the National Banking Act, which fostered a cozy relationship between banking interests and Republicans, as nationally chartered banks were eligible to secure interest-bearing government bonds to support the war effort.[9] The expanded scope of the general government continued into the war's twilight, including the Freedmen's Bureau Bill in 1865, which charged federal officials with feeding, clothing, educating, and employing emancipated slaves.[10]

Republicans' predilections for policies that prodded self-made success were not anathema to a bold, active federal government. To the contrary, mid-nineteenth-century Republicans roused the federal government to take up an expansive policymaking role, which supported a free labor vision of national growth and a ramped-up war machine to defeat the Confederacy. For the North's economy, the growth of the federal government and the proliferation of taxpayer-funded initiatives created a wealthy class of bankers and industrialists whose interests were firmly moored to the Republican Party. Stephen Skowronek has described the long-term effect of this governing period: "[s]eeds were planted here that would gradually blossom into a new, more pluralistic form of politics in which leaders of private-sector organizations would bargain over the shape of national policy with the leaders of government."[11] The Republican Party would have to recalibrate itself to accommodate a platform that held together the interests of wealthy businessmen, western farmers, and civil rights radicals under an ideological umbrella of equal economic opportunity, strong national government programming, and suspicious attitudes toward regulation.

THE RECONSTRUCTION HOUR

After Abraham Lincoln's assassination in 1865, Andrew Johnson's ascension to the presidency posed an existential threat to the free labor vision. Johnson, a Southern Democrat whose presence on the presidential ticket was intended to serve as a sign of unity, opposed Confederate secession. Johnson shared a disdain with Northern Republicans for slave power. However, unlike his Republican counterparts, the Tennessean believed the slave-owning oligarchy's primary harms fell on poor whites—like his own family. Moreover, Johnson harbored deep racial animus against Blacks, whom he believed colluded with their former masters to deprive white yeomen of their due profits. He was quick to make amends with the upper echelon of the defunct Confederacy in part because of his Southern sympathies and, in part, because he could now command respect from the slave-owning elites who long looked down on him as a lowbrow, backwoods politician. As one Republican congressman succinctly said, Johnson was "no poor white trash now."[12]

While the Republican Congress was out of session in early 1865, Johnson pursued a postwar policy of presidential restoration, which permitted conditions in the South that were acutely incompatible with principles of free labor. At a rapid clip, Johnson issued presidential pardons to ex-Confederates, particularly to those who owned property over $20,000 who were specifically required to seek a presidential pardon. Johnson's generous amnesty, in conjunction with the president's order that federal authorities return dispossessed Confederate property to those pardoned, hampered free labor ideals from taking root in the defeated South for two significant reasons. First, Johnson diminished the Freedmen's Bureau's capacity to lease out the congressionally approved forty acres of abandoned and confiscated lands for former slaves' use, making newly freed Americans beholden to the old planter class once again. Second, Johnson's tepid rebuke of ex-Confederates failed to create a sharp break from the antebellum ruling class when new state governments in the South formed in 1865. These governments began working earnestly to impede Black civil rights and expropriate Black labor.

In 1865 and 1866, lawmakers in Mississippi, Alabama, South Carolina, Florida, Virginia, and Louisiana adopted severe laws, known as Black Codes, to resubordinate former slaves to a new status of quasi-enslavement. Among other things, these laws required Black persons to enter annual labor contracts with a white person, denied Blacks the right to enter certain occupations, restricted movement away from plantations, outlawed the rental of property, empowered white employers to settle work disputes unilaterally, and required employment relationships to cover entire family units. Contractless persons were deemed unlawful vagrants and subject to fines and indentured servitude as punishment. Worse yet, the planter class could take away children who were deemed abandoned by destitute parents. Not only did this pernicious practice deny the dignity of familial unity, but it also robbed Black Southerners of the labor contributions of children and, so long as the family could not travel together, the freedom of mobility. Stealing children into servitude was an acute problem in places like breakaway North Carolina and unionist Maryland. To command total dependence on white employers, in 1866, Georgia restricted hunting and foraging rights on Sundays in counties with large Black populations[13] and proscribed the taking of "any timber, wood, rails, fruit, vegetables, corn, cotton, or any other article, thing, produce or property of any value whatever, from the land, enclosed or unenclosed, of another, without the consent of the owner."[14] Presidential restoration readily allowed for the suppression of free Black labor.

There were grim warning signs for the South's future political economy, signs that came to fruition in late 1865 and 1866. In July 1865, Louisiana governor James Madison Wells wrote to Johnson that the Freedmen's Bureau risked allowing former slaves to become idle and congregate for nefarious purposes by "allowing the negroes to go where they please and work for whom they please."[15] Andrew Johnson sent General Carl Schurz, a committed Republican, on a fact-finding mission to survey conditions in the South in May 1865. Schurz's observations were prescient, warning of the dangers the antebellum political elites posed to free labor principles in the former Confederacy:

> The question arises, what policy will be adopted by the "ruling class" when all restraint imposed upon them by the military power of the National Government is withdrawn, and they are left free to regulate matters according to their own tastes? It would be presumptuous to speak of the future with absolute certainty; but it may safely be assumed that the same causes will always tend to produce the same effect. As long as a majority of the Southern people believe that "the Negro will not work without physical compulsion," and that "the blacks at large belong to the whites at large," that belief will tend to produce a system of coercion, the enforcement of which will be aided by the hostile feeling against the Negro now prevailing among the whites, and by the general spirit of violence which in the South was fostered by the influ-

ence slavery exercised upon the popular character. It is, indeed, not probable that a general attempt will be made to restore slavery in its old form, on account of the barriers which such an attempt would find in its way; but there are systems intermediate between slavery as it formerly existed in the South, and free labor as it exists in the North, but more nearly related to the former than to the latter, *the introduction of which will be attempted.*[16]

While Schurz surveyed the Deep South, concluding that Southerners were waiting out federal forces so that "free labor [could] be avoided,"[17] military administrators on the ground echoed concerns about the leveraging of white ex-Confederate power against the free movement of Black labor. Major General Steedman conveyed to Schurz from his vantage point in Augusta, Georgia, that the planter class's "political principles, as well as their views on the slavery question, are the same as before all the war . . . I believe that the planters of this region have absolutely no conception of what free labor is. I consider them entirely incapable of legislating understandingly upon the subject at the present time."[18] Texan colonel John L. Haynes echoed similar thoughts, writing to the assistant adjutant general:

> The present orders recommend that freedmen remain with their former masters so long as they are kindly treated. This, as a temporary policy, is the best that could be adopted, but I very much doubt its propriety as a permanent policy. It will tend to rebuild the fallen fortunes of the slaveholders, and reestablish the old system of class legislation, thus throwing the political power of the country back into the hands of this class, who love slavery and hate freedom and republican government. . . . They should be able to discuss the question of free labor as a matter of political economy, and by reason and good arguments induce the employers to give the system a fair and honest trial."[19]

It was evident to adherents of the free labor ideology on the ground that the old slave power stood to reconstitute itself if the planter class continued to have a stranglehold on property and a free hand to unilaterally manipulate the Southern economy's labor supply. The end of the slave power compelled, as Major General Peter Joseph Osterhaus observed in Mississippi, the destruction of the "peculiar notions of the southern gentlemen," which could only be achieved if the "southern States regenerated on a real free labor basis."[20] That is precisely what presidential restoration under the Johnson administration would not achieve, and it put the president at loggerheads with congressional Republicans whose resistance to lenient sectional reunification had percolated since 1863. Andrew Johnson's decision to rapidly pardon former Confederates and then return the title to their property shaped the political economy in the South for decades to come, rigging it against freedmen and reinforcing structural inequalities incompatible with free labor ideals.[21] The Black Codes acutely doubled down on that offense against the reigning political order in Congress by restricting occupational opportunities, possession of property, and commandeering labor.

Against this backdrop, Congress returned to Washington with rage and wrested control of Reconstruction away from the president. The Radical Republicans enacted the first federal civil rights legislation over President Johnson's veto.[22] The revolutionary law defined citizenship to include Black men and eviscerated the Black Codes by proscribing apartheid laws.[23] State lawmakers were required to "subject to like punishment, pains, and penalties" all persons no matter their race, color, or antebellum status when legislating and afford to all equitable access to the courts without regard to race.[24] Beyond the regulation of state power, Congress also commanded the equal treatment of nonwhites in all contract formations[25] and property transactions.[26]

Congress passed the Civil Rights Act of 1866 with near unanimity among Republicans but not without considerable concerns about the lawfulness and durability of the law. A federal statute protecting Black participation in the public square was vulnerable to repeal by a later Congress; it was not a fundamental legal change with permanence like the recently adopted Thirteenth Amendment abolishing slavery. While constitutionalizing the Civil Rights Act of 1866 would give it long-term staying power, some supporters and detractors questioned the general government's authority to preempt state and local measures and delineate standards of equal citizenship without a new constitutional amendment. In June 1866, Congress proposed the Fourteenth Amendment to clarify congressional power and safeguard the rights of Black citizens against hostile majority coalitions in the future. Ratified in 1868, the Fourteenth Amendment constitutionalized the Civil Rights Act of 1866. However, the act's broad pronouncement of racial equality, which included private actors, was fixed in terms of state power, putting daylight between the sweep of the act and the amendment that the Supreme Court would later exploit.

The Civil Rights Act of 1866, the forerunner to the Fourteenth Amendment, must be understood in terms of the dominant coalition's free labor ideology. The protections afforded by federal legislation spoke to the heart of the Republican Party's overarching vision for the national project: the elimination of an entitled oligarchy and the empowerment of the individual worker to take control of their economic destiny, which, if successful, would allow individuals to lift their standard of living and *earn* improved social status. Social status—the dignity extended to persons in the public square—was not on the same footing as the opportunity to contract and gain access to land. The regulation of social rights versus civil rights was a cleavage issue within the party regime. Reconstruction governments in the South and labor disputes in the North reinforced the wall separating civil rights from social rights. Republicans' legislative agenda and constitutional interpretation reflected that division.

As early as the late 1860s, Republican legislators in the South initiated earnest attempts to enact measures reflecting more contemporary understandings of civil rights. The mixed fate of this legislation presaged the fracture in the Republican Party over "social equality" legislation. In 1868, Louisiana's Republican governor, Henry Warmoth, vetoed a public accommodations antidiscrimination bill, arguing, in line with a free labor narrative, that legislation could not solve the problems of marketplace discrimination but that time would. Warmoth's veto met with scathing rebuke from his co-partisans, especially Black Republicans, in the Louisiana House who "denounced the governor as an apostate and a traitor, worse, if possible, than [Andrew] Johnson."[27] The harsh rebuke was not, however, unanimous among Republican legislators. One Republican house member supported the governor's veto, arguing that the Civil Rights Act of 1866 was sufficient and social legislation beyond the act risked inflaming racial tensions.

Similar events unfolded in 1870 in Mississippi, where the Republican governor rejected legislation barring segregation on the railroads. "The railroad conductor should not look into the face of a man to determine from the color of his skin whether he has a right to travel on his train. He should look to the ticket," the governor argued.[28] South Carolina experienced like fissures among the Republican caucus. As one legislator put it: "I am willing to give the Negro political and civil rights, but social equality never."[29] Indeed, while South Carolina Republicans debated a measure to require that businesses like hotels and inns offer equal access without regard to race as a condition of licensure, many white Republicans lingered in the hallways of the statehouse to avoid speaking or voting on the bill. Meanwhile, Democrats attacked it as militant social legislation and some Republicans as a bridge too far.

The late 1860s and early 1870s strained the Republican coalition. World events and Reconstruction governments stoked fears that the working class rejected free labor ideals and were beginning to demand more than they earned through social legislation, taxation, and property redistribution. Deteriorating labor relations in Europe and the United States triggered fears about anticapitalist power grabs among American businessmen. South Carolina, which had adopted aggressive measures to equalize land ownership, tax burdens, and access to public places of business, became a flashpoint of concern for Northern Democrats and more moderate Republicans. South Carolina's legislature, which had a Black majority between 1867 and 1876, was attacked as the epitome of socialism—the working class gone amuck—a charge that resonated acutely with many Americans wearily watching socialist movements in Europe unfold.

As Heather Cox Richardson describes it, "Northerners gradually came to accept the idea that black workers were plundering South Carolina landowners in a class struggle against capital."[30] At this point, the 1870s also marked the beginning of the Republican coalition's more cautious approach to further government expansion. Even large structural changes to the federal government, like the creation of the Department of Justice in 1870, were muted compared to earlier legislative initiatives in the 1860s. Angst over domestic working-class organizations and the splintering of some Republicans in 1872 over internal personality conflicts, Reconstruction fatigue, and civil service reform caused bankers and business owners to rally behind Ulysses S. Grant and fortified the industrialist and financier elites' status within the Republican ranks.

THE REPUBLICAN REGIME AND JUDICIAL TRANSITIONS

By Reconstruction's advent, the Republican Party worked through considerable ideological growing pains—from Lincoln's tempered moderation to congressionally led radicalism to coalitional fissuring over Reconstruction governments' policies and congressional hostility toward ex-Confederates. The Chase Court's constitutionalism reflected the uncomfortable transition from the old regime to the new regime and the Republican Party's maturation between 1864 and 1870.

Until 1870, Democrats held significant sway on the Supreme Court. Former slaveholding Jackson appointees, Tennessean John Catron and Georgian James Moore Wayne, served until 1865 and 1867, respectively. Samuel Nelson, a Tyler appointee, was on the bench until 1872. Robert Cooper Grier, a Polk appointee, served until 1870 alongside antiabolitionist Nathan Clifford, a Buchanan pick, who remained on the court until 1881. In 1863, Lincoln chose Unionist Democrat Stephen Johnson Field from California for the Court. Field had no connection to the antislavery movement before the war and disfavored Reconstruction. Even while serving as chief justice, Lincoln appointee Salmon Chase actively flirted with Democratic Party politics and plotted with the breakaway Liberal Republican Party that opposed President Ulysses Grant's reelection and Reconstruction, notwithstanding his long history of supporting abolition and Black suffrage.

Given the partisan and ideological predispositions of the justices, it is unsurprising that the Chase Court dragged its heels and resisted some Reconstruction measures like loyalty oaths[31] and congressional power to establish military tribunals,[32] while avoiding deeper conflicts with Reconstruction policy[33] and reaffirming the illegitimacy of secession in terms more aligned with Lincoln's conciliatory vision for healing sectionalism than in terms of the view held by some radicals that secession was "state suicide."[34] Congress pushed back against the Court, stripping it of jurisdiction ahead of a challenge to the Reconstruction Acts.[35] Congress passed the Judicial Circuits Act of 1866, reducing the Supreme Court's full complement from ten seats to seven.[36] The court-shrinking scheme denied Andrew Johnson vacancies to fill, though a Grant victory in the 1868 election would change Republican fortunes. The early Chase Court was Marbury-Laird redux, as it picked fights where it had disagreements with Congress while avoiding the most combustible confrontations with the dominant coalition, which, if realized, would foment a constitutional crisis that would put the Court in Republicans' political crosshairs. The greatest friction between the Court and the solidifying Republican regime erupted in the first year of Ulysses Grant's presidency.

The Supreme Court was stripped naked of any apolitical veneer between 1870 and 1871 in a series of cases that signaled the long-term ideological trajectory of constitutional law in the Republican-made regime. The sequence of events that played out over these cases about federal currency was described aptly by one legal historian as "a circus."[37] In *Hepburn v. Griswold*, the eight-member Supreme Court decided a narrow challenge to the constitutionality of the Legal Tender Act.[38] That 1862 law created fiat money, paper notes not backed by a fixed amount of gold and silver, to finance Northern war efforts. While debates brewed over the wisdom of the gold standard and paper currency, the almost decade-old law stood for the federal government's power to act not just in a time of emergency but more broadly to support economic growth. The Supreme Court delivered a sucker punch to the national government's authority to govern economic affairs by hammering away at the law's constitutionality. The Court's decision in *Hepburn* would not last beyond the next term.

When the Court heard *Hepburn*, five justices had some affiliation with the Democratic Party, three of whom were affiliated with the old Jacksonian regime. But with the aging of Democrats Justices Nelson, Grier, and Clifford, and unbroken Republican control of federal power since 1860, the opportunity for the Court to strike a blow against expansive federal power was waning—and it was an opportunity that would ingratiate Chase with conservatives. To the former point, Congress expanded the Supreme Court's membership to nine with the Judiciary Act of 1869. This law also provided the first retirement benefit for judges who wanted to leave judicial service after ten years at age seventy. The timing of the new retirement provision was fortuitous as Robert Grier's mental faculties were in rapid failure, rendering him particularly susceptible to coercive influence and confusion. In conference discussions about *Hepburn*, Grier's initial vote was inconsistent with his thinking on the question, resulting in a tied vote. Eventually, Grier switched his vote to join his four colleagues to void the Legal Tender Act as applied to debts owed before Congress passed it. However, Grier's participation would matter little. He retired from the Court before the decision was handed down, so the final vote against the greenbacks was 4–3 in an opinion written by Chief Justice Chase.

With Grier's retirement and the additional associate justice seat restored by Congress, President Grant had a significant opportunity to shift the Court's ideological disposition even absent additional retirements, though Samuel Nelson left the bench in 1872. On the same day the first legal tender case was published, February 7, 1870, Grant nominated William Strong and Joseph Bradley. With Strong and Bradley confirmed to the Court, a Republican majority was in place to dramatically overrule *Hepburn* and sustain the war measure against constitutional attack. In 1871, the Court did just that in *Knox v. Lee*, splitting 5–4. Chief Justice Chase penned a blistering dissent, disparaging the Court's about-face as the work of raw politics:

> A majority of the court, five of four, in the opinion which has just been read, reverses the judgment rendered by the former majority of five to three, in pursuance of an opinion formed after repeated arguments, at successive terms, and careful consideration; and declares the legal tender clause to be constitutional; that is to say, that an act of Congress making promises to pay

dollars legal tender as coined dollars in payment of pre-existing debts is a means appropriate and plainly adapted to the exercise of powers expressly granted by the Constitution, and not prohibited itself by the Constitution but consistent with its letter and spirit. And this reversal, unprecedented in the history of the court, has been produced by no change in the opinions of those who concurred in the former judgment. One closed an honorable judicial career by resignation after the case had been decided, after the opinion had been read and agreed to in conference, and after the day when it would have been delivered in court, had not the delivery been postponed for a week to give time for the preparation of the dissenting opinion. The court was then full, but the vacancy caused by the resignation of Mr. Justice Grier having been subsequently filled and an additional justice having been appointed under the act increasing the number of judges to nine, which took effect on the first Monday of December, 1869, the then majority find themselves in a minority of the court, as now constituted, upon the question.[39]

The *Legal Tender Cases* were nothing less than jurisprudential whiplash, the likes of which would be repeated in the mid-1930s during fights about the New Deal. More importantly, however, the Court's 1871 ruling was a signal of what was to come from the justices now that Republicans had a firmer grasp on power. Exercises of national power that would be a boon to economic development and business interests would be treated with favor. This would be especially true when the primacy of national authority could be invoked to snuff out local regulations.[40] But the two incongruous outcomes also highlight the reality of constitutional law: constitutional jurisprudence is a byproduct of coalitional development and pure voting strength. Though the question of paper money was a grave one that carried national significance, the next decade presented the Supreme Court with multiple opportunities to test and shape legal doctrine that would impose their understanding of the meaning and scope of the Civil War amendments into constitutional doctrine. This newly fashioned Supreme Court held the power to make law at a critical juncture. These nine men did so in a way that reflected the public mood and that was profoundly influenced by international affairs in addition to goings-on in the Reconstruction South. The South Carolina Reconstruction government brought these two issues together, creating a political firestorm that affected the national political mood. The story of South Carolina is important beyond its outsized influence on the thinking of political elites. It is also important because South Carolina offers a parallel vision of constitutionalism that never gained traction nationally and was not able to be sustained in the wake of state party–building failures and political violence.

RACIAL CAPITALISM AND THE TRAGEDY
OF SOUTH CAROLINA

One cannot understand the postwar Constitution without understanding the politics of the rice fields of South Carolina. On a map of
the United States, the area between Charleston and Savannah hardly
registers a finger-length's distance. But it was there, and it was in the
cotton-growing Palmetto backcountry where the promise of a radically
reconstructed American constitutional order drew brief breath in the
1860s and 1870s. It is also there where Reconstruction was dealt fatal
blows. Black statesmen representing a political majority, mainly consti-
tuting citizens freed from enslavement, held the power to remake this
region in the aftermath of civil war and constitutional upheaval. These
men laid the path for a legal regime grounded in principles of egalitarianism and substantive equal protection. This revolutionary democratic
experiment agitated a national backlash as white Northerners soured
on Black Reconstruction.

During this same period, the United States Supreme Court began to
develop postwar constitutional law, embracing the state action doctrine, limiting federal power, and adopting a narrow concept of equality. Black constitutionalism and Radical Republican constitutionalism
were inapposite to the Court's doctrine. The tenets of Black constitutionalism diverged from what would become the foundation of national
constitutional law—an abandonment of the federal Constitution's true
promise—not just because of disagreement over abstract jurisprudential
commitments but because of industrialization. The emancipatory state
was incompatible with the rise of the nineteenth century's system of
racial capitalism in which the racialized exploitation of labor and the
accumulation of wealth mutually reinforced each other. The coalitional
aspirations of Radical South Carolina and the foundations of Black
constitutional thought that might have taken hold from these aspirations and the intervening cataclysm of social, economic, and political
events were a critical juncture for American constitutionalism, which
allowed the supremacy of contract rights and formalistic ideas of equality to gain a foothold in federal jurisprudence.

In 1868, after an election held under the mandate of the Reconstruction Act, South Carolina gaveled in its state constitutional convention
to establish a framework for state government and prepare the Palmetto
State to return to the union. The constitutional convention comprised
forty-nine white delegates, a supermajority of which were lifelong South

Carolinians, and seventy-two Black delegates, most of whom were previously enslaved. The document they produced was revolutionary. The South Carolina Constitution transformed the state government from a parliamentary system to a gubernatorial system. The new constitution created local governments for the first time. Liberal social views from a declaration of rights, mandates for public education, support for the poor, protections for women's property and marriage rights, and universal suffrage were incorporated into the document. The most cardinal idea animating these radical changes was the right to vote with provisions intended to enshrine universal male suffrage. Supporting a broad entitlement to the franchise included protections limiting the justifications for disenfranchisement to "treason, murder, robbery, or duelling;" the popular election of presidential electors; freedom from arrest for electors; and amnesty for crimes of free persons while they were enslaved.

The 1868 South Carolina Constitution leaned toward a constitutional theory of vulnerability whereby the state had an obligation to protect citizens and a duty to preserve dignity over other values. Northern-born Jonathan Jasper Wright, who would become the first Black member of the South Carolina Supreme Court, captured the essence of a constitutional vision for active government when debating a rejected constitutional proposal to ban extending state credit to individuals, organizations, or businesses. To be sure, the relatively moderate Wright was supportive of state investments for internal improvements, which aligned with business interests; but blocking a strict limitation on state policymaking was essential for land redistribution and ensuring the power to establish a state land commission that was authorized to buy, subdivide, and resell land.[41] Wright echoed a sentiment that embraced a more robust role for government, saying, "The welfare of the people is to be cared for by the Legislature ... This is a progressive age. The Legislature will be responsible to the people, and the people will see that they do their duty."[42]

The debates at the state constitutional convention, the constitution produced in 1868, and the subsequent years of Republican governance produced the best look into postwar Black political thought and the potential Black Republican constitutionalism held. Delegate Richard Harvey Cain, a Black minister and recent transplant to South Carolina after the war, during a debate about debt relief, offered a constitutional vision for the state that embraced universal and substantive legal protections:

I hope we will take hold high upon the highway of human progress, lay the foundation broad and deep, and rear a superstructure whose grand proportions shall give shelter and justice to the rich man as well as the poor. I want to see this State take its place in the Congress of the United States. I want to see internal improvements, the railroads rebuilt, and, in fact, the whole internal resources of the State so developed that she shall be brought back more happy and prosperous than she ever was. I believe, under the aegis of freedom and liberty, she will take such a bound forward as has never before been witnessed in this country.[43]

The South Carolina Constitution championed several affirmative protective obligations of the state. In the Declaration of Rights, a "duty" was imposed on the General Assembly "to pass suitable laws to protect every religious denomination in the peaceable enjoyment of its own mode of worship."[44] Another section delineated specific equal protection guarantees with respect to punishment and all matters of government for witnesses, property holders, students, and convicts.[45] Like the Mississippi Constitution, South Carolina's adopted more abstract language on the permissibility of racial classifications than Louisiana, which expressly banned racial discrimination in public services. The new state constitution stipulated that "[d]istinction on account of race or color, in any case whatsoever, shall be prohibited, and all classes of citizens shall enjoy equally all common, public, legal, and political privileges."[46] Notably, the original verbiage proposed for this clause did not include the term "public." Convention delegates advocating for the right argued that the federal Constitution was designed to choke slavery out of existence, but its lack of clarity became an obstacle. Thus, the meaning of equality needed to be exceedingly clear to resolve any doubt. In the words of one delegate, the provision was offered to "destroy distinction" although the state constitution's Bill of Rights "secure[d] perfect political and legal equality to all the people of South Carolina."[47]

The South Carolina Constitution also created social safety-net obligations. The constitution required that "[i]nstitutions for the benefit of the insane, blind, deaf, and dumb, and the poor, shall always be fostered and supported by this State, and shall be subject to such regulations as the General Assembly may enact;"[48] it also required support for juvenile offenders as a matter of an educational guarantee within the state's penal system.[49] And in the subsequent years, the General Assembly enacted laws to this end, establishing agricultural work programs for indigent persons,[50] authorizing counties to provide medical care to the poor and provide hospital accommodations,[51] securing financial benefits for the victims of Klan violence,[52] establishing a school for prisoners in the state penitentiary,[53] and providing "for the care, correction, education and instruction of juvenile offenders."[54]

The educational benefits granted as a constitutional right were sweeping. South Carolinians were provided a right to "a liberal and uniform system of free public schools,"[55] which, if assisted by the state in their entirety or in part, had to be "free and open to all the children and youths of the State, without regard to race or color."[56] The General Assembly would later pass legislation that provided $200 annual stipends for no fewer than 124 students to attend the University of South Carolina based on a "free, competitive examination."[57] Critically, the state constitution stipulated that state law must ensure compulsory primary-education attendance, a rare idea in the United States. However, it was also provided for in Arkansas's 1868 constitution and by law in Massachusetts.

A unique element of South Carolina's 1868 constitution that would eventually help doom the coalition that breathed life into it was taxation. Before the war, South Carolina's tax system demanded very little of the planter class and disproportionately taxed nonproducers. A provision in the Declaration of Rights yoked the constitution's equalitarian instructions to a constitutional obligation that citizens contribute to the public treasury. Equitable taxation of property was necessary and just because "each individual has a right to be protected in the enjoyment of life, liberty, and property according to standing laws. He should, therefore, contribute his share to the expense of his protection and give his personal service when necessary."[58]

Francis Lewis Cardozo, who would eventually become the first Black man to hold statewide office in American history as South Carolina's secretary of state, argued that a constitutional command for compulsory education was vital for dismantling the old power structure. Cardozo told the convention that the aristocracy's "power is built on and maintained by ignorance" and that constitutionalizing education rights would be essential if the planter class held power again because the old ruling elite would "take precious good care that the colored people shall never be enlightened."[59] Notably, only South Carolina managed to integrate higher education meaningfully. While the University of Arkansas admitted Black students when it opened in 1872, they received instruction on a segregated basis; they were taught after hours by the university president. The University of South Carolina's first Black student was admitted in 1873, resulting in an exodus of white students and faculty from the school. The legislature countered the backlash, recruiting new faculty from the North who educated a biracial student body.

The South Carolina government during Reconstruction embraced a vision akin to that of Senator Charles Sumner of Massachusetts, a radical, who believed that egalitarian policymaking was not just a benchmark to measure Reconstruction's success but also a constitutional principle. In 1866, Sumner offered a largely ignored resolution that declared that "the work of Reconstruction" required aggressive oversight by Congress to ensure that the former Confederate states were governed "according to the requirements of a Christian Commonwealth, so that order, tranquility, education, and human rights shall prevail within their borders." For Sumner, this was not just a run-of-the-mill political necessity but a constitutional command issued by the guarantee clause, which mandates states maintain a republican form of government. On this clause, which Sumner described as the "sleeping giant of the Constitution," Sumner expounded:

> That in determining what is a republican form of government, Congress must follow implicitly the definition supplied by the Declaration of Independence, and, in practical application of this definition, it must, after excluding all disloyal persons, take care that new governments are founded on the two fundamental truths therein contained: first, that all men are equal in rights; and secondly, that all just government stands only on the consent of the governed.[60]

South Carolina's constitution and subsequent legislation to enforce state constitutional protections reflected the Sumner position. Universal male suffrage, noncitizen property ownership rights,[61] and the equal access to the courts[62] reflected a strong desire to safeguard political and civil rights. Like the Louisiana Constitution, South Carolina's embraced a fundamental guarantee to access public accommodations and common carriers as a "public right" without which dignity could not be preserved. While the South Carolina Constitution specifically protected the right of "all classes of citizens" to "enjoy equally all common, public, legal and political privileges," legislators enforced this provision in 1870 with a new law that created strong legal protections in the public square. They described the law as enforcing the federal civil rights legislation and the federal constitution's guarantee of a republican form of government in the states. The legislative preamble for Act 279, "An Act to Enforce the Provisions of the Civil Rights Bill of the United States Congress, and to Secure to the People the Benefits of a Republican Government in this State," read as follows:

Whereas, in this State the Government is a Democracy, the people ruling, and the government is also a Republican one, in which all things pertaining to the government are in common among all the people; and whereas it follows that no person is entitled to special privileges, or to be preferred before any other person in public matters, but all persons are equal before the law; and whereas these propositions lie at the very foundation of our policy, and the American people have embodied the same, in the most emphatic manner possible in their organic and statute laws, and the same do by their sovereign will and pleasure sustain; and whereas notwithstanding all these great and glorious facts, there are found some brutal, ill-disposed and lawless persons in the State who persist in denying and tramping upon the sacred rights of certain of the people . . .

The law barred common carriers from "discriminat[ing] against persons on account of race, color, or previous condition," as well as theaters and places of public amusement from doing the same. But beyond the possibility of imprisonment and a stiff financial penalty, if persons aided and abetted in an unlawful public-accommodation denial, they would be stripped of the right to vote and disabled from holding elected office. However, such an extreme punitive consequence as disenfranchisement likely ran afoul of the state's constitution suffrage protections.[63]

Between the joints of Reconstruction, South Carolina lay a paramount right to dignity that covered both state and private actors. South Carolina deemed this right essential for a republican form of government, inseparable from the liberty, equal protection, and citizenship guarantees of the three Civil War amendments to the United States Constitution. This emerging governing philosophy also opened the possibility that the right to contract could be subordinated to other dignitary interests. This was central to the course of debates at the constitutional convention because delegates were forced to grapple with the status of slave contracts, which the 1868 constitution declared void and nonjusticiable in state courts.[64]

On this point, future state supreme court justice Jonathan Jasper Wright argued that voiding slave contracts was a moral imperative: "It is our duty to destroy all the elements of the institution of slavery. If we do not, we recognize the right of property in man. We are not to recognize the right of our Courts to go on contending and fighting over these matters."[65] (Ironically, Wright would vote while on the South Carolina Supreme Court to overturn the provision as a violation of the federal contract clause.)[66] Robert B. Elliott asked fellow delegates to "put our stamp of condemnation upon this remnant of an abominable institution. . . . this bastard of iniquity."[67] One of the most radical, progressive members of the convention, William J. Whipper, offered a rousing speech backing the voiding clause for, if nothing else, keeping South Carolina's courts an arm's length from any disputes:

> I am zealous to see this Ordinance passed, to see the last vestige of that hated institution buried so deep in the sea of oblivion that no resurrection air shall ever breach it in its loathsome walls. . . . The facts are simply these: men in this portion of the country, for a long period of time, had been conniving at wholesale robbery—robbing, stealing, and selling human plunder. . . . We are told, also, [by those in opposition to nullifying slave contracts] that this is a quarrel between two gentlemen and it is proposed to let them fight it out. I am willing they shall, and that the buyer and seller shall settle upon whatever terms they choose, but I am not willing that the machinery of our Courts should be used for the purpose of wringing the bone from the two dogs. I ask, then, that we wipe out this thing forever.[68]

In the thrust of Reconstruction, federal courts considering the adoption of the Thirteenth and Fourteenth Amendments snubbed the theory that dignitary interests might alter the state of contract enforcement. The Supreme Court held in *Osborn v. Nicholson* that slave contracts were "valid when executed," and it concluded, therefore, that as "a court of justice, we have no choice but to give it effect." The Court explained, "We cannot regard it as differing in its legal efficacy from any other unexecuted contract to pay money made upon a sufficient consideration at the same time and place."[69] A few years later, however, the Court refused to entertain a prewar contractual claim made by a Black man in Mississippi on the presumption that he could not enter into an agreement as a Black person. In that case, *Hall v. United States*, the Court reasoned that it was necessary to "roll back the tide of time, and to imagine ourselves in the presence of the circumstances by which the parties were surrounded when and where the contract is said to have been made."[70] In what might well be deemed a prelude to the public interest doctrine and the supremacy of contract that developed in the mid-to-late 1870s, the jurisprudential murmurings of contract law in this period suggested that dignitary interests were subordinate to formal contract enforcement, and they especially shunned any dignitary interest in contractual relationships that could result in wealth redistribution from owners to workers.

Not all contractual relationships were viewed in this dignitary light, though a percolating Black labor movement scored a few small legislative victories early in the postwar period. An 1869 law to improve agricultural contracts required each document to be witnessed by "one or more disinterested persons" and, on the demand of either party, executed before a judge to read and explain the terms and conditions. The law required a detailed listing of the obligations, including work conditions, time of service, and the wage or crop share owed. This seemingly attempted to recalibrate the power imbalance between planters and laborers. However, it included a disparately onerous remedy on laborers for contractual breach who could be imprisoned for failing while their employers were only subject to financial penalties.[71] Two later laws adopted in 1872 further regulated labor relations. One of the laws restricted plantations from paying in self-made scrip instead of government currency without a special contract, and the other barred private profiteering off prison labor.[72]

These measures fell short of the calls for a more activist government that would promulgate a series of rules to manage employment relationships in the state. Black labor conventions, which demanded greater intervention on behalf of Black workers, were held during Reconstruction in Georgia, South Carolina, and Alabama—a symptom of what Eric Foner described as "Black dissatisfaction with the failure of Reconstruction governments to do more for plantation laborers, as well as the difficulty even among black leaders of transcending free labor precepts."[73] In South Carolina, the labor convention adopted seven platform points that demanded a fundamental reordering of South Carolina laws to benefit the working class: preferential liens for workers on land, a commissioner of contracts (appointed by the governor) to oversee labor contracts, expedited judicial procedures for labor suits, fair representation among laborers in jury pools, the division of lands into smaller parcels by sheriffs executing estate sales to democratize land holding, a nine-hour workday for manufacturers, and a repeal of taxation on cotton and rice sales.

The egalitarian vision laid out by Black Republicans in the state's constitutional convention and through public policy adopted during regular legislative sessions to further that constitutional regime conflicted with elite monied interests in the state. A slow-boiling combination of toxic racial and class-based animus in South Carolina weakened the biracial Republican coalition and undermined Northern support for Reconstruction. Just a few years after the South Carolina Constitution was adopted, opponents of the Republican Reconstruction state legislature, bemoaning the large amount of public spending for the general welfare and the more equitable postwar tax structure, lodged complaints about the General Assembly. In 1871, the *New York Times* framed the matter as fundamentally about the definition of majoritarian politics:

> Taxes are imposed without adequate representation. In South Carolina, as in many other States, the voting outnumbers the taxable population ... The enfranchisement of the negro has for a time transferred political control from the master to his former chattel. This is the chief grievance. Taxation without representation is a catch-word to conceal the real purpose of the movement, which is to deprive the negro, as far as may be possible, of the right of suffrage, and augment the strength of the Democratic Party.[74]

In late 1870, the *Charleston Daily News* stated plainly that elite grievances were about the old aristocracy's displeasure at being placed on equal political footing with Black laborers:

> The members of the Legislature represented only one class—that of negro labor. Accumulated capital, landed estate, personal property, intelligence, experience, and station had no voice in their deliberations. The ninety thousand poor laboring colored men could have what they liked, because four-fifths of the law-makers were themselves negroes, or were elected solely by the negro vote.[75]

White conservatives across South Carolina organized to make their displeasure with the state's political biracial leadership, budgeting priorities, and tax policies known. Twice, once in 1871 and again in 1874, white men of means convened a statewide taxpayers' convention to protest Republican policy and Black rule in the state legislature. International news rendered the 1871 meeting's timing ideal for the reactionaries in South Carolina. In March and May 1871, socialists took over Paris and established the Paris Commune. The Commune's failure that spring would mark the violent end of the age of revolution in Western Europe. All the while, Americans were gripped by the Parisian workers' attempt to form a working government. As one historian described it, "Few American media, from small-town newspapers to the New York state, proved immune to the excitement [the Paris Commune] generated. For years the Commune remained a vital issue in American culture because it had the power to mask and illuminate domestic concerns."[76] Indeed, the events in Europe gripped the attention of Justice Stephen Johnson Field, who wrote to another federal jurist, "For months the stirring events occurring in Europe have absorbed my thoughts to the exclusion of almost everything else, except the duties which I have been obliged to discharge from day to day."[77]

Northern journalists covering American politics below the Mason-Dixon directly and indirectly connected French socialism and the Reconstruction South. Writing about the prospect of uneducated white Southerners and freedmen joining together, the *New York Tribune* reported, "Many thoughtful men are apprehensive that the ignorant voters will, in future, form a party by themselves as dangerous to the interests of society as the Communists of France" unless public schooling could educate a substantial proportion of poor whites and freed Blacks in the South. On the same pages that the *New York Daily Herald* reported on socialist unrest and the Paris Commune, the paper also told readers about the Taxpayers' Convention, adopting the South Carolina conservatives' framing that they gathered to resist a "mass of corruption and robbery" by Republican leaders whose budgetary policy worked to "gratify the pocketbooks of a score or so of scoundrels."[78]

Wealth redistribution and the usurpation of power by the uneducated masses was top of mind for many in the United States, and it was the language adopted by anti-Black conservative South Carolinians. Scottish journalist Robert Somers observed of the South Carolina legislature that "a proletariat Parliament has been constituted, the like of which could not be produced under the widest suffrage in any part of the world save in some of these Southern States."[79] White elites seized upon this idea and weaponized it. Members of the 1871 Taxpayers' Convention blasted the Republican government, alleging that their "aim seems to be to acquire wealth by the most unblushing corruption."[80] Similarly, another antitaxation white supremacist proclaimed, "The task before" white South Carolinians was to "surrender the wealth which they inherited or acquired" and "to feel that henceforth their social position was to be of sackcloth and ashes, in which they would be compelled to recognize their former slaves as their equals, and receive them as visitors in their parlors."[81]

The rhetoric brewing in South Carolina was later echoed in Congress, where opposition to civil rights and Radical Reconstruction was framed as the protection of property rights, which, it was argued, provided a bulwark against disruptive laborers who, like the radicals in Europe, posed a danger to capitalism and the freedom of contract. Georgia senator Thomas Norwood conjured up images of the Paris Commune to oppose Senator Charles Sumner's proposed rider to the Amnesty Act of 1872 that would have banned race discrimination in places of public accommodations. Whereas Sumner had aspired to forge a coalition that would remove political disabilities imposed on former

Confederates and shore up Black civil rights, moderate Republicans began to abnegate the radical elements of Reconstruction. Norwood argued that services in places of public accommodation were just another form of contract indistinguishable from labor contracts, thus painting a picture for lawmakers that the proposed federal civil rights law was the first step toward regulating labor relations in favor of workers' rights:

> The principle [that the government can regulate public accommodations and labor relations] is the same . . . You have established the principle, therefore, and you have invited into these halls an organization whose voice has already been heard in this land, whose vanguard has already appeared on the streets of New York city, and whose thunder was heard in Paris just after its surrender. When 'the commune,' when 'the international,' who represent labor, shall come back here and ask to be protected against capital . . . where will be the limit to their power[?][82]

The rhetoric planted in 1871 and 1872 continued into 1874 as South Carolina's wealthy elite gathered again for a second Taxpayers' Convention. Again, opponents of Black rule drew a connection between calls for workers' rights and the redistribution of wealth. One tax revolter argued, "Now that the negroes were free. . . they refused to work on unhealthy plantations, unless paid a rate of wages which rendered it impossible for the planter to realize a profit on his crop, so the lands were allowed to go to waste."[83] The president of the 1874 convention blasted the Reconstruction legislature's policymaking as a "process of confiscation and legalized plunder."[84] Up north, the *New York Times* repeated Southern newspapers' negative portrayals of the legislators, describing them as laughing while eating peanuts and exchanging personal barbs while "law-making and money-grabbing" at the expense of "honest citizens."[85] The *Times* reported:

> The Legislature of South Carolina is apparently a gang of thieves, intent only upon plundering the people whom it is supposed to serve. Long practice had made the Legislature of the State a perfected system of brigandage. Ignorant negroes, transplanted from the cotton fields to the halls of the Capitol, where they have been drilled by unscrupulous white adventurers, have naturally made a mockery of government, and bankrupted the State.[86]

This argument had staying power. Similar themes emerged in Supreme Court doctrine twenty years later when the justices struck down a federal income tax in the famous *Pollock* decision. Indeed, Joseph Hodges Choate, the attorney arguing against the 1894 income tax, sounded the alarm to the Court, explaining to justices that they were a last defense against the "Communist march," which needed to be choked off "now or never."[87] And when the Court did Choate's bidding, Justice Henry Billings Brown wrote in his dissent, "Even the specter of socialism is conjured up to frighten congress from laying taxes upon the people in proportion to their ability to pay them. It is certainly a strange commentary upon the constitution of the United States and upon a democratic government that congress has no power to lay a tax which is one of the main sources of revenue of nearly every civilized state. It is a confession of feebleness in which I find myself wholly unable to join."[88]

Grumblings about Southern labor relations predated the American panic over European socialism and organized white resistance to egalitarian social policy. In 1867, three years before President Grant nominated him to the Supreme Court, Joseph Bradley sympathetically repeated concerns "that the Freedman's Bureau is an engine of mischief; that it teaches the negroes to be discontented; gives them false notions; and utterly incapacitates them from labor." Suggesting that a chief cause of concern after the war was restoring a balance of power between labor and capital, Bradley wrote: "This is the great question of the day—how to restore the labor of the Southern States to a normal condition."[89] Expressing a similar genre of thought, Georgetown, South Carolina, planter Ralph Middleton griped about the inability to control labor in 1870: "[t]he difficulties seem to thicken around us" because in the emancipation state, the "planter is all the time at a great disadvantage." Middleton bemoaned how Black workers did "pretty much as they please" and failed to respond to coercive labor pressures, "laugh[ing] at threats of dismissal as there are any number of places where they can go."[90]

Northern reports reflected glowingly on Black labor when signs suggested that the balance of power between worker and employer in the South was not agitated: "The actual result [of Reconstruction] has been that the blacks have never worked harder or better under slavery than they do now. The South was never richer or more prosperous than the present moment."[91] Reports from Colleton County, South Carolina, noted that some large plantations were run by Black cooperatives, which distributed tracts of land to dues-paying members, provided benefits to sick members, and handled disputes through internal arbitration. Historian Brian Kelly observed, "By late Reconstruction the party had ditched its prewar emphasis on the liberating aspects of free labor in favor of sermons about the mutual interests of employers and employed and admonishments against unruly workers."[92] The fissure between class interests cannot be divorced from broader racial conflicts, but "elite hostility was based not merely on a perceived affront to white racial sensibilities, but on resentment over the disruption of their authority as employers that emancipation had introduced."[93] The friction between Black laboring Republican foot soldiers and more elite business interests was something Southern Democrats were willing to exploit. As one Georgia Democrat from neighboring Savannah argued, the more radical Republican egalitarian vision, specifically as it related to civil rights and social equality, would "subvert capital to labor."[94]

Perhaps no incident better captures the strain placed on the Republican Party because of tensions between Black political philosophy and business interests than the Lowcountry rice strikes of 1876. Reports of severe food insecurity began to surface from two Lowcountry counties, Colleton and Beaufort, in May 1876. Locals sent pleas to the governor in spades, begging for food assistance, relaying that many ate one meal a day and had neither cash on hand nor sufficient credit to boost their dwindling food supplies. As the laboring class hungered, planters on some ten plantations reduced worker pay, citing the Reciprocity Treaty of 1875 that allowed the free trade of Hawaiian rice and sugar into the United States and consequently depressed the domestic rice market. Workers employed on a day-to-day basis initiated the labor strike after planters reduced their daily wages from fifty cents per day to forty cents. The strike grew to include regular workers who opposed their low compensation and being paid in checks that were only redeemable at plantation stores where goods were sold at high prices.

Black plantation farmhands saw the state as having a crucial role in protecting the right to organize and improve labor conditions. The strikers wrote to Governor Chamberlain and explained: "We the undersigned do hereby strike, from this day forward, and until we receive full wages for a day's services, and we further agree not to return to work until the planters agree to pay us for hoeing the rice from 50 cts to 75 cts per half acre, according to the quality and conditions of the land . . . Our reasons for striking is our employers reduced our wages to 40 cts per day, a figure at which we cannot live."[95]

The May strikes subsided after planters agreed to return to paying the original daily rate of fifty cents. However, the peace did not last. Much more widespread, intense, and unruly strikes broke out in August and September as the harvest season began. The August strikes were initially triggered by one plantation's check system, in which workers were compensated with scrip that could be used to purchase items at a marked-up rate at a plantation store or that were redeemable for cash more than three years later. Although the upcoming election enhanced the friction of the late summer's disputes, the May strikes had already exposed the ideological fissures that would grow deeper during the second and third rounds of protests. Republican governor Daniel Henry Chamberlain's sympathies were as divided as his politics, an ominous sign for the health of the South Carolina Republican coalition and the future of Reconstruction politics in the Palmetto State. Chamberlain campaigned that year for reelection, advocating for fiscal restraint and anticorruption in the wake of white property owners' protests against swelling tax burdens that were imposed to support the expanded footprint of the state's welfare programs. His appeals appeased the more conservative elements of the Republican Party and business interests in particular at the expense of his core constituency—Black Republicans.

Chamberlain and statewide leaders' continued straddling of their base's interests while courting conservative interests fueled intra-party opposition against him. For example, the appointment of judges frayed the relationship between the laboring class and Chamberlain. While Black workers found support from one local Black judge, Chamberlain installed a white rice planter who was averse to workers' interests as a trial judge in Colleton County and refused to remove another white planter judge at the behest of Black leaders. To appease conservative business interests without turning his back on the Republican Party's Black voting base, the governor offered sympathetic word for workers' plight and acts of amnesty to striking workers but also urged for a hardline approach to those who blocked others from working. This was in line with the advice of Republican attorney general William Stone, who advocated that the governor quell the unrest by arresting a handful of the main organizers.

The problems were not just local. It was a nationalized question that implicated core constituencies of the national Republican Party. One Charleston official wrote to Governor Chamberlain in blunt terms that the many stood to lose if the rice workers continued to disrupt the harvest, telling him that "the planters would be ruined, the factors and bankers in Charleston would suffer enormous losses, and the capitalists of New York who have made the advances would join them in one general outcry against the state administration."[96] By 1876, the interest convergence of the Republican Party and Southern planters forged a critical juncture in American politics. Chamberlain and others in the upper echelons of Republican leadership shared a resentment toward organized labor, much like the Democratic Party–aligned *Charleston*

News and Courier, which said of the organized strikers, "The freedman has only exchanged one master for many masters, if he is not at liberty to work where and when and on what terms he will."[97] But whatever might be said of the 1876 rice strikes, they would never be repeated in South Carolina after the state's Republican Party disassembled in the wake of violent voter suppression and coalitional stress and Redeemer Democrats seized power. Moreover, white Democrats would continue to dissuade Black activism with violence and intimidation to an extent that an anonymous writer for the *Atlantic* proclaimed in 1878 that "Republicanism is dead, and the old intolerance has revived."[98] The promise of Black constitutionalism died in the South Carolina Lowcountry, but the fears it ignited reverberated in constitutional jurisprudence nationally. It is difficult to understate the ripple effect of South Carolina and the threat of Black constitutionalism on the national stage.

LUKEWARM POLITICAL EQUALITY AND THE ORIGINS OF CONTRACTS AND PROPERTY

American constitutional law mirrored the ideological commitments of the Republican Party with greater intensity in the 1870s and 1880s. With judicial turnover in the early 1870s and Ulysses Grant kicking off sixteen years of uninterrupted Republican control of the presidency, free labor constitutionalism took root at the Supreme Court. Now armed with the Thirteenth, Fourteenth, and Fifteenth Amendments, the Court made interpretative choices informed by free labor ideology as shaped by salient political controversies. This inflection point in the Court's history limited the war amendments' full potential and laid the path for the Court to become a deregulatory juggernaut. The decisions of the Chase, Waite, and White Courts could be easily confused as disjointed pronouncements but have a greater degree of cohesiveness taken together and read against the mainstream Republican credo.

The remade Constitution protected a right of enterprise access that would enable the self-made man to earn social equality. What the Constitution would not do was affirmatively guarantee a right to public dignity or countenance "unnatural" governmental intervention—regulators picking winners and losers—in economic affairs. Class consciousness was viewed as anathema to the natural forces of social mobility, which allow for today's indigents to become tomorrow's independent producers. In this sense, proworker legislation was received by the Court as a type of social stagnation, not unlike the kind of rigged system in the

South that stirred Republicans in 1866 to action. The Constitution enabled the government to take action that might safeguard a person who sold their labor for wages to contract and improve their condition by securing economic independence. Constitutional jurisprudence reflected this view that the government had an obligation to not artificially constrain workers' access to the labor market. In the decades after the Civil War, the courts nationalized economic policy to limit business-related regulations and dulled the egalitarian promise of the Reconstruction amendments as a consequence. The tragic paradox is that constitutional development in the wake of Radical Reconstruction diverged from the vision held by the brain trust behind the new constitutional architecture in significant ways, partially evidenced by their contemporaneous protests. It nonetheless tracked with the baseline ideology, political flashpoints, and the shifting demographics of the coalition's stakeholders.

The *Slaughterhouse Cases* was an inflection point in constitutional law because of how it interpreted the Fourteenth Amendment. It pitted two Radical Republican principles against one another: the nationalization of citizenship and the success of free labor under Southern Reconstruction governments.[99] The *Slaughterhouse Cases* emerged from a long history of nonexistent public health policy in New Orleans. Antebellum New Orleans was an unsanitary necropolis, beleaguered by deadly epidemic after deadly epidemic. Union general Benjamin Butler, who took the city over in 1862, found that "the streets were reeking with putrefying filth" and acted to reverse the city's public health nightmare.[100] Union forces cleared the canals and the streets, which had been used to dump decomposing animal parts and household refuse in pools of standing water. Butler's success reportedly caused even some of the most diehard secessionists to confess that "the federals could clean the streets, if they couldn't do anything else."[101] Problems with the city's white-owned abattoirs nevertheless persisted.

In 1869, Louisiana's biracial Reconstruction government passed "An Act to Protect the Health of the City of New Orleans, to Locate the Stock Landings and Slaughter Houses, and to incorporate the Crescent City Livestock Landing and Slaughter-House Company," which created a private-public-partnership utility to improve the city's sanitation and perhaps appeal to the city's white moderates by showing that the Republican state government could effectively address long-standing problems.[102] The law issued a franchise to a specially chartered corporation made of private investors to run a centralized slaughterhouse where the city's butchers could rent space downstream from the city's water supply.[103] The legislation set fees and implemented health inspections.[104] Critically, the new slaughtering facilities were open equally to Black butchers. White butchers claimed their right to pursue their trade was infringed, and white New Orleanians who once despised the unsanitary butchers now backed their protests in light of the biracial Reconstruction government's egalitarian policies, including school integration, antidiscrimination, and protecting a wide array of civil liberties.

The white butcher's constitutional challenge charged that the monopoly violated their fundamental right to engage in a chosen profession because the Fourteenth Amendment's privileges or immunities clause was intended to forbid states from discriminating among their own citizens. Indeed, many Radical Republicans believed the clause was important for either applying the Bill of Rights to the states or as embodying the free labor protections of the Civil Rights Act of 1866. A broad reading of the Fourteenth Amendment, as advocated by the white butchers, could presumably hamstring states and especially Reconstruction governments from drawing any distinctions necessary to rebuild the South, safeguard public health, and protect Black free labor. In what historian Michael Ross called "a vote of confidence for a biracial reconstruction government,"[105] a 5–4 Supreme Court sided with Louisiana by holding that the monopoly was permissible under the state's police powers and that the privileges or immunities clause only protected national citizenship guarantees like conducting business with the federal government or engaging in interstate or international trade.[106]

While the decision was inexplicable in its cramped reading of national citizenship in the wake of the Civil War's defeat of sectionalism, it was nonetheless a ruling that was supposed to give greater latitude to Reconstruction state governments to allow biracial democracy to succeed, preserve police powers to address public harms, and protect free labor interests. Though the *Slaughterhouse Cases* fell devastatingly short of the intended effect of the Civil War amendments, it nonetheless is not inconsistent with free labor ideology and can be understood as fitting within the parameters of the partisan regime's triple aims of empowering Black freedom, feeding large-scale industrial growth, and permitting police power regulation that benefited the public interest without seeming to engage in wealth redistribution—an idea echoed by elected officials commenting on the decision in the months and years after the Supreme Court issued it.

The Supreme Court's decision in *Slaughterhouse* and the proposition that state discrimination because of race was impermissible, at least when it came to direct relationships between the state and the citizen that did not upset private social inequities, reverberated five years later in *Strauder v. West Virginia*. There, the Supreme Court held that a West Virginia law limiting jury service to white men was incongruous with the equal protection clause and cited the butcher case for the idea that the Civil War amendments were designed primarily for the protection of Black citizens' free labor and access to the basic functions of government. In *Strauder*, the Court was unafraid to highlight the problem constitutional indifference could pose to white men in the South in jurisdictions with Black majorities:

> That the West Virginia statute respecting juries—the statute that controlled the selection of the grand and petit jury in the case of the plaintiff in error— is such a discrimination [intended to be eradicated by the Civil War amendments] ought not to be doubted. Nor would it be if the persons excluded by it were white men. If in those States where the colored people constitute a majority of the entire population a law should be enacted excluding all white men from jury service, thus denying to them the privilege of participating equally with the blacks in the administration of justice, we apprehend no one would be heard to claim that it would not be a denial to white men of the equal protection of the laws. . . . The very fact that colored people are singled out and expressly denied by a statute all right to participate in the administration of the law, as jurors, because of their color, though they are citizens, and may be in other respects fully qualified, is practically a brand upon them, affixed by the law, an assertion of their inferiority, and a stimulant to that race prejudice which is an impediment to securing to individuals of the race that equal justice which the law aims to secure to all others.[107]

The jurisprudential flow from *Slaughterhouse* and *Strauder* extended to property rights in the next century. In *Buchanan v. Warley*, the Court invalidated a Louisville ordinance mandating segregated neighborhoods. Louisville prevented Buchanan, a white man, from selling his property to a Black man. In this sense, *Buchanan* was a decision tethered to the free labor idea of the right to contract and enjoy property. In the Court's view, the Constitution protected a white man's right to alienate property—a right unlike claims to social equality that the Court has previously deemed to lie outside the ambit of the Fourteenth Amendment. The Court explained, "this court has held laws valid which separated the races on the basis of equal accommodations in public conveyances, and courts of high authority have held enactments lawful which provide for separation in the public schools of white and colored pupils where equal privileges are given. But in view of the rights secured by the Fourteenth Amendment to the federal Constitution such legislation must have its limitations, and cannot be sustained where the exercise of authority exceeds the restraints of the Constitution."[108] Indeed, the Court affirmed the rights of persons in Washington, DC, to create private racially restrictive covenants through nongovernmental agreements, which Louisville was not permitted to do in *Buchanan v. Warley*.[109] Decisions in this area that embraced racial equality were a mirage of progress, hewed to a narrow construction of equality that had little meaning outside of state-backed discrimination to impede property, contract, or core political rights.[110] The progress made in political equality along the lines of *Strauder* and *Warley* was dwarfed by regressive rulings in the free labor era on social and economic matters. These other rulings reflected a libertarian ethos that held social equality at the bottom of the constitutional hierarchy and most prized the right to contract's doctrine disfavoring any regulation that could be cast as wealth redistribution.

THE SOURED TURN AGAINST EQUALITY

The party's appetite for Reconstruction soured. Free labor ideology morphed to embrace the proposition that the economy grew from the top down. As a consequence, antiregulation became vogue, and government regulation was skeptically viewed as a redistribution of wealth. This was at odds with the mid-1870s Granger Movement, which was comprised of disaffected farmers in the Midwest who sought, with the help of Democrats, to regulate railroads. To Republicans, the antimonopoly reformers were veering dangerously toward communism. Bitter debates over legislation in 1875 indicated the same held for legal regimes requiring full access to public places of business. These shifts foreshadowed what C. Vann Woodward described as the economic underpinnings of Reconstruction's untimely end once the emerging business interests of the South found common ground with Republican industrialists, particularly within the railroad sector.[111]

The cooled engines of war and the faded sideshow of Andrew Johnson's presidency revealed contested areas of an underdeveloped governing philosophy within the dominant coalition. This was acutely true with respect to the coalition's splintering over federal civil rights legislation in the 1870s. Senator Charles Sumner introduced a major civil rights bill in 1870 protecting against race discrimination at several types of public accommodations, including railroads, steamboats, theatres, public schools, churches, and cemeteries. But Republicans failed to move Sumner's antidiscrimination bill until after his death in 1874.

Notwithstanding contentious public debate over the bill during the election season prior and Republicans' losing control of Congress, Benjamin Butler led the charge to pass the legislation during the lame-duck session in 1875. Congress watered down the Civil Rights Act of 1875 from the original proposal by removing provisions to desegregate schools and cemeteries,[112] illustrating the delicate balance even the most ardent supporters of the act had to embrace to avoid the accusations of legislating social equality. Some Republicans like Simeon Chittenden voiced concerns that the legislation was "impolitic" because its passage would "unnecessarily . . . vex white men, North and South."[113] Chittenden's rhetoric echoed the sentiment in the Republican *Chicago Tribune* the year before, mocking the proposal as requiring "that every white man in the South shall love every Negro" only by a matter of "degree, not kind."[114] Democrats decried it as a measure with de minimis support, which Republicans wanted to foist on the public during their majority's twilight.

Despite passing with large majorities, President Grant signed the bill into law without fanfare. The president and members of Congress had little to say about the law after its approval. The lukewarm reception was matched by a reluctance to enforce the law. In John Hope Franklin's words, it was "a dead letter from the day of its enactment."[115] The Grant Administration barely informed federal authorities about their responsibilities under the law. Federal judges, including those with Republican affiliations, were quick to declare the 1875 Civil Rights Bill unconstitutional or undermine it by narrowing its scope. Unionist judge Thomas Duval in Texas and Democrat-turned-Republican judge Robert Paine Dick of North Carolina took positions that the act might license separate-but-similar accommodations. Michigander and Grant appointee to the Court of Appeals for the Sixth Circuit, Judge Halmor Hull Emmons, a staunch Republican, declared the act unconstitutional.

Democrats made hay especially of Emmons's decision, speculating that the law was responsible for softening white support for Republicans in the South. The *Memphis Daily Avalanche* declared that "[n]o Republican journal has dissented from Judge Emmons' declaration. . . . The truth is, the Republican leaders are anxious to be rid of the Civil Rights business law, law or no law, and are rejoiced that a Republican Judge has been the first to knock the life out of it."[116] Emmons's ruling was praised in the *Detroit Free Press* as one informed by legal principle over partisan allegiance.[117] The Civil Rights Act of 1875 was orphaned in a matter of weeks. Reconstruction's end in 1877 was telegraphed well before federal troops left the South.

The Republican orthodoxy that understood the liberty right under the Fourteenth Amendment as protecting a right to access economic opportunity for public benefit and not as an affirmative obligation to secure dignity or trammel private decision-making became a core component of constitutional law. The Court previewed this position in 1875, explaining that the Fourteenth Amendment "adds nothing to the rights of one citizen as against another."[118]

A parallel development in the state-action-doctrine philosophy emerged from the *Civil Rights Cases* in 1883. Here, the Supreme Court held that the Civil Rights Act of 1875, which regulated equal access to public accommodations operated by private parties, fell outside congressional Fourteenth Amendment enforcement powers not because states neglected basic rights but because Congress failed altogether to identify a Fourteenth Amendment violation by the state that Congress had the power to address.[119] Or, as the Court put it, the Civil Rights Act "ma[de] no reference whatever to any supposed or apprehended violation of the Fourteenth Amendment on the part of the States."[120]

Social equality was not the sort of constitutional interest Congress could vindicate in the same way it could intervene to even the economic playing field. Justice Bradley's opinion in the *Civil Rights Cases* mirrored the debate over social equality versus politics and civil rights that embroiled the late 1860s and 1870s. Bradley offered stinging commentary to this effect, writing, "When a man has emerged from slavery, and by the aid of beneficent legislation has shaken off the inseparable concomitants of that state, there must be some stage in the progress of his elevation when he takes the rank of a mere citizen, and ceases to be the special favorite of the laws, and when his rights as a citizen, or a man, are to be protected in the ordinary modes by which other men's rights are protected."[121]

The same logic extended to state-mandated segregation in *Plessy v. Ferguson*, where the Court parsed the kind of free labor equality mandated by the Constitution from claims that aimed to secure more egalitarian social standing. The *Plessy* Court explained that constitutional theory long understood a difference between the impermissible act of "interfering with the political equality of the negro" and state-mandated segregation, a question of social standing.[122] Echoing earlier arguments that date back to the first days of Reconstruction and the moderate wing of the Republican Party, the Court rejected the notion that Jim

Crow laws like the one challenged in *Plessy* injured Black Americans. Social equality was not bestowed; it had to be earned. Thus, in the Court's view, if the "two races are to meet upon terms of social equality, it must be the result of natural affinities, a mutual appreciation of each other's merits, and a voluntary consent of individuals."[123]

The caveat, however, was that the Constitution still obliged governments not to interfere with the right to contract or use property along racial lines—vehicles through which social equality was achievable. For the majority, this distinguished *Plessy* from the Court's earlier decision in *Yick Wo* where the Court held San Francisco's unequal enforcement of an ordinance to block Chinese residents from operating laundries violated the Fourteenth Amendment.[124] The Court ruled that state actors could not use "an evil eye" and implement racially neutral laws in a racially discriminatory manner under the Fourteenth Amendment. But far from a radical statement of racial justice, the court's ruling is best viewed in free labor terms. The Court protected economic enterprise from government-backed racial animus, which was consistent with the lowest common denominator of what supporters of the Civil Rights Act of 1866 and the Fourteenth Amendment intended to safeguard: a right to make a livelihood.[125] Under free labor constitutionalism, *Plessy*, a significant decision in the modern constitutional anticanon, and *Yick Wo*, a celebrated opinion in the modern constitutional canon, were not at odds. The Court's protection of racial minorities vulnerable to white supremacy would only go as far as the claims fit within the partisan regime's core tenets.

THE LAW OF PUBLIC INTEREST AND THE SUPREMACY OF CONTRACT

In 1874, the Court heard a challenge to a Topeka municipal tax designed to fund corporate subsidies.[126] The Court deemed the taxpayer-funded grants unlawful for want of a public purpose in *Loan Association v. Topeka* because the city's attempt to attract business to the city "was purely in aid of private or personal objects" and "an unauthorized invasion of private right."[127] Here, Topeka sinned by picking winners and losers in doling out public funds to benefit "leeches."[128] Justice Samuel Miller wrote in private correspondence a few years later about these beneficiaries of corporate welfare in terms that placed them well outside the free labor ideal because "[t]hey engage in no commerce, no trade, no manufacturing, no agriculture. They *produce nothing*."[129]

In not so many words, the Court, in *Loan Association*, gestured toward a free labor idea of substantive due process that invoked natural law principles colored by Miller's description of the useless, parasitic business. Striking down the municipal tax, the Court explained: "There are limitations on such power which grow out of the essential nature of all free governments. Implied reservations of individual rights, without which the social compact could not exist, and which are respected by all governments entitled to the name."[130] The opinion failed to identify the constitutional provision from which this natural law principle emanated. Justice Clifford, in dissent, attacked the vagueness of the reasoning: "Courts cannot nullify an act of the State legislature on the vague ground that they think it opposed to a general latent spirit supposed to pervade or underlie the constitution, where neither the terms nor the implications of the instrument disclose any such restriction."[131] The Republican free labor principle won over the objections of Clifford, who owed his seat to the old Democratic order.

Whatever *Loan Association* may have set in motion, economic substantive due process was long in the making. The Court continued to gesture toward robust judicial review of economic policy under the new amendments in the decades after the Topeka case. In *Munn v. Illinois*, the Court upheld a state law setting maximum rates for grain storage warehouses, which the Illinois Constitution classified as a public good (and it was similarly embraced as such by the Court).[132] The Court established the "affectation with a public interest" test.[133] In doing so, the Court warned that the state's interest in private contracts was different and subject to constitutional scrutiny.[134] The Court further articulated this principle of substantive due process in the economic sphere in the *Railroad Cases*, explaining that the "power to regulate is not a power to destroy, and limitation is not the equivalent of confiscation."[135] However, these cases more immediately presaged the state action doctrine that would manifest in the *Civil Rights Cases*: regulations that interfered with private matters outside the public interest violated the free labor principle.[136]

The Court breathed life into the free labor–informed dicta that gestured to an economic liberty principle under the Fourteenth Amendment in *Loan Association*, *Munn*, and the *Railroad Cases*. In *Allgeyer v. Louisiana*, the Supreme Court gave the theory teeth and struck down a Louisiana law that regulated marine insurance policies.[137] In doing so, the *Allgeyer* decision set the stage for the notorious Lochner Era. The Court explained the protections afforded by the Fourteenth Amendment by tapping into the free labor ideal that the state must protect individual industriousness:

> The 'liberty' mentioned in that amendment means, not only the right of the citizen to be free from the mere physical restraint of his person, as by incarceration, but the term is deemed to embrace the right of the citizen to be free in the enjoyment of all his faculties; to be free to use them in all lawful ways; to live and work where he will; to earn his livelihood by any lawful calling; to pursue any livelihood or avocation; and for that purpose to enter into all contracts which may be proper, necessary, and essential to his carrying out to a successful conclusion the purposes above mentioned.[138]

In *Lochner v. New York*, the Court went full bore into economic substantive due process, striking down a New York law that proscribed an employer from "requir[ing], or permitt[ing], [an employee] to work in a biscuit, bread, or cake bakery, or confectionery establishment, more than sixty hours in any one week," in order to protect bakery employees' health and safety.[139] Holding that the baker law violated a right to contract, the *Lochner* Court expounded a few significant propositions. First, workers should be free from "unreasonable, unnecessary, and arbitrary interference with the right of the individual to his personal liberty, or to enter into those contracts in relation to labor which may seem to him appropriate or necessary for the support of himself and his family."[140] Second, the state should retain police powers to constrain the right to sell labor to advance public health, provided the regulation has a "direct relation" to public health.[141] Finally, the judiciary had the power to scrutinize legislative enactments and enjoin those that unreasonably impaired the right to contract.[142]

The Court chastised the New York law, saying it was "impossible" "to shut our eyes to the fact that many of the laws of this character, while passed under what is claimed to be the police power for the purpose of protecting the public health or welfare, are, in reality, passed from other motives."[143] The Court explained that contrary to the public health rationale proffered, the "real object and purpose were simply to regulate the hours of labor between the master and his employees."[144] Thus, for the *Lochner Court*, "the state redistribution of existing entitlements violate[d] liberty."[145]

Scholars often cast *Lochner* as an inflection point, which led to something radically new. It was. And it was not. The *Lochner* Era did not usher in a new period that jettisoned an old constitutional order. The *Lochner* Era pumped steroids into the preexisting constitutional order's long-standing ideas and power structures. The right to contract without unnatural impediments was at the heart of the free labor vision that led to the passage of the Civil Rights Act of 1866 and the adoption of the Fourteenth Amendment. Constitutional jurisprudence flirted with the idea of substantive due process for three decades, and the dominant Republican Party had long been weary of aggressive policies that could be plausibly construed as usurping unearned status or redistributing wealth, perhaps most visible in the rebuke of the economic and taxation policies adopted by South Carolina's Reconstruction government. In this sense, *Lochner* was simply a reflection of free labor principles hitched to the Republican Party's capitalist marriage to the American industry—the very industry it breathed life into during the Civil War.

CONCLUSION

The Supreme Court, in the interregnum between Reconstruction and the New Deal, wiped out the constitutional promise of egalitarian liberation to build a constitutional bulwark against socialism. The full promise of America's constitutional reformation never arrived. The jurisprudential choices made during this period were overwhelmingly probusiness, prowork (though not proworker), and pro–wealth accumulation in service of the coalitional interests that supported the dominant political order—big business whose stakeholders objected to anything that whiffed of wealth redistribution or the assisted reallocation of social clout. As a result, the Court limited federal intervention in civil rights, expanded federal dominion over commerce, imposed severe limitations on the regulatory authority of states and municipalities, and protected some core political exercises but refused to intervene in invidious forms of state-enabled discrimination. The Supreme Court's jurisprudence structurally limited the capacity of the state to regulate economic or social inequality. Of course, it need not have been this way, as the nascent Black constitutionalism of Reconstruction South Carolina demonstrates. Ironically, however, the emergence of a Black governing vision and the fear it inspired across the country influenced the constitutionalism the political regime adopted considerably.

As with all constitutional orders, the era Lincoln and the Republicans kicked off in 1860 did not last forever. The onset of the Great Depression created a crisis within the order. A hollowed-out federal government and state governments hamstrung by economic jurisprudence were inept in addressing economic collapse. The laissez-faire orthodoxy of national government policymaking could not respond to or address the dire economic crises it helped create. From this moment, a new regime rose in 1932 with President Herbert Hoover's reelection defeat, one that embraced a larger governmental footprint with a commitment to liberal democracy, forged from the hard-wrought experiences of economic catastrophe and international conflict.

CHAPTER 4

New Deal Constitutionalism

The old Republican order made the nation and itself a victim of its success. The antiregulation and probusiness politics of the era created highly concentrated markets with coercive labor structures that resulted in wild increases in production output. Laissez-faire politics and the attendant constitutional doctrine it created ushered in the Great Depression. Without regulation, the economy suffered from overproduction and underconsumption. Employment opportunities were constrained as few jobs were created even when consumer demand rose. Mass production came at the expense of craft labor. Tensions between the working and business classes grew sharper as a result. Farmers and miners protested the repossession of farms, the control of company towns, and the costs of essential services—sometimes violently. However, this was not the only social strife brewing in American society. The Republican vision of economic growth benefited from immigration, though it was only welcomed to the extent that subordinated immigrant labor furthered business interests. Ironically, the success of their economic program fueled urbanization and the development of a diverse working class to whom their regressive policies did not appeal.

"Let it be from now on the task of our Party to break foolish traditions. We will break foolish traditions and leave it to the Republican leadership, far more skilled in that art, to break promises," Franklin Roosevelt said in his acceptance speech for the Democratic presidential nomination in 1932.[1] For Roosevelt, jettisoning the old Republican order meant forming a new "economic constitutional order" that embraced an "economic declaration of rights," including the protection of Americans' right to work and enjoy financial security.[2] Now a new order was needed that recognized the complexities of an interconnected national economy that would be built "from the bottom up and not from the top down" to improve the welfare of "the forgotten man at the bottom of the pyramid."[3] Roosevelt argued for expansive government that valued the power of yet unorganized labor, ensured the right to secure employment, and safeguarded individual monetary security as a property right. Unlike the reconstructive moments spearheaded by Jefferson, Jackson, and Lincoln, however, Roosevelt did not subscribe to a stringent view of what the Constitution meant; instead, he emphasized constitutional flexibility.

The New Deal order jettisoned the cramped, formalistic deployment of governmental power that was the mainstay of the Republican order that preceded it. Of primary importance, the New Deal order endorsed an active role for the state whereby the federal government was obligated to provide basic social welfare needs, intervene in social and political crises, and provide public policy resolutions for widespread problems. The Democratic Party regime embraced group-based mobilization and organization to enable a greater assertion of individual rights. The new regime rejected the strict separation of public and private spheres that Republicans adhered to for the old order's purpose of shielding private affairs from governmental intervention and regulation. The coalition would also tether itself to preserving liberal, democratic values in the middle of an era when such values were threatened. Roosevelt made this well known in his first inaugural address, warning Americans "that the only thing we have to fear is fear itself—nameless, unreasoning, unjustified terror which paralyzes needed efforts to convert retreat into advance."[4] Eventually, the onset of world war and a global fight against totalitarianism became a feature of the new Democratic Party regime. Foreign policy would not be an affair of pure self-interest but one where ideology was part of the calculus and democratic principles were key to national security.

THE INTERVENTIONIST STATE

The Democratic order's embrace of robust government intervention in social and economic affairs starkly contrasted with the old Republican order. Democratic majorities enacted sweeping legislation between

1933 and 1934, known as the First New Deal, including the National Industrial Recovery Act, the Securities Act of 1933, the Tennessee Valley Authority Act, the Emergency Banking Relief Act, the Glass-Steagall Act, and the Agricultural Adjustment Act. The Second New Deal saw longer-lasting legislative successes, including the passage of the Social Security Act and the National Labor Relations Act. Roosevelt also created the Works Progress Administration by executive order during this period. Later major legislative successes included the Housing Act of 1937 and the Fair Labor Standards Act of 1938.

Underpinning these sweeping legislative measures was the reigning coalition's conception of what constitutes a public good, which differed vastly from the prior coalition's. The constitutionalism of Lochnerism fixated on line drawing between what policy spaces were of a public versus private nature. The intervention-heavy policies of the New Deal reflected a new understanding that saw greater degrees of interconnectedness in society where Lochnerists saw sets of private acts. Thus, constitutional doctrine constrained the government's power to act unless a measure regulated a monopoly or something deemed intrinsically immoral. This hands-off approach was justified because government regulation was often characterized as a redistribution of wealth, a non–public interest. Consequently, many labor and economic policy prescriptions were off limits for federal and state lawmakers.

The Supreme Court showed some softening of *Lochner*'s edges in the early 1930s. In *Home Building & Loan Association v. Blaisdell*, the Court ruled that a Minnesota law imposing a moratorium on foreclosure remedies met constitutional muster.[5] Taking care to note that the state law did not impermissibly redistribute wealth, the majority reasoned that the law must be judged under a reasonableness standard given the economic emergency that was satisfied.[6] Similarly, the Court upheld the New York Milk Control Board's setting a minimum price for milk sales in *Nebbia v. New York*.[7] There too, the Court was effectively giving its constitutional blessing to a law preserving the status quo—that is, keeping milk producers afloat—rather than redistributing economic power from business interests to workers or consumers. The four most conservative members of the Court dissented in both *Blaisdell* and *Nebbia*.

However, lest it be believed that the Court had turned its back on *Lochner*, the Court struck down part of the New York Milk Control Act of 1933 (the same law at issue in *Nebbia*) for permitting price differentials that the Court determined were intended to create barriers to entry and disadvantaged larger milk dealers.[8] The Court reaffirmed the baseline principle of *Lochner* when it invalidated New York's minimum wage law for women and workers under twenty-one-years-old in *Morehead v. New York ex rel. Tipaldo.*[9]

Even when the Supreme Court signaled openness to greater governmental power as it did in *United States v. Butler*,[10] the majority suggested a limiting principle was necessary to hedge against governmental redistribution of wealth, with only Brandeis, Stone, and Cardozo in dissent. In *Butler*, the Court reasoned that the federal government's taxing power was not limited to Congress's enumerated powers in Article I, Section 8.[11] However, the Court invalidated the Agricultural Adjustment Act, which taxed agricultural product processors to subsidize farmers and reduce crop output, as violating the Tenth Amendment by intruding on the states' authority to regulate agriculture, thus opening the door for Congress to redistribute wealth.[12]

The rigid formalism of the *Butler* decision was endemic to the pre-1937 Hughes Court. The Court struck down controls implemented under the National Industrial Recovery Act's provision allowing the president to regulate the interstate transportation of oil products unlawfully produced under state law.[13] The Court held that the broad grant of authority was a constitutionally impermissible grant of legislative power under the nondelegation doctrine because Congress failed to establish standards to guide how administrative action should be taken to block the transportation of hot oil.[14] In *Carter v. Carter Coal Company* and *A. L. A. Schechter Poultry Corp. v. United States*, in order to prevent the federal government from regulating industry, the Court doubled down on a tradition of tortured commerce-clause readings that parsed out the production of goods from interstate commerce and applied granular analyses of local, individual commercial transactions that ignored chains of interstate transactions.[15] The Court's resistance to New Deal legislation was deeply rooted in the old order's turn-of-the-century extreme formalism, which worked to keep business safe from the ambit of the federal government's regulatory power.[16]

The Supreme Court was on course to become a vestigial organ because of the stickiness of free labor ideology until 1937, when it abruptly reversed course, upholding the crowning legislative achievements of the Second New Deal. After Roosevelt's landslide election in 1932; the Democrats' performance in the 1934 congressional elections, which yielded expanded congressional majorities; and the Democratic Party's dominance with Roosevelt's reelection in the 1936 presidential cycle, the Court faced a crisis of Marshallian proportions. The Court could continue to obstruct liberals in the coordinate branches and expose itself to political retribution in the wake of repeated, sweeping defeats for conservatives, or the Court could acquiesce to the new political order and bring constitutional doctrine in line with it. As it was in *Marbury*, so it was in *West Coast Hotel*. The Court folded, 5–4, upholding a Washington state minimum wage law.

Justice Owen Roberts held a decisive vote in the Court's 5–4 decisions against liberal initiatives in *Morehead* and *Carter Coal* and in decisions invalidating laws providing for railroad worker pensions[17] and federal bankruptcy relief for municipalities and state political subdivisions.[18] In response to Roosevelt's blowout reelection in 1936 and the ratcheting up of political pressure from the Democratic coalition, Roberts made a sharp, though brief, jurisprudential turn left. In a series of 5–4 decisions starting with *West Coast Parrish*, the Supreme Court upheld the National Labor Relations Act of 1935[19] and the Social Security Act of 1935's unemployment insurance protections.[20] With five fresh Roosevelt appointees added to the Court, the Fair Labor Standards Act of 1938 was unanimously deemed a valid exercise of the federal government's regulatory powers under the commerce clause.[21]

The binary formalism of commerce-clause jurisprudence, which parsed commerce from manufacturing, things that had a direct effect on commerce from things that merely had an indirect effect, and interstate transactions from local transactions, insulated business from the unfriendly hand of the federal government. The doctrine of binary oppositions at the heart of the old order's constitutional brand was anathema to the Democratic order's deemphasizing of formalism and rejection of narrow conceptions of the public good that failed to appreciate the interconnectedness of modern society. Society's interconnectedness required breaking down the distinctions between what was once divided up into private and public, and the aggregation principle—the idea that individual actors' seemingly isolated acts were actually interconnected—was adopted in commerce-clause cases like *Wickard v. Fillburn*, *Katzenbach v. McClung*, and *Daniel v. Paul*.[22] Constitutional doctrine was less concerned with whether any actor's conduct individually had a substantial effect on interstate commerce, thus subjecting them to federal regulation, but rather whether the effect of similarly situated parties in total had a discernible impact on interstate commerce. And just as the Court rejected the dual classification system in the commerce-clause arena, the Court similarly turned away from the idea that the federal government could not impose taxes to regulate by penalty[23] and expanded the federal government's taxation power.[24]

GROUP RECOGNITION, ORGANIZATION, AND INDIVIDUAL RIGHTS

A tenant of New Deal politics was the idea that group power enhanced individual rights. The government, which had previously been quiescent on providing a legal apparatus for harnessing the power of mass organization, had to affirmatively provide vehicles in statutory law and the constitutional space to recognize groups and enable individuals to organize without veering off into central planning. Part and parcel of this new governmental aim was that things the old regime saw as private affairs were now deemed part of the public interest. The first manifestation of this idea in New Deal policy was union rights. The federal government needed to inject democracy into an industrial world.

The early roots of the right to organize grew out of the Norris-LaGuardia Act of 1932, which declared that each worker should "have full freedom of association, self-organization, and designation of representatives of his own choosing . . . for the purpose of collective bargaining or other mutual aid or protection"[25]—rights that were then affirmatively codified in the National Industrial Recovery Act in 1933.[26] Section 7(a) of the NIRA laid down the basic principle of the right to organize, which was subsequently expounded upon by regulations promulgated by the National Labor Relations Board:

(1) That employees shall have the right to organize and bargain collectively through representatives of their own choosing and shall be free from the interference, restraint, or coercion of employers of labor, or their agents, in the designation of such representatives or in self-organization for the purposes of collective bargaining or other mutual aid or protection;

(2) That no employee and no one seeking employment shall be required as a condition of employment to join any company union or to refrain from joining, organizing, or assisting a labor organization of his own choosing; and

(3) That employers shall comply with the maximum hours of labor, minimum rates of pay and other conditions of employment, approved or prescribed by the President.[27]

Federal labor law continued to develop over the next twenty-six years. In 1935, Congress passed the National Labor Relations Act. The

NLRA (commonly known as the Wagner Act) banned employers from interfering with organizing employees and laid down the parameters within which employers had to live while bargaining with unions. The Wagner Act was critical for state building under the New Deal order as it fundamentally restructured the relationship between the government and workers. A coalition of Republicans and conservative Democrats on an override of President Truman's veto amended federal labor law, enacting the Taft-Hartley Act, which restrained unions from engaging in certain types of strikes, proscribed coercive organizing tactics, permitted the adoption of state right-to-work laws, and authorized injunctions to enjoin strikes that endangered public health or national security. In 1959, Congress passed the Landrum-Griffin Act, which provided greater protections for individual labor union members by enshrining democratic norms in unions' internal operations, including the right to a secret ballot and free speech rights.[28]

Constitutional jurisprudence during the New Deal era also embraced for the first time a right to association as an outgrowth of the right to organize. The initial articulation of the principle came down from the Court in 1937 in *DeJong v. Oregon*, where the justices ruled that the "holding of meetings for peaceable political action cannot be proscribed" by states.[29] In *Thomas v. Collins*, the Supreme Court invalidated a Texas statute that mandated union officials secure an official organizer's card from the Texas Secretary of State before soliciting workers to join their organizations.[30] In distilling the reasons why the Texas law was noxious to constitutional values, the Court linked association and organization as a right protected under the Constitution that was necessary for individuals to work and improve their station:

> As a matter of principle a requirement of registration in order to make a public speech would seem generally incompatible with an exercise of the rights of free speech and free assembly. Lawful public assemblies, involving no element of grave and immediate danger to an interest the state is entitled to protect, are not instruments of harm which require previous identification of the speakers. And the right either of workmen or of unions under these conditions to assemble and discuss their own affairs is as fully protected by the Constitution as the right of businessmen, farmers, educators, political party members or others to assemble and discuss their affairs and to enlist the support of others.[31]

The doctrinal evolution set in motion in *DeJong* and *Collins* undergirded a "social democratic" conception of the freedom to associate that understood the interactive effect of free speech values and civil rights. In some measure, they constitutionalized the 1936 Democratic Convention speech given by Roosevelt in which the president explained how the marvels of industrialization and modernization corrupted American democratic values and corroded individual rights by placing power in the few rather than the many:

> Since [the American Revolution] man's inventive genius released new forces in our land which reordered the lives of our people. The age of machinery, of railroads; of steam and electricity; the telegraph and the radio; mass production, mass distribution—all of these combined to bring forward a new civilization and with it a new problem for those who sought to remain free.
>
> For out of this modern civilization economic royalists carved new dynasties. New kingdoms were built upon concentration of control over material things. Through new uses of corporations, banks and securities, new machinery of industry and agriculture, of labor and capital—all undreamed of by the fathers—the whole structure of modern life was impressed into this royal service.[32]

For Roosevelt, the old order's division of private and public affairs insulated the inequitable distribution of power, which the public rejected by defeating Herbert Hoover in 1932 and legislators rejected by passing popular legislation that protected the right to organize:

> Against economic tyranny such as this, the American citizen could appeal only to the organized power of Government. The collapse of 1929 showed up the despotism for what it was. The election of 1932 was the people's mandate to end it. Under that mandate it is being ended.
>
> The royalists of the economic order have conceded that political freedom was the business of the Government, but they have maintained that economic slavery was nobody's business. They granted that the Government could protect the citizen in his right to vote, but they denied that the Government could do anything to protect the citizen in his right to work and his right to live.[33]

The ideological underpinnings of the prolabor legal regime that emerged in the first years of Roosevelt's tenure and that was later proselytized in the 1936 Democratic Convention foreshadowed doctrinal developments that were cornerstones of constitutional jurisprudence during the last three decades of the New Deal coalition: first, that the liberty interest in organized labor outweighed constitutional claims challenging pro-union laws[34] and second, that there is a liberty interest based in the due process clause that secured a right to group membership—a right to association that was first expressly recognized by the Supreme Court in NAACP v. Alabama.[35] Citing DeJong and Collins, the Court quashed an Alabama trial court's contempt order against the NAACP for refusing to provide a membership list as required under state law: "Effective advocacy of both public and private points of view, particularly controversial ones, is undeniably enhanced by group association, as this Court has more than once recognized by remarking upon the close nexus between the freedoms of speech and assembly."[36] The Court invalidated similar mandatory production and disclosure laws in *Bates v. City of Little Rock*[37] and *Shelton v. Tucker*.[38]

AMERICAN LIBERALISM AND CIVIL RIGHTS

While the Supreme Court's jurisprudence of the 1950s and 1960s, which embraced civil rights and racial liberalism, were heroic constitutional developments that made American law more just, these rights must also be understood through the lens of realpolitik. Civil rights were fundamental to state building for the Democratic Party in the New Deal era, and the federal judiciary was a coalitional partner in that undertaking.

The Roosevelt and Truman administrations favored civil rights more than any presidential administration since Reconstruction. However, the New Deal coalition's national-level approach to expanding civil rights for Black Americans was tepid, resulting from Democratic leadership's fears that accelerating attacks on Jim Crow and other forms of private racial discrimination would peel off Southern Democrats from the Democratic Party fold. The most notorious example was FDR's refusal to support federal anti-lynching legislation publicly. Notwithstanding the Party's balancing act, which stayed rapid progress on racial equality in the early 1930s, the Democratic order's ideological tenets were a natural home for a civil rights movement. The regime's focus on radical democracy fit with the broader goals of the civil rights movement, as evidenced by some of the early progress secured at the Supreme Court in the white primary cases, most notably *Smith v. Allwright*. The case for civil rights as critically needed for a healthy democracy at home and for the credible exportation of democratic values abroad materialized as a theme in the coalition program. Democrats' belief that organized interests were essential for harnessing political rights also made the civil rights movement an easy fit within a coalition in which "Blacks were conceived as an ethnic interest group rather than one side of a racialized social division."[39]

A careful reading of the New Deal coalition's treatment of race is complicated (and crucial) because much of the New Deal's evolution on racial equality and civil rights is misunderstood. The focus on federal action at the expense of greater attention to more local developments and misapprehension about the extent of Southern Democrats' role in forming the coalition's identity have obscured some key aspects of what it meant to be a New Dealer. Consequently, the federal judiciary's early cases addressing race discrimination have been wrongly described as courts applying judicial review in a muscularly countermajoritarian fashion.

The New Deal coalition contained multitudes on the question of race. Civil rights were not part of the 1932 Roosevelt campaign. Even the New Deal's formative years between 1933 and 1935 did not produce a tight-knit connection between American liberalism and racial equality. Indeed, civil rights concerns were relegated to the back burner. A constellation of stars aligned to dislodge the coalition from its earlier lukewarm relationship to progressive racial politics: the movement of Black voters towards Democrats in the mid-1930s, the emergence of pro–civil rights labor forces that became a cornerstone of the Democratic Party constituency, and the coalition's underlying ideological commitments to group organization and radical democracy. The Supreme Court's increasingly aggressive disposition against racial discrimination in the 1940s and early 1950s should be read within this context as a coextensive outgrowth of the coalition that made it.

The coalition's interventionist inclinations were also critical for the advancements of racial equality, though gravely imperfect and sometimes actively destructive for Black Americans. This is the paradox of the New Deal for civil rights and racial equality. The Works Progress Administration, which provided jobs for millions of Americans between 1935 and 1939, employed some 350,000 Black Americans. Black Americans were underrepresented in terms of economic need but were employed at rates double their share of the national population. A similar pattern unfolded within the Civilian Conservation Corps, which provided work improving public lands for single jobless men between the ages of eighteen and twenty-five. The Tennessee Valley Authority, which provided a substantial number of jobs to Black workers, nevertheless underpaid those workers relative to their white counterparts and failed to offer housing on equal terms.

Long-term-oriented social safety programs also failed in their implementation. When Congress passed the Social Security Act in 1935, agricultural workers and domestic workers were excluded from the law's old-age insurance and unemployment insurance benefits, disproportionately harming Black workers. Truman pushed for the expansion of

Social Security as part of his administration's fair deal agenda. Congress failed to act on Truman's proposal to widen Social Security's footprint during Truman's time in office. However, legislation to expand Social Security to cover farmers, domestic workers, state and local employees, among others, later received near-universal support in Congress and was signed by President Eisenhower in 1954. Federal housing policy was decentralized to subordinate it to localized interests, which stymied any promise of racial progress, with disastrous consequences for entrenching racial inequality. Similar decentralization resulted in the discriminatory administration of G.I. benefits under the Servicemen's Readjustment Act of 1944. As historian Eric Rauchway summed up New Deal programming and race, "If the New Deal's efforts to assist black Americans were halting and small and always coupled with some slight or setback, they nevertheless existed . . . The inequitably distributed benefits of the New Deal nevertheless did, as the Roosevelt campaign had promised in 1932, go principally to poor and needy people, among whom black Americans were numerous."[40]

Though slow in the coming, a few key players in the federal government tackled racial discrimination in employment, housing, and federal programming, with varying degrees of success. In 1933, Roosevelt's interior secretary, Harold Ickes, instituted a nondiscrimination policy for all Public Works Administration projects and promulgated racial quotas for Public Works Administration contractors. Roosevelt issued an executive order in 1935 barring discrimination against workers qualified for Work Progress Administration jobs "on any grounds whatsoever."[41] Labor Secretary Frances Perkins took various progressive actions to advance racial equality. She even threatened Georgia governor Eugene Talmadge with suspending federal programming in the state unless he permitted Black participation. Future secretary of Housing and Urban Development Robert Weaver, who was part of the Public Works Administration until the Housing Act of 1937, created the Public Housing Administration as a permanent, free-standing subdivision of the Department of the Interior in 1937 and imported similar quota systems. At the behest of William J. Trent Jr., who argued that segregated national park facilities constituted "a contradiction in democratic government," federal officials began eroding racial discrimination at national parks, which culminated in the end of segregated park facilities in 1942.[42] In 1940, the Civil Service stopped requiring job applicant photographs, which were used to discriminate in federal employment. As New Deal scholar William Leuchtenburg described it, while some of them were "minimally enforced," the racial equality measures put into place by prominent New Dealers within the Roosevelt administration "gave the white South an indication of a new attitude in Washington."[43]

Without minimizing the value of these developments, racial liberalism needed more than one-off victories to become anchored in the New Deal Coalition. Beginning in the 1930s, Northern Democrats on the state and local level and organized labor—not Democrats in Washington—centered racial liberalism in the heart of the New Deal. This emerging trend punctuated party infighting between New Deal progressives and Southern reactionaries.[44] In 1935, the Congress of Industrial Organizations (CIO) formed a federation of industrial unions to help organize unskilled laborers. Unlike the American Federation of Labor's interests, which represented workers whose skill base constituted a barrier to entry, the CIO was a strong supporter of Black civil rights partially because it needed the support of Black workers who could otherwise easily serve as strikebreakers. The CIO, which juxtaposed civil rights as a democratic value to fascism, became the most significant force in supporting Northern Democrats and a major supporter of the New Deal and FDR's efforts to oust conservatives from the Democratic Party in 1937 and 1938. That effort punctuated the coalition's development, leading to a perception that the true New Deal believers were liberals fighting against Southern reactionaries.

However, the 1940s brought some significant federal policy changes, which helped to cement the civil rights movement's home in the New Deal coalition. Two catalyzing dynamics, rooted in World War II, contributed to the mainstreaming of racial liberalism in the dominant coalition. First, the influence of Black voters continued to expand, and second, given the totalitarian ideologies the United States was fighting abroad, the war created the opportunity to critique the treatment African Americans received at home. As one early commentator assessed, the "ideological nature of the war" pitted fascism against American democracy, challenging the tenability of permitting discriminatory practices to continue and necessitating public policy "more consistent with the tenets of American democracy."[45]

In 1941, Roosevelt issued Executive Order 8802, banning "discrimination in the employment of workers in defense industries or government because of race, creed, color, or national origin."[46] Roosevelt established the Fair Employment Practices Committee to investigate discrimination claims, though it lacked enforcement power. In 1946, Truman established the President's Committee on Civil Rights by Executive

Order 9808 to investigate the state of civil rights and make recommendations to secure them. The committee's report, issued in 1947, condemned Jim Crow by calling for "[t]he elimination of segregation, based on race, color, creed, or national origin, from American life" and concluded that "[t]here is no adequate defense of segregation."[47]

The committee also recommended that the Department of Justice take a more proactive role in civil rights litigation, including submitting "briefs amicus curiae in private litigation where important issues of civil rights law are being determined."[48] The following day, the Department of Justice decided to participate in *Shelley v. Kraemer* as an amicus supporting the NAACP, the first time the federal government voluntarily waded into civil rights litigation. The United States' brief, leaning into the New Deal's emphasis on radical democracy and parroting Truman's speech earlier in 1947 to the NAACP, urged the Court in *Shelley* to block judicial enforcement of racially restrictive covenants on property sales because they could not "be reconciled with the spirit of mutual tolerance and respect for the dignity and rights of the individual which give vitality to our democratic way of life."[49]

The 1948 Democratic Party platform fully embraced civil rights for the first time, including language that said: "The Democratic Party commits itself to continuing its efforts to eradicate all racial, religious and economic discrimination. We again state our belief that racial and religious minorities must have the right to live, the right to work, the right to vote, the full and equal protection of the laws, on a basis of equality with all citizens as guaranteed by the Constitution."[50] In the wake of the Committee on Civil Rights recommendations and just days after the Democratic Party Convention and the addition of a civil rights plank to the Party's platform, President Truman signed Executive Order 9980 and Executive Order 9981. The orders created an antidiscrimination regime for federal employees and desegregating the military, respectively. Notably, Truman's desegregation order tapped into the theme of radical democracy, proclaiming that nondiscrimination in the nation's military was necessary to maintain the "highest standards of democracy."[51] Truman himself was indicative of how racial equality was an ever important identity marker for American liberalism. Truman, while Roosevelt's running mate, proclaimed that "I am a liberal, as proved time and again by my record in the Senate, and I dare anyone to challenge these facts. I am for a permanent FEPC. I am for a Federal law abolishing the poll tax. I am for a Federal anti-lynching law."[52] As Truman's earlier statement and presidential policy positions show, racial liberalism's seedlings during the Roosevelt years took root during the mid-1940s and early 1950s.

It is essential to step away from the Democratic Party's national leadership and drill down into state-level party development in the 1940s to understand the relationship between Democrats' commitment to racial equality and the coalition's ideological maturation. The Democratic Party's economic liberalism continued to bring Black voters into the fold, generating a robust coalition of civil rights supporters in the North that included union workers, Jews, white urban elites, and Black constituents. As this coalition of voters began to capture the state party apparatuses outside the South, racial equality became more prominent in state party platforms, and state lawmakers placed civil rights on the legislative agenda. National Democratic Party officials in the 1960s, who have been long hailed as leading the coalition on civil rights, in reality were negotiating the path forward for the core of the coalition's already established appetite for racial liberalism, which culminated in federal laws, including the Civil Rights Act of 1964, the Voting Rights Act of 1965, and the Fair Housing Act of 1968.[53]

Equality as a democratic value was a major theme in Northern New Dealers' state agendas in the 1940s and 1950s. In 1943, legislators in Michigan proposed the first modern antidiscrimination law in employment. As David Freeman Engstrom has noted, such a legislative initiative was possible because of the new order's ideological tenets: the Michigan bill "applied to private acts of discrimination—an unthinkable intrusion into the principle of liberty of contract that had prevailed during the Lochner era just one decade earlier."[54] The Michigan bill was followed by several legislative proposals in more than twenty state legislatures and multiple proposals in Congress in 1945. Notably, support for these measures was framed as necessary to advance and preserve American democracy.[55] In Northern states where employment antidiscrimination laws were adopted, liberal Democrats drove the legislative bus and Republicans lagged in their support. Elsewhere there were failures. In 1946, California voters considered a proposition that would have prohibited employment discrimination because of an individual's race, religion, color, national origin, or ancestry,[56] though it was met with defeat, as were so many of the bills introduced in state legislatures.

In 1940, the Court faced the question of whether nonviolent forms of police coercion violated Black defendants' due process rights when the police and community at large were whipped into a racist frenzy to solve a white man's murder. Writing for a unanimous Court in *Chambers v.*

Florida, Hugo Black tapped into the theme of radical democracy, alluding to the dangers of antiminority prejudice in collapsed European democracies:

> Today, as in ages past, we are not without tragic proof that the exalted power of some governments to punish manufactured crime dictatorially is the handmaid of tyranny. Under our constitutional system, courts stand against any winds that blow as havens of refuge for those who might otherwise suffer because they are helpless, weak, outnumbered, or because they are non-conforming victims of prejudice and public excitement. Due process of law, preserved for all by our Constitution, commands that no such practice as that disclosed by this record shall send any accused to his death. No higher duty, no more solemn responsibility, rests upon this Court, than that of translating into living law and maintaining this constitutional shield deliberately planned and inscribed for the benefit of every human being subject to our Constitution—of whatever race, creed or persuasion.[57]

The Court articulated the idea that intentional discrimination against racial groups was anathema to democratic ideals and theorized that the application of strict scrutiny in race discrimination claims was appropriate in the wartime cases *Hirabayashi v. United States* and *Korematsu v. United States*.[58] Of course, the Court's principles in the Japanese internment cases rang hollow given the Court's decisions to uphold racist wartime measures that restricted Japanese-Americans' freedom of movement as exigencies of military necessity. The colossal damage inflicted by *Hirabayashi* and *Korematsu* was blunted only by the Court's pressuring the Roosevelt administration to end race-based detentions of loyal citizens in *Ex parte Endo*, a nonconstitutional decision that rejected racial stereotypes as a lawful basis for the detention of loyal citizens.[59]

In the years following the exclusion cases, the Court's jurisprudence gingerly winnowed out racially discriminatory laws, favoring an as-applied challenge to California's anti-Japanese Alien Land Act in *Oyama v. California*, where the state denied an American citizen, Fred Oyama, property purchased in his name by his noncitizen father[60] and striking down California's anti-Japanese fishing ban in *Takahashi v. Fish and Game Commission* as impermissibly frustrating federal immigration power while issuing a restrained acknowledgment of the racial animus at play.[61] Randall Kennedy has remarked that *Oyama* reached the correct decision but lacked a "broader educative force."[62] So too with *Takahashi* in the sense that the Court was hesitant to engage in a full frontal attack on the racial discrimination motivating California law—

which Justice Frank Murphy pointed out in his *Takahashi* concurrence.[63] At the same time that the Court unwound racial discrimination against people of Japanese ancestry, the Court took a more aggressive posture against racially segregated educational institutions.[64] In a sense, the justices were negotiating within constitutional and statutory decisions how to combat race discrimination in a manner parallel to the way that the Democratic coalition was navigating the party's civil rights agenda. By the time the Supreme Court handed down its anti–school segregation decision in *Brown v. Board of Education* the cause of racial equality as a necessary condition for democracy had already found itself at the core of American liberalism and was concurrently evolving in jurisprudence.[65]

RADICAL DEMOCRACY

Constitutional flexibility, an idea espoused by Roosevelt, was a potentially dangerous proposition in an era broiling with antidemocratic sentiments. And the use of executive authority was key to undoing the economic stagnation that plagued the nation. Pliable constitutionalism, however, ran the risk of unchecked power, which was a precarious disposition to hold in light of 1930s world affairs. Indeed, many European democracies fell victim to the perils of totalitarianism in the 1930s; as Felix Frankfurter observed, "Epitaphs for democracy are the fashion of the day."[66]

American democracy was not without domestic critics either. Pundits called for soft presidential dictatorial powers and congressional bypasses so that the executive could wrestle the nation out of economic calamity. Recent experience with a Congress divided closely along party lines did not make matters easier. Indeed, Hoover tussled with Congress between 1931 and 1932 while showing signs of openness to innovations that departed with traditional Republican policy positions, but he remained unwilling to repudiate the Republican order. However, even as the Great Depression deepened, Congress failed to respond in the lame duck session between Herbert Hoover's defeat in November 1932 and Roosevelt's inauguration in March 1933, further imperiling the public's trust in democratic institutions. Roosevelt's first Inaugural Address warning about the danger of fearing "fear itself" was, of course, a warning about the dangers of inaction, which could cause the nation to slide into a state sympathetic to dictatorial power and threaten democratic institutions and values. Unlike the tide of demagoguery seen elsewhere, of Americans, Roosevelt proclaimed, "We do not distrust the future of essential democracy."[67]

But even as some of the New Deal's landmark accomplishments were enacted, fears about the potential for economic anxiety and social unrest to upend liberal democracy in the United States simmered. University of North Carolina at Chapel Hill sociology professor Howard Odum, weary of regional economic disparities and inequality, wrote in 1935 that the United States was not immune from the kinds of totalitarian impulses that swept the European continent. Odum warned that even in America the "combination of demagogic leadership and mass social pathology . . . may easily result in anything but orderly transitional democracy."[68] A year later, Joseph P. Kennedy echoed Odum's observation. In the wake of America being "catapulted" into "an economic morass," Kennedy suggested that the harsh reality remained that "[d]emocracy will not be safe for this country unless we constructively deal with causes of dictatorships."[69] Indeed, as late as 1938, Roosevelt made the case that the New Deal's economic plan was also a means of protecting democracy itself.

Roosevelt issued dire warnings to Congress about the perils of Fascism in an April 1938 speech after weeks of press coverage about the tide of illiberalism spreading across Europe. Reports splashed the pages of the *New York Times* with news about Nazi Germany's discrimination against Jews, demands that Christian pastors submit to the Nazi regime, and censorship of literary materials deemed racially impure. A rise in anti-Semitism was reported in Greece at the same time as Fascists threatened stability in Romania. In Russia, Stalin worked to consolidate power as the Soviets initiated a purge of the religious faithful.

Four days before Roosevelt's April 1938 speech to Congress and in the midst of global turmoil, the New Deal order's central focus on preserving democracy against the dangers of illiberal regimes through the exercise of governmental economic regulatory power was articulated in constitutional jurisprudence. In *United States v. Carolene Products,* the Supreme Court laid the path for the future of equal-protection jurisprudence. In a challenge to a federal law regulating the sale of filled milk, the Court laid down the principle that "legislation affecting ordinary commercial transactions is not to be pronounced unconstitutional unless in the light of the facts made known or generally assumed it is of such a character as to preclude the assumption that it rests upon some rational basis within the knowledge and experience of the legislators."[70] This idea was reiterated in 1955 in *Williamson v. Lee Optical* where the Court, in contrast to earlier decisions from the Lochner era, endorsed the power of states to similarly regulate ordinary commercial transactions provided the legislature had a rational basis.[71]

The Court's pronouncement reaffirmed a core tenet of the New Deal coalition—that the government's power to regulate commerce, industry, labor, and public health were essential for the preservation of democracy. In this sense, *Lochner* and its ideological underpinnings from the old Republican order were understood to pose a danger to democracy. At the same time, the Court provided a constitutional rebuke to the threat to liberal democratic values brooding across the Atlantic. In the famous footnote four, the *Carolene Products* decision signaled that unlike ordinary economic regulations, heightened judicial scrutiny was warranted where a law restricted the civil liberties enumerated in the Bill of Rights, discrimination against "discrete and insular minorities" was present, laws infringed on the right to vote, or extraordinary burdens threatened an open and fair political process.[72]

Footnote four presaged a divorce from the Republican order's marriage to formalistic constitutionalism with respect to the state action doctrine. In 1941, the Court triggered a path toward greater voting rights protections and the New Deal order's undermining of Southern authoritarian enclaves. In the 1920s and early 1930s, the Court invalidated laws in Texas that prohibited Black participation in the Democratic Party primary or permitted political parties to exclude Blacks from voting in primaries. The Court held in *Nixon v. Herndon* and *Nixon v. Condon*, respectively, that the mandatory exclusion law constituted state action in violation of the Fourteenth Amendment and the delegation of exclusion authority similarly was state action in violation of the Fourteenth and Fifteenth Amendments.[73] However, the Court's old-order formalism was disastrous for Black voters in *Grovey v. Townsend*.[74] There, the Supreme Court held that the Texas legislature's decision to recede from political party affairs and defer to party convention decision-making about party nominations was not state action.[75] Indeed, no constitutional problem existed, notwithstanding the fact that the Democratic Party's selection process was the de facto general election.

The Court's about-face in 1944 in *Smith v. Allwright* struck at the heart of white supremacy in the South. Because party primaries were designated by the state as a vehicle for candidates to secure their names on the ballot, the Court held that Texas had sufficiently engaged in state action and, thus, party-run primaries needed to meet constitutional muster.[76] The days of lawfully denying Black participation in Democratic Party primaries were over. The decision in *Smith v. Allwright* was possible because of the rejection of rigid, hyperformalist constitutionalism that drew more restrictive delineations between the private and public spheres. The Court, however, also noted the importance of eliminating white primaries as a democratic value:

> The United States is a constitutional democracy. Its organic law grants to all citizens a right to participate in the choice of elected officials without restriction by any state because of race. This grant to the people of the opportunity for choice is not to be nullified by a state through casting its electoral process in a form which permits a private organization to practice racial discrimination in the election. Constitutional rights would be of little value if they could be thus indirectly denied.[77]

The path set off by the white primary decision led to a greater infusion of democratic norms as part of the New Deal constitutional tradition. In 1960, the Supreme Court declared that racially motivated forms of gerrymandering violated the Fourteenth and Fifteenth Amendments.[78] In 1966, the Court struck down state poll taxes in *Harper v. Virginia State Board of Elections*, overruling a relic of the Hughes Court that upheld the ability of states to impose costs on voting.[79] The Court ended the practice of the county unit system in Georgia, which weighed primary results in rural counties heavier than urban counties to prevent city voters from outvoting the rest of the state. In *Gray v. Sanders*, the Court laid down the principle of one person, one vote: "The conception of political equality from the Declaration of Independence, to Lincoln's Gettysburg Address, to the Fifteenth, Seventeenth, and Nineteenth Amendments can mean only one thing—one person, one vote."[80] The Court applied that principle to state legislative districts in Reynolds v. Sims.[81] Carrying on the theme from *Smith v. Allwright*, the Court explained vote dilution was an affront to democratic values:

> The right to vote freely for the candidate of one's choice is of the essence of a democratic society, and any restrictions on that right strike at the heart of representative government. And the right of suffrage can be denied by a debasement or dilution of the weight of a citizen's vote just as effectively as by wholly prohibiting the free exercise of the franchise.[82]

The New Deal coalition's support for an interventionist state, radical democracy, and the attendant decay of discrete spheres of public and private domains was also reflected in the jurisprudential evolution of the state action doctrine. The Supreme Court's decision in *Newberry v. United States* embodied the old regime's hardline differentiation between public and private functions.[83] There, the Court rejected Congress's purported constitutional authority to regulate primary contests, striking down the 1911 amendments to the Federal Corrupt Practices Act's campaign-expenditure limits as it applied to candidates before the general election because Congress's power stopped short of regulating non–state actors, and partisan primaries were in no way dispositive of general election results.[84]

The Court in *Newberry* chose formalism over functionalism, which was a core criticism FDR and his allies lodged against Hoover and the old regime. The state action doctrine in the New Deal period was not so constrained. Rather, the Supreme Court took a functionalist turn by finding state action nexuses that formalism ignored, justifying judicial interventionism in affairs now declared as public. The Court's notable first pivot toward functionalism was in *United States v. Classic*, where the Court rejected *Newberry*'s rule that Congress's election-clause powers fell short of reaching primaries, reasoning that Congress could regulate partisan primaries because they are fundamental to the election process.[85] Born out of a commitment to radical democracy, the Court expanded on this fundamentality principle, finding state action where private constraints on voting preferences imperiled democracy.[86]

The coalition's formative years also informed constitutional law concerning the separation of powers. New Dealers watched the decay of free societies abroad because of an attrition of power from legislative institutions to executive leaders turned dictators. Consequently, fears of institutional rot dominated many policy debates throughout the mid-1930s. Concerns about the separation of powers comprised a theme used by opponents of Roosevelt's court-packing plan. In 1937, the House dealt what William Leuchtenburg described as "the worst rebuff Roosevelt was ever to suffer . . . " when, citing fears of too much executive power, members rejected legislation authorizing the president to reorganize executive agencies to promote efficiency.[87] Even modern administrative law grew out of New Dealers' weariness. Anti-totalitarianism was a major driving force behind the Administrative Procedures Act, which prescribes processes and procedures for administrative agencies.

The era's heightened concerns about the slow creep of authoritarianism manifested in constitutional law in 1952 after President Harry Truman seized steel mills by executive order in the wake of a labor dispute that threatened national steel production. Citing steel manufacturing as indispensable for national security and the prosecution of the Korean War, the government argued that Truman's executive order was a lawful exercise of the president's Article II powers as commander-in-chief. The Supreme Court rejected Truman's steel seizure in *Youngstown Sheet &*

Tube v. Sawyer.[88] The Court's decision in *Youngstown* was an out-growth of the New Dealer apprehension about going down the slippery slope of dictatorial power, something specifically noted in concurring opinions by Justice Robert Jackson[89] and Justice Felix Frankfurter.[90]

The commitment to radical democracy also informed the federal government's urging to transform the state action doctrine in the Court's landmark decision in *Shelley v. Kramer*, where the Court held it was impermissible under the Fourteenth Amendment for courts to enforce racially restrictive property covenants between private parties.[91] The Court similarly held that where states were entangled with discriminatory actors, a sufficient link could be established to impose constitutional limits on private action.[92] In *Marsh v. Alabama*, the Court held that constitutional rights applied in privately owned company towns that functionally served the same public purpose as any other municipal corporation and that clearing the way for the free marketplace of ideas in places that served a public function was necessary for a healthy democratic society:

> Many people in the United States live in company-owned towns. These people, just as residents of municipalities, are free citizens of their State and country. Just as all other citizens they must make decisions which affect the welfare of community and nation. To act as good citizens they must be informed. In order to enable them to be properly informed their information must be uncensored. There is no more reason for depriving these people of the liberties guaranteed by the First and Fourteenth Amendments than there is for curtailing these freedoms with respect to any other citizen.[93]

The short-lived peak of the Court's expansive approach to state action came in 1968, when the justices held that the principle in *Marsh* was applicable to a privately owned suburban shopping mall. Whereas in *Marsh*, the Court determined a company town essentially served the same function as a state-created municipality, in *Amalgamated Food Employees Union v. Logan Valley Plaza*, the Supreme Court reasoned that shopping centers serve as a kind of town square. Thus, when protesters arrived on shopping center property to protest one of the stores onsite, the mall owners could not petition the courts to keep peaceful protesters from mall property and impede protesters' free expression because the area was generally open to the public.[94]

CONCLUSION

New Deal constitutionalism placed a premium on approaching government with a sense of pragmatism, because it held that government's capacity to adapt and respond to the public need was also indispensable for preserving democracy. This meant relaxing the constraints on government power and reconceptualizing the meaning of public versus private matters. New Dealers professed that political mobilization was a vehicle for the preservation of rights and took measures to enhance the organizing capacity of workers. This idea metamorphized into constitutional doctrine, which shielded various political activities. To understand the New Deal order's constitutionalism, one must understand that the coalition's formative years were imbued with a concern for preserving and advancing democracy. Even the prosecution of the Second World War was markedly different because of the partisan regime's ideological predisposition—the war effort was framed not just as an issue of national security for territorial defense or protection of resources but rather as a war about the principled defense of democracy. While modern observers may take that for granted, the ideological nature of the American war experience was not inevitable. Fears of authoritarianism and the defense of democratic institutions' integrity were core to the coalition, setting constitutional law down a path of expanding the franchise and equalizing voting rights. Nevertheless, as with all coalitions, success came at a price for the New Deal order. The democratization of Southern enclaves, dramatic changes in immigration law, and the expansion of civil rights brought a fractured Democratic Party, resentment, and backlash.

CHAPTER 5

The Reagan Revolution and the New Right's Order

THE ORIGINS AND RISE OF MOVEMENT CONSERVATISM

American politics' center of gravity was left of center between 1932 and 1980. The forces of liberalism, dominant in American political thought, did not inhibit Republican victories but produced triangulating GOP presidencies seeking a middle path of policy moderation with a baseline acceptance of the New Deal. The era produced two two-term Republican victories. The administrations of Dwight Eisenhower and Richard Nixon were drawn leftward because of the Overton window that resulted from the New Deal. While decidedly more muted than Democrats, each administration favored an active role for the federal government and rejected foreign policy isolationism. Not all Republicans, however, were so enthusiastic about the party standard-bearers' ideological flavor.

Indeed, Dwight Eisenhower's "middle way" agenda accepted the idea that trade unions provided a net benefit to American society, approved a modern social safety net, lamented the dangers posed by income inequality, and embraced business regulations to "prevent or correct abuses springing from the unregulated practice of a private economy."[1] This is not terribly surprising to careful observers of American political history. Eisenhower, after all, was a preemptive president in the New Deal order. However, his posture angered the hyperconservative wing of the Republican Party, which had rallied around presidential bids made by Senator Robert Taft of Ohio in the 1940s and in the run-up to the 1952 presidential election. Taft and his followers formed the core of what would become movement conservatism. Conservative activists opposed the New Deal, foreign policy interventionism, American involvement in World War II, labor unions, and the burgeoning rights revolution.

Race relations and civil rights emerged as a sticking point for the right-wing Republican Party faithful. In particular, the Eisenhower administration's enforcement of school-desegregation orders in Little Rock, Arkansas, provided conservative hardliners a high-profile vehicle to attack Republican moderation as insufficiently defensive of American values. The civil rights movement was a useful foil. Movement conservatives depicted it as a communist-inspired betrayal of American principles to entice new members into the fold. And from this struggle emerged the first nationally prominent arguments in favor of constitutional originalism from political conservatives—albeit from Democrats prior to the partisan realignment in the years following the 1964 presidential election—who maintained that the Supreme Court erred in *Brown v. Board of Education* because the justices failed to appreciate the original intent, meaning, and historical practice of school segregation at the time of the Fourteenth Amendment's ratification.

Using race as a cleavage issue in the way movement conservatives did was increasingly possible because of the interactive effect of the successes and the particular implementation choices of New Deal order policies. Just as, in the early twentieth century, Republican policy successes opened opportunities for the opposition, here too opponents made gains. Many once impoverished whites now comfortably joined the middle-class ranks, but not all Americans felt the riches of the era uniformly. Indeed, socioeconomic mobility was not enjoyed equally by Black Americans. The racial wealth gap persisted, and thus Black Americans still benefited from robust government intervention, which white voters now looked at with heightened skepticism. Movement conservatives seized on these expansive government interventions as a racially charged cudgel to be used against the New Deal coalition and liberalism within the Republican Party. At the same time, an influx of Northern conservatives moving South due to New Deal programming investments in the region helped put the Democratic South into play for Republicans. Population shifts towards the South and West helped movement conservatism, which flourished with appeals to suburban voters in particular. From this developing strategic position, movement conservatives railed against the New Deal, arguing that the primary role of government should not be egalitarianism but protecting property. In their view, America required a return to free-market capitalism, elite-driven politics (radical democracy was overrated and organized labor was ill-advised), traditional morality, and religious dedication.

The movement conservative wing was kept at bay during the 1950s and early 1960s. However, they made significant inroads in 1964 by securing one of their own, Arizona senator Barry Goldwater, for the 1964 Republican presidential nomination over the moderate governor Nelson Rockefeller of New York. Goldwater, arguing that the nation suffered from "moral decline and drift,"[2] tapped into the movement conservative ethos, campaigning on the idea that the vast federal bureaucracy and "cancerous growth" of the federal government more generally threatened Americans' control of their own destiny.[3] The average voter was "in danger of becoming the forgotten man;" instead, Goldwater insisted, "the private man" should displace the New Deal bureaucrat and reclaim his place "as the center of the family, the state, and as the prime mover and molder of the future."[4] In a rejection of Eisenhower's "middle way," Goldwater famously pronounced in his nomination acceptance speech that "extremism in the defense of liberty is no vice . . . [and] moderation in the pursuit of justice is no virtue."[5]

Goldwater's sharp turn right and unvarnished language in defense of uncompromising conservative positions did not sit well with the American public or liberal Republicans. Indeed, the New York Times reported that the speech "aroused a widespread disquiet in the nation" and "cost Mr. Goldwater the support of several leading liberal Republicans."[6] Goldwater's hardline messaging and hostile positions towards civil rights and the social safety net did curry favor with voters in the South, which handed him nearly all of his Electoral College votes (from Alabama, Georgia, Louisiana, Mississippi, and South Carolina; he also won Arizona). But Lyndon Johnson routed Goldwater in the popular vote too, winning 61.1 percent to 38.5 percent.

The slow dissolution of the Solid South indicated that structural changes that could create openings for Republican success after 1964 were on the horizon. Nonetheless, Richard Nixon's successful election strategy in 1968 did not challenge the fundamentals of the American electorate. Nixon understood that liberalism remained popular and that New Deal Democrats would have to fall victim to their success before a substantially different, more conservative vision for government might gain currency with the public. Yet, in the wake of tumultuous years in 1967 and 1968 during which Martin Luther King Jr. and Senator Bobby Kennedy were assassinated, mass protests broke out over the war in

Vietnam and other social causes, and civil unrest erupted in major American cities, including Washington, DC; Detroit; Newark; Chicago; and Baltimore, Republicans campaigned on restoring "law and order" in the smoldering nation, swaying just enough of the electorate to clinch the White House from Hubert Humphrey.

Still, throughout the Johnson, Nixon, Ford, and Carter administrations of the late 1960s and 1970s, liberal policies carried the day. Lyndon Johnson's Great Society program expanded the federal government's social policy footprint with the passage of Medicaid, federal funding for primary schools, federal college tuition support, support for the working poor, and expanded federal housing initiatives. The rights revolution continued to garner successes in Congress with the passage of the Fair Housing Act of 1968, Title IX of the Education Amendments of 1972, Equal Employment Opportunity Act of 1972, the Rehabilitation Act of 1973, Employee Retirement Income Security Act of 1974, the Education for All Handicapped Children Act of 1975, the Age Discrimination in Employment Act of 1975, the Voting Rights Act Amendments of 1975, Indian Child Welfare Act of 1978, and the Pregnancy Discrimination Act of 1978. Congress expanded the regulatory state, enacting the National Traffic and Motor Vehicle Safety Act 1966, the Clean Air Act of 1970, the Occupational Health and Safety Act of 1970, Federal Election Campaign Act of 1971, the Clean Water Act of 1972, the Consumer Product Safety Act of 1972, and the Endangered Species Act of 1973. Congress passed legislation to curb the abuse of executive power at home and abroad with the Congressional Budget and Impoundment Control Act of 1974 and War Powers Resolution, respectively.

Meanwhile, the turmoil of the late 1960s accelerated throughout the 1970s, which empowered movement conservatives and undermined the New Deal partisan regime. In what Kevin Kruse and Julian Zelizer identify as four crises—of legitimacy, identity, equality, and confidence—the old partisan regime and its ideological tenets could not grapple with the cascading political upheavals of the decade. Trust in government and the liberal order's capacity to provide policy solutions for national problems was called into question by Watergate, the Pentagon Papers, stagflation, rising crime, a decay in race relations, the antiwar movement, fights over women's rights, urban violence, a major energy crisis, and international debacles in Vietnam and Iran. The wisdom of New Deal–inspired programming like Johnson's Great Society was questioned. One historian, Bruce Schulman, described the decade as rocking the national consciousness and faith in liberalism: "Americans developed a deeper, more thorough suspicion of the instruments of public life and a more profound disillusionment with the corruption and inefficiency of public institutions. The ideal of social solidarity, the conception of a national community with duties and obligations to one's fellow citizens, elicited greater skepticism during the 1970s, while the private sphere commanded uncommon, and sometimes undeserved, respect."[7] The seventies eroded the liberal order's standing as the nation continued to decline, and leaders ham-handedly responded with ineffective solutions. The alarming times gave cachet to simmering arguments made by movement conservatives assailing the Warren Court and New Deal liberalism: the Constitution required redemption and restoration—a return to first principles à la originalism. The door was open for movement conservatives to establish a new partisan regime.

SLOW-BOILING CONSERVATIVE CONSTITUTIONALISM

The liberal political regime of the 1970s remained intact, though it was disintegrating at a slow burn. As the New Deal order unraveled from numerous destabilizing crises, the constitutional jurisprudence of the decade was similarly in flux and less clear eyed than in years prior. Bungled timing, scandal, conservative electoral gains, and liberal entrenchment in the Senate created the conditions to nudge the Supreme Court rightward in the 1970s, resulting in a soft conservative jurisprudence. In 1968, nearly three months after Lyndon Johnson announced he would not accept the Democratic nomination for president and instead focus on managing the war in Vietnam, the leading liberal in the jurisprudential arm of the partisan regime, Chief Justice Earl Warren, tendered his resignation. With Johnson as a lame-duck president and the very real prospect of Richard Nixon defeating the sitting vice president in November, senate conservatives were determined to sink a liberal successor to Warren. Senate conservatives had a ripe target in Johnson's nominee, sitting associate justice Abe Fortas. As historian Joshua Zeitz described it, "From the start, it all went wrong."[8]

Democratic senator Robert Byrd of West Virginia, a former Klansman who filibustered the Civil Rights Act in 1964, pledged to do "everything in [his] power" to oppose the "leftist" Abe Fortas. Russell Long of Louisiana, another segregation stalwart, denounced the nominee as one of the "dirty five" who sought to expand the rights of the accused. James Eastland of Mississippi, an ardent racist and chairman of the Senate Judiciary Committee, told the president that he had "never seen so much feeling against a man as against Fortas." He might have been thinking in part of his colleague, John McClellan of Arkansas, who ironically *wanted* that "SOB formally submitted to the Senate" so that he could take the fight public.[9]

With resistance from Republican members of the Senate and anti–civil rights Democrats, the Fortas nomination was the first to be defeated by a filibuster. The Fortas saga was not yet over, however, as the justice resigned under pressure over financial dealings. With Warren and Fortas leaving the Court, Nixon could reshape the Court by replacing two liberals with more conservative jurists. Nixon nominated a moderate conservative, Warren Burger, to fill the chief justice's seat. Though right-wing senators held sufficient power to impede the continuation of the Warren Court tradition, they were still on the outside of the dominant regime looking in. Nixon failed to replace Fortas with Clement Haynsworth and Harrold Carswell, judges known for their strong opposition to the rights revolution but also assailed for their lack of personal integrity and professional credentials. Nixon eventually replaced Fortas with the moderate Harry Blackmun and selected moderate Lewis Powell and conservative William Rehnquist to fill additional vacancies left by Hugo Black and John Marshall Harlan II, respectively. Though only three years had passed since Warren's retirement, by 1972, the Supreme Court, though ostensibly not conservative, was but a shell of its former liberal self.[10]

What resulted in the 1970s was a country club jurisprudence that was business friendly and cool, but not hostile, to the rights revolution. Unlike the Court of the 1930s, which stood against the tides of change, constitutional doctrine reflected the planted but weakening liberal order of the 1970s. Several salient decisions reflected the internal ideological tensions and line-straddling that signified constitutional law's new bent. The Burger Court pumped the brakes on the rights revolution. On racial equality, the Supreme Court championed some important tools to combat discrimination while closing the door on others. An early sign of the Burger Court's reserved appetite for race discrimination claims came in 1971. In *Palmer v. Thompson*, a 5–4 Court rejected the argument that, despite evidence that Jackson, Mississippi, closed public swimming pools to circumvent a district court order mandating their integration, the city could be compelled to operate the pools on a desegregated basis.[11]

In 1971, the Court, in a unanimous opinion written by the chief justice, held that student assignment remedies that required busing Black students to predominantly white schools within the Charlotte-Mecklenburg County School District were permissible in order to dismantle segregated schooling.[12] However, the Court struck a blow to educational parity in 1973 when it ruled that inequitable funding of public schools within a state did not violate equal protection guarantees.[13] A year later, the Court took away some arrows in the quiver of federal courts when fashioning equitable remedies in school segregation cases—the first time the Supreme Court declined to act in a school desegregation case since *Brown*. In *Milliken v. Bradley*, the Court held that absent evidence of school districts colluding to discriminate, interdistrict remedies like busing were inappropriate.[14] Thus, the demographic effects of white flight to the suburbs, driven in some measure by the desire of white parents to avoid integrated urban schools, insulated suburban schools from federal court intervention and undermined the project of diversifying city schools. Finding himself on the losing side of a school discrimination case for the first time since having argued *Brown*, Justice Thurgood Marshall acknowledged that the Court's decision was a pivot that tracked with the national attitude:

> Today's holding, I fear, is more a reflection of a perceived public mood that we have gone far enough in enforcing the Constitution's guarantee of equal justice than it is the product of neutral principles of law. In the short run, it may seem to be the easier course to allow our great metropolitan areas to be divided up each into two cities—one white, the other black—but it is a course, I predict, our people will ultimately regret. I dissent.[15]

Parallel to the justices' approach to school busing, the Burger Court interpreted Title VII of the Civil Rights Act of 1964 as prohibiting tests or policies that have a disparate impact on job seekers because of race.[16] Intent was not the touchstone of legality, but effect. But in *Washington v. Davis*, the Burger Court laid down precedent that disparate impact theory could not form the basis of a cognizable constitutional equal protection claim.[17] The 7–2 decision left the liberal stalwarts William Brennan and Thurgood Marshall on the outside looking in on the major decisions of the day. The Court extended the rule to constitutional claims under the Fifteenth Amendment in 1980.[18]

The coup de grâce of the 1970s' meandering race jurisprudence was handed down in *Regents of University of California v. Bakke*.[19] There, the Supreme Court on a divided 4–1–4 count upheld race-conscious affirmative action plans in public higher education with a controlling opinion authored by Justice Lewis Powell. The Powell opinion reasoned that affirmative action plans could meet constitutional muster if race was considered as a "plus factor" in admissions decisions without race-based quotas[20] because holistic affirmative action plans furthered an academic freedom–related interest in diversity.[21] Affirmative action as a tool of remedial racial justice was not legitimate in the eyes of the majority's judgment.[22] The Powell diversity rationale was a compromise made for the times. Powell sought the path of least resistance, which hedged the waning liberal order's egalitarian principles against intensifying politics of racial resentment.

The rights revolution's arrested development in the 1970s was similarly felt in one of the decade's landmark rights-expanding decisions, *Roe v. Wade*.[23] On the one hand, the Supreme Court's ruling in *Roe* recognizing a woman's fundamental right to abortion was an extension of liberal thinking on civil rights. On the other hand, the Court's reasoning in *Roe* stepped away from the more familiar egalitarian principles of the rights revolution. The Harry Blackmun–authored opinion was steeped in gendered language, couching the right to reproductive healthcare not as a pure matter of radical feminism but as a medical decision made by a physician—presumptively a man—and a pregnant woman.[24]

The Burger Court in the 1970s was discernibly more conservative than the Court had been in years prior. Yet, the Court during this period cabined liberalism's reach and slowed expansions of the rights revolution rather than challenging it head-on with new interpretive lenses, like a solid commitment to originalism or strict textualism. The first half of the Burger Court's life laid the groundwork for new constitutional line-drawing that would result in institutional rearrangement and a shift in the window of constitutional discourse. Unlike the 1860s or 1930s courts, the slow burn toward conservative constitutionalism avoided an acrid institutional standoff between an oppositional judiciary and a new regime. While the Court's jurisprudence of the 1970s was anchored in the unraveling liberal order, it is best understood as a milquetoast preview of the Reagan revolution.

THE REAGAN REVOLUTION AND THE NEW CONSERVATIVE ORDER

The 1980 elections swept Republicans into power in the White House and the Senate. The ninety-seventh Congress was divided, with the House of Representatives remaining in Democratic hands. However, Republicans netted thirty-five seats by primarily defeating moderate and liberal Democrats.[25] Like FDR and Lincoln before him, Ronald Reagan labored to reset the conditions of policy legitimacy and to reorder institutional arrangements—but in this case with a vision that rejected key elements of the liberal regime that had dominated American life since 1932. The Reagan revolution was characterized by its emphasis on moral hegemony—at home and abroad—and rugged individualism. Reagan projected himself as the protector of the nation, stepping into the breach to restore order by undoing the New Deal's excesses and to renew the country's international standing. Reagan's campaign and tenure as president assaulted the New Deal's social welfare ideals and the Great Society's programming as misguided and unsuccessful. Reagan made this case by tapping into race-based stereotypes and antagonizing civil rights liberals, casting poverty as a personal moral failure and tying his antistatism to originalist principles. The interests of religious conservatives, disaffected white voters, and big business converged to buoy support for a new conservative governing commitment: state interventionism was not to be trusted. Indeed, in a famous 1986 Reagan press conference, the president summed up the sentiment by proclaiming, "I think you all know that I've always felt the nine most terrifying words in the English language are: 'I'm from the government, and I'm here to help.'"[26]

More than a briefing room quip, the notion that the problem with the liberal order was not that government action was just mismanaged but that it was inherently suspect was plainly articled in 1980 and 1981. The 1980 Republican Party platform pronounced that "[f]or too many years, the political debate in America has been conducted in terms set by the Democrats," who "spawned" an era of "big government" that threatened individual freedom.[27] Reagan's inaugural address in 1981 echoed the message:

> In this present crisis, government is not the solution to our problem; government is the problem. From time to time, we have been tempted to believe that society has become too complex to be managed by self-rule, that government by an elite group is superior to government for, by, and of the people. But if no one among us is capable of governing himself, then who among us has the capacity to govern someone else? All of us together, in and out of government, must bear the burden.[28]

Not only was the federal government's footprint too large, but the new movement pointed to the excesses of the rights revolution as a vector of America's social decay. The new regime was unreceptive to civil rights expansionism and stood against feminism, gay rights, racial justice, environmentalism, and organized labor, which undergirded the countercultural movements of the 1960s and 1970s. Reagan wrapped up these arguments in his famous 1980 Neshoba County Fair speech outside Philadelphia, Mississippi, where he made a tacit appeal to disaffected white voters and argued for a new arrangement for America's government institutions with language that gestured toward Southern opposition to civil rights:

> I believe in states' rights; I believe in people doing as much as they can for themselves at the community level and at the private level. And I believe that we've distorted the balance of our government today by giving powers that were never intended in the Constitution to that federal establishment. And if I do get the job I'm looking for, I'm going to devote myself to trying to reorder those priorities and to restore to the states and local communities those functions which properly belong there.[29]

There are three overlapping touchstones of the Reagan revolution to which conservatives returned to convey governmental distrust and moral interventionism: the diffusion of power (an emphasis on states' rights, dual federalism, and privatization), regulatory skepticism (deregulation, the unitary executive, antibureaucracy, and cynicism of expertise), and rights retrenchment (a souring on radical democracy while embracing an opposition to civil rights liberalism, social conservatism, and "law and order"). While Reagan could usher in a dramatic reorientation of the national mood, the nation's reliance on New Deal programming limited Reagan's reconstruction. As Stephen Skowronek observed, "Reagan closed off a prior course of development;" but his reconstruction was somewhat more bark than bite because "the institutional commitments of the liberal regime, though battered and starved, were not decisively dislodged, and their 'entitlements' would continue to determine the range of political possibilities."[30] While it did not effectively unwind the liberal order's landmark achievements in full, the Reagan revolution stopped the growth of the social welfare state, delegitimized government intervention, and discredited rights expansion.

Reagan's 1984 Republican Convention nomination acceptance speech represented the New Deal liberal order as anathema to the founders' vision: "Isn't our choice really not one of left or right, but of up or down? Down through the welfare state to statism, to more and more government largesse accompanied always by more government authority, less individual liberty and, ultimately, totalitarianism, always advanced as for our own good. The alternative is the dream conceived by our Founding Fathers, up to the ultimate in individual freedom consistent with an orderly society."[31] Reagan's message coincided with an emerging conservative legal movement intent on hitching constitutional law to a legal theory that would unravel major pieces of liberal constitutionalism and stall progressive government programming.

Unlike older regimes, movement conservatives focused on developing a legal theory to provide the imprimatur of faithful and dispassionate application of constitutional principles. Before he became a member of the Supreme Court, Lewis Powell authored a memorandum in 1971 for the Chamber of Commerce about the business communities' interests in the waning years of the New Deal era. Among other corners of society that Powell identified as problematic for corporate interests, he noted business leaders had neglected the courts. "Other organizations and groups . . . have been far more astute in exploiting judicial action than American business," he wrote. Powell urged the chamber and its allies to build a pool of business-friendly lawyers to bring suits and intervene in litigation through amicus briefs: "[l]abor unions, civil rights groups and now public interest law firms are extremely active in the judicial arena. Their success, often at business' expense, has not been inconsequential."[32]

Legal theories like law and economics and originalism gained favor as conservative lawyers organized. The same year as Powell's memorandum, then Yale Law School professor Robert Bork decried in a law review article the "disturbing" and "deplorable" state of constitutional law's "lack of a theory," which meant that judges were "without effective criteria" for assessing rights claims.[33] Bork's broad-based attack on the judiciary in the near wake of the liberal Warren Court would be taken up by conservative scholars, judges, and lawyers. While an associate justice on the Court, William Rehnquist echoed Bork's critique, panning the idea of a living constitution in favor of an interpretive approach that hinged on the "language and intent of the framers" and rejecting the notion that "nonelected members of the federal judiciary may address themselves to a social problem simply because other branches of government have failed or refused to do so."[34] A year later, Harvard law professor Raoul Berger penned a famed book, *Government by Judiciary*, arguing that constitutional text should be interpreted consistently with the original intent of its provisions' framers. Originalists were part of a broad conservative social movement searching for a legal theory.

In the early-to-mid-1980s, a right-wing constitutional vision coalesced into a firmer ideological identity, and originalist ideas metastasized through the formation of professional networks and vocal advocates within the federal government. The Federalist Society is a notable example of this development. Established during a three-day symposium at

Yale Law School in 1982, the group pronounced that it was "founded on the principles that the state exists to preserve freedom, that the separation of governmental powers is central to our constitution, and that it is emphatically the province and duty of the judiciary to say what the law is, not what it should be."[35] It would become one of the most effective legal-oriented groups in the 1980s and decades after Reagan left office.

During his tenure in the Reagan administration, Attorney General Edwin Meese also advocated for originalism. In 1986, Meese addressed the American Bar Association, saying, "It has been and will continue to be the policy of this administration to press for a Jurisprudence of Original Intention. In the cases we file and those we join as amicus, we will endeavor to resurrect the original meaning of the constitutional provisions and statutes as the only reliable guide for judgment."[36] With appointees like Meese at the helm of the Department of Justice, the Reagan administration used the DOJ to shift legal thought dramatically. Over time, and at the urging of significant figures in conservative circles like Justice Antonin Scalia, originalists gravitated toward embracing the original public meaning of constitutional text. Through its growth, originalists fundamentally committed themselves to the idea that, as Lawrence Solum has described it, "The communicative content of the Constitution (the linguistic meaning in context) is fixed at the time each constitutional provision is framed and ratified."[37] These ideas, far from the neutral principles they were purported to be, were operationalized within the federal judiciary at a greater rate to give cover for the Reagan revolution's paradigm-shifting agenda to enhance presidential authority, cripple the administrative state, embrace an anticlassificationist view of constitutional safeguards against racial discrimination, adopt social conservative views on matters of sexuality and bodily autonomy, and limit the reach of the federal government's powers under the commerce clause.

UNWINDING FEDERAL POWER

In 1980 and 1984, the Republican Party platform emphasized the need to shrink the size of the federal government. The platform denounced sprawling federal regulation at the expense of localized governing and generally backed a more limited role for the federal government. In 1980 the GOP pledged "to restore the family, the neighborhood, the community, and the workplace as vital alternatives in our national life to ever-expanding federal power."[38] With Reagan's victory, Republicans attacked the size and scope of the federal government and, in 1981, pursued a series of tax cuts aimed to "starve the beast." As economic sociologist Monica Prasad has explained, "Reagan and his administration wanted tax cuts because they would lead to less revenue (thus forcing government spending down) and because they would lead to more revenue (thus paying for themselves)."[39] The platform in 1984 called for sustained efforts to pare down the federal government: "The role of the federal government should be limited. We reaffirm our conviction that State and local governments closest to the people are the best and most efficient."[40]

Reagan closed out the eighties with his 1989 Farewell speech, recounting to the public that his mission to reverse the New Deal's course had triumphed. Reagan told the nation, " . . . back in the 1960s, when I began, it seemed to me that we'd begun reversing the order of things—that through more and more rules and regulations and confiscatory taxes, the government was taking more of our money, more of our options, and more of our freedom. I went into politics in part to put up my hand and say, 'Stop.'"[41] The notion that limited government was a good unto itself permeated the politics of the 1990s. After Reagan departed from the White House, the national mood was predisposed against active government. Though a Democrat, President Bill Clinton tapped into the Reagan revolution. There may be no single moment that captures the conservative mood that enmeshed the opposition party in Reagan's revolution than the State of the Union speech Clinton delivered in 1996:

> We know big government does not have all the answers. We know there's not a program for every problem. We have worked to give the American people a smaller, less bureaucratic government in Washington. And we have to give the American people one that lives within its means.
>
> The era of big government is over. But we cannot go back to the time when our citizens were left to fend for themselves. Instead, we must go forward as one America, one nation working together to meet the challenges we face together. Self-reliance and teamwork are not opposing virtues; we must have both."[42]

Just a year before Clinton's pronouncement confirming that the nation had abandoned New Deal liberalism, Republicans captured control of Congress in the 1994 midterm elections. In that campaign, Republicans, led by soon-to-be speaker of the House Newt Gingrich, announced a "Contract with America." Riding the wave of Reaganism's paradigm-shifting politics, redistricting that diluted Black voting power, vulnerable conservative Democrats who would lose or might likely switch parties, and the thermostatic nature of being the opposition party to the White House incumbent, Republicans seized the moment to push a profoundly conservative vision of government policy. Republicans pledged Social Security reform, small business investments, tort law reform, socially conservative tax policies, enhanced parental rights in schools, antipornography laws, a policy to deny welfare benefits to minor mothers, welfare work requirements, funding for prison construction, expenditures for more law enforcement, and pro-prosecution criminal procedure reform. Republican hopefuls also banded together to support new institutional constraints on the federal government, including congressional term limits, an amendment to the Constitution requiring a balanced budget, and a legislative line-item veto that would empower the president to reject congressional appropriations line-by-line.

When Republicans announced their plan, the *New York Times* called it "a throwback to the Reagan era."[43] And it was. Unmistakably, the force behind it had a spirit originating with Republican members of Congress who were elected as true believers in the Reagan revolution in 1980. As Julian Zelizer has explained, this group comprised "devout followers of Ronald Reagan, whose election in 1980 symbolized to them a watershed moment akin to the election of Franklin Roosevelt for liberals."[44] The substance was a real outgrowth of the Reagan years, with much of the pledge directly drawn from Reagan's 1985 State of the Union Address.

The entire thrust of the first fifteen years into the Reagan revolution centered on curbing and downsizing the federal government. However, the building blocks of the New Deal Order made a wholesale supplanting of federal programming and governmental entities impossible. Despite the antistatist tilt of the Reagan years and Reagan's earlier opposition to the program, reliance on Social Security could not be displaced; environmental law was deprioritized, but the Environmental Protection Agency remained in what was described as a "stalemate" between environmentalists and Reagan,[45] and the Department of Education continued to operate despite Reagan's demands for its abolition. Many of the programmatic reliance interests and much of the institutional inertia that the New Deal order created were firmly rooted, even if they could be constrained by administrative staffing decisions, enforcement policies, and slash-and-burn budgets. Hollowing out the federal government and repurposing it was vital to second-stage Reaganism. While antistatism could only go so far, social conservatives could capture the federal government's infrastructure to promulgate national reforms.

The irony of the Reagan revolution is that it was less revolutionary in its achievements than in its rhetoric when it came to limiting the reach of the federal government. Reaganism successfully ate away at the edges of the federal government's power. However, it did not gut it because, in addition to the difficulty of dislodging established institutions, its power proved useful. Nevertheless, curtailing Congress's power to enforce constitutional rights under the Civil War amendments was more valuable because the enforcement power had minimal value for anti–civil rights elements of the Reagan coalition. The Supreme Court's jurisprudence tracked this dynamic by limiting the federal government's spending power to bolster state control and constrain commerce-clause powers while slashing the power of rights enforcement.

The first major Supreme Court decision to mirror the Reagan revolution's antistatist attitude came in 1995. In *United States v. Lopez*, the Court struck down a federal law, The Gun–Free School Zones Act of 1990, which made it a federal crime "for any individual knowingly to possess a firearm at a place that the individual knows, or has reasonable cause to believe, is a school zone." Notably, the law did not target an activity that touched on any commercial or economic transaction, nor did the law constrain a jurisdictional hook that tied criminal activity to some interstate activity. The question before the Supreme Court was whether the commerce clause empowered the federal government to criminalize weapons possession in school zones. The government argued that the law was permissible because Congress rationally concluded that crime depresses economic development and that the "impediments to the educational process" because of gun violence "have substantial deleterious effects on the functioning of the national economy."[46] The Supreme Court rejected the government's arguments, holding that "[w]here economic activity substantially affects interstate commerce, legislation regulating that activity will be sustained" but that a law punishing gun possession was too attenuated from the commercial area to be justified under Article I powers.[47]

The Court struck a second blow to the commerce-clause power in 2000, invalidating part of the 1994 Violence Against Women Act that provided a private cause of action for victims of gender-motivated violence. Unlike the Gun-Free School Zones Act, Congress went to great lengths to document how sex-based violence impaired the national economy's productivity and growth. As a group of law professors argued in an amicus brief in *United States v. Morrison*, "The direct effects of violence against women on their participation in the national economy were thoroughly documented—grown women lost jobs, time from work, economic opportunities."[48] To this end, the federal government argued that the record compiled by Congress outlining the tight link between violence and participation in the commercial marketplace was appropriate because "[i]t is not the character of the activity, but the substantiality of its impact on interstate commerce, that determines whether the activity may be regulated under the Commerce Clause."[49] The Supreme Court rejected the federal government's claim, holding that the evil Congress legislated against was a noneconomic activity that fell outside the ambit of the body's enumerated powers. Just as the Court did in *Lopez*, the *Morrison* Court found no value in the federal government pointing to the "costs of crime" or reduction in "national productivity" in defense of what the Court viewed as strictly social policy.[50]

The Court's commerce-clause jurisprudence tightened further when the Court upheld the Affordable Care Act (ACA) in 2012 in *National Federation of Independent Businesses v. Sebelius*.[51] There, the justices faced a constitutional challenge to the individual mandate contained in the ACA that required Americans who did not have employer-supplied healthcare insurance to purchase and maintain a minimum level of insurance, enforced by a tax penalty. Congress adopted this regulatory regime to ensure that the millions of uninsured Americans who nevertheless participated in the healthcare marketplace, either by seeking emergency medical care at no cost or by tapping into the healthcare system later in life and thereby driving up costs across the board, were forced to contribute to the insurance market. However, a majority coalition of all the justices appointed by Republican presidents corked the commerce-clause power and held that Congress could only regulate commercial activity that was already happening—Congress had no authority to compel individuals into undertaking commercial marketplace activity.[52]

Taken together, *Lopez*, *Morrison*, and *NFIB*, capture the ambitions, limitations, and pivot of the Reagan revolution. The Court did not drag commerce-clause jurisprudence back from its high-water mark but still capped it from expanding. The Court starved Congress's capacity to enact some forms of social policy through loose ties to commerce, but the Court also followed through on the era's general civil rights hostility by strangling the Fourteenth Amendment's Section-Five enforcement-clause power in *Morrison* and an earlier decision, *City of Boerne v. Flores*. In *Morrison*, the Supreme Court doubled down on the notion that private violence alone, absent state action, was not a matter that fell under the purview of Congress's Fourteenth Amendment power to adopt legislation to enforce equal protection guarantees—and they included an approving citation to *Cruickshank v. United States*, a 1876 Supreme Court decision holding that the federal government could not protect Black citizens from private violence in Reconstruction Louisiana.[53]

The Supreme Court held in *Boerne* that Congress could not proactively protect against state encroachment of civil rights and civil liberties if those interests were not also constitutional rights. In other words, Congress can protect preexisting rights but cannot define rights beyond the federal judiciary's Fourteenth Amendment jurisprudence. In a 6–3 decision, including three of Reagan's four appointments, one of Bush's two appointments, and one of Clinton's two appointments, a conservative shift on matters of federal civil rights enforcement was cemented.[54]

One of the most important mechanisms of federal policymaking that emerged from the New Deal was the government's spending power for the general welfare. In 1936, the Supreme Court signaled in *United States v. Butler* that Congress could appropriate monies to support programs uncoupled from its enumerated powers.[55] This also meant that the federal government could expend funds backing conditional grants designed to induce states to adopt policies favored by Congress, but it was outside the federal government's constitutional authority to adopt directly. Congress thus held the "power to fix the terms upon which its money allotments to states shall be disbursed"[56] so long as the exchange was not "coercive."[57] Even here, the creep of Reaganism's emphasis on state control seeped into constitutional law. While the power to spend was not gutted, the Roberts Court imposed artificial constraints on conditional grants akin to what the Rehnquist Court undertook with the commerce-clause power. In the Affordable Care Act case, the Court refused to permit Congress to withdraw massive funding from states according to a new set of conditions tantamount to "economic dragooning that leaves the States with no real option but to acquiesce."[58] In so doing, the Supreme Court hamstrung the ability of Congress to change the terms and conditions of major social welfare programs and other preexisting federal programs.

The Reagan revolution was firmly entrenched in American constitutional doctrine, dealing substantial blows to rights-based legislation and other liberal causes. The Supreme Court suppressed Congress's ability to tie social policy to economic productivity. It raised the floor to protect civil rights and liberties, limiting the power to proactively protect the full citizenship of minorities or other politically vulnerable groups. There were fewer constitutionally permissible paths for federal officials to exert power to defend rights and protect the vulnerable. Reaganism could not dislodge the 1937 constitutional revolution because path dependence would not let it, but that programmatic and institutional inertia was less an encumbrance when it came to constricting civil rights measures consistent with the backlash to the New Deal's rights revolution.

REGULATORY SKEPTICISM

Part of the Reagan revolution's antigovernment pivot against the New Deal bureaucracy was grounded in skepticism of the regulatory state. Reagan's hostility toward regulation by federal agencies was key to his political maturation into a conservative stalwart. In his 1964 speech in support of Barry Goldwater's presidential campaign, "A Time for Choosing," which launched Reagan's national political profile, Reagan laid out a broadside attack on the New Deal administrative state as a threat to liberty:

> These proliferating bureaus with their thousands of regulations have cost us many of our constitutional safeguards. How many of us realize that today federal agents can invade a man's property without a warrant? They can impose a fine without a formal hearing, let alone a trial by jury? And they can seize and sell his property at auction to enforce the payment of that fine.[59]

When in office, Reagan followed through and operationalized his antiagency stance by blaming a "virtual explosion in government regulation" for "higher prices, higher unemployment, and lower productivity growth," as well as slow job growth.[60] Among his first acts as president, in 1981, Reagan issued an executive order that mandated federal agencies undertake cost-benefit analyses for major rulemaking efforts and centralized oversight of rule promulgation within the Office of Management and Budget. He nominated viciously anti–administrative state heads to the Department of the Interior and the Environmental Protection Agency. Reagan Department of Justice officials plotted taking down independent agencies as unconstitutional. Reagan's administration issued statements to advocate for a unitary executive theory—the idea that agencies and their personnel must be subject to presidential oversight and removal without limitations imposed by Congress.

Reagan used presidential signing statements to wrestle the focal point of statutory interpretation away from Congress and toward the executive branch by offering the administration's position on the meaning, scope, and constitutionality of legislation being enacted into law. When he was a DOJ lawyer in the 1980s, future Supreme Court justice Samuel Alito advocated for presidential signing statements to supplement legislative history and constrain liberal interpretations of federal law, opining, "From the perspective of the Executive Branch, the issuance of interpretive signing statements would have two chief advantages. First, it would increase the power of the Executive to shape the law. Second, by forcing some rethinking by courts, scholars, and litigants, it may help to curb some of the prevalent abuses of legislative history."[61] These statements, rarely used before Reagan came to power, proliferated in successive administrations and peaked with the George W. Bush administration, when the president signaled opposition to nearly seven hundred congressionally approved statutory provisions.

The Supreme Court's doctrine reflected the Reagan revolution's antipathy toward the administrative state; it expanded executive control over agency officials and undercut the capacity of agencies to regulate in *Free Enterprise Fund v. Public Company Accounting Oversight Board* and *Seila Law LLC. v. Consumer Finance Protection Bureau*. In *Free Enterprise Fund*, the Court undercut Congress's power to limit the president's authority to remove agency officials, consolidating executive power.[62] In a 5–4 decision authored by Chief Justice John Roberts, the Court held that Congress could not create multiple layers of protections for government officials who could only be terminated for cause. The Court determined that, because the Constitution gives the president the duty to take care that laws are faithfully executed, Congress could not create an agency board whose members were removable only for good cause if those members were overseen by other agency officials who were also only removable from their positions for cause. As such, a president must retain some at-will authority to shape the administrative state at their pleasure, free of statutory constraints. Notwithstanding a sweeping construction of presidential power, the Court acknowledged that Congress could still impose for-cause limitations on removing both high-ranking officers and rank-and-file employees within the administrative state, but Congress could not do both. The Supreme Court expanded this principle in *Selia Law*, holding that a president must retain the ability to fire an agency headed by a powerful single director at will. While not eliminating the capacity of Congress to define administrative officers' terms of service to the executive, the Court's separation of powers doctrine subjected administrative agencies to the whims of a presidential administration determined to bring the regulatory state to heel.

In addition to the Court's appointments-clause jurisprudence, the administrative-law rules the Court crafted in the age of Reaganism resisted giving significant deference to administrative agencies' judgment. These bodies of case law acted as a pincer movement that opened agencies to increased influence by antiregulation presidential administrations while simultaneously pressuring Congress to draft exceedingly specific statutory authority for agencies to act. Previously, Congress often delegated its legislative authority to agencies to regulate on its behalf. A 1984 case, *Chevron U.S.A., Inc. v. Natural Resources Defense Council, Inc.*,[63] addressed instances in which the scope of Congress's statutory delegation was not entirely clear. The Court held that courts should defer to an agency's interpretation of their own authority if it is a reasonable one, thus allowing agencies to lawfully act and promulgate regulations in spaces where Congress did not legislate with granular specificity or imprecisely. However, beginning in the mid-1990s, in keeping with the Court's more conservative bent, the justices developed what Court watchers have dubbed the "Major Questions Doctrine": the Court instructed federal agencies that they may not regulate issues of "vast economic and political significance" in absence of express statutory authority.[64]

The Court refused to allow the Federal Communication Commission to waive certain requirements for long-distance telephone companies;[65] the Food and Drug Administration to regulate the tobacco industry;[66] the Environmental Protection Agency to consider implementation costs while establishing ambient air quality standards;[67] the United States attorney general to regulate drugs used for assisted suicides;[68] the Environmental Protection Agency to regulate greenhouse gases that imposed permitting requirements "over millions of small sources [of greenhouse gas emissions], such as hotels and office buildings;"[69] the Center for Disease Control to prohibit evictions during the coronavirus pandemic in 2020 and 2021;[70] the Occupational Health and Safety Administration to require emergency vaccinations to prevent the transmission of COVID-19 at large workplaces;[71] and the Environmental Protection Agency to apply its formulation of emissions caps to coal-fired and natural-gas-fired power plants to combat climate change.[72]

A key juncture in the Reagan coalition's development came at the intersection of regulatory skepticism and free speech absolutism, which gave rise to spaces of nonintervention for conservative media outlets to flourish. In 1949, the Federal Communications Commission stated a policy that media outlets held licenses to broadcast "under an obligation to insure that opposing points of view will . . . be presented."[73] Thus, as a condition for media outlets to maintain broadcast licenses, broadcasters' programming needed to "devote a reasonable percentage of broadcast time to the coverage of public issues" and the coverage of those public issues had to "be fair" and provide "an opportunity for the presentation of contrasting points of view."[74] Twenty years after the FCC introduced the concept, the Supreme Court upheld the fairness doctrine, under the idea that media outlets' paramount duty was to serve the public because they served as "fiduciaries" of public airwaves with "obligations to present those views and voices which are representative of [one's] community and which would otherwise, by necessity, be barred from the airwaves."[75]

In 1987, the FCC ceased enforcing the fairness doctrine after deciding that the policy was no longer in the public interest and, despite Supreme Court precedent in *Red Lion*, concluding that the rule was an unconstitutional restriction on free speech.[76] Congress responded with legislation to codify the policy, which Reagan vetoed on constitutional grounds. Reagan's veto message reasoned that the First Amendment's design was intended to "promote vigorous public debate and a diversity of viewpoints in the public forum as a whole, not in any particular medium, let alone in any particular journalistic outlet" and that any concerns about balance in media coverage could not be remedied by "bureaucratic regulation, but only through . . . freedom and competition."[77] In the wake of the doctrine's demise, conservative media outlets exploded and created echo chambers of information that helped radicalize the Republican base to rally against the expanse of government regulation and stoke a culture war against progressives in the hopes of curtailing the successes of the civil rights revolution.

RIGHTS RETRENCHMENT

The Reagan revolution called for the retrenchment of the rights revolution ushered in by New Dealers and the Warren Court, in particular, as Americans soured on the principles of radical democracy, the civil rights revolution, and labor unions in favor of social conservativism and "law and order."

The waning years of the New Deal order and the emergence of Richard Nixon's strategy to court Southern voters with a conservative message of "law and order" signaled opposition to civil rights in the wake of major legislation passed in 1964 and 1965 as well as a hardline hostility toward protest movements opposing the war in Vietnam, all of which helped forge a new coalition of Republican voters. The realignment Nixon helped usher in brought voters holding socially conservative views into the Republican Party's core, incentivizing the Republican Party to cater to opponents of the New Deal's vision of civil rights and to build this constituency by standing in strong opposition to simmering demands for another wave of civil rights in the way of women's rights, gay rights, and secular public education—even if opposition to women's equality and sexual liberation required manufacturing controversies for social conservatives to rally around.

This development preceded the Supreme Court's decision in *Roe v. Wade*, as Linda Greenhouse and Reva Siegel have masterfully studied. They note that "between 1970 and 1972, the Republican Party's interest in raiding the Democratic Party's traditional coalition of voters supplied reason for President Nixon to take a stand on abortion at odds with positions staked out by his own administration and allies" and enabled Republicans to adopt an alternative "framing [of] abortion in terms that helped change its social meaning" from one about public health or individual decision-making "into a symbol of partisan identity bearing on questions of sex, religion, and even race."[78] To this end, Evangelicals—who were by and large dispassionate about issues like abortion even at the time the Supreme Court decided *Roe v. Wade*—used sex equality as a rallying point to attack the federal judiciary and liberalism in order to energize churchgoers and inconspicuously avenge the IRS's move to strip the tax-exempt status of religious conservative schools that refused to admit Black students. Now abortion was recast as part of a broader unraveling of family values that social-conservative organizations like Rev. Jerry Falwell Sr.'s Moral Majority and other conservative interest-group leaders like Phyllis Schlafly and Paul Weyrich claimed were under attack by feminists, gay rights advocates, and secularists.

The Republican evolution on abortion is captured by the radicalization of Ronald Reagan, who as governor in 1967 signed legislation in California to permit abortions if there was a physical and mental health threat to the mother or if the mother was a victim of rape or incest. By 1980, Reagan called the law "a mistake" and vowed to support a federal constitutional amendment overturning the Supreme Court's decision in *Roe v. Wade*.[79] Throughout the 1970s and 1980s, the GOP platform plank on abortion drifted considerably rightward too. When the GOP first included an antiabortion plank, the party position was that "the question of abortion is one of the most difficult and controversial of our time," and notwithstanding a wide array of positions among Republicans, the party supported the "enactment of a constitutional amendment to restore protection of the right to life for unborn children."[80] The 1980 platform reaffirmed the 1976 position, with the added support for a ban on taxpayer-funded abortions. In addition, the platform tied abortion to broader social conservative interests under a mission to reshape the federal judiciary: "We will work for the appointment of judges at all levels of the judiciary who respect traditional family values and the sanctity of innocent human life."[81] In 1984, language was added stating that the "Fourteenth Amendment's protections apply to unborn children."[82]

The Supreme Court's forty-year trajectory during the era of movement conservatism's gravitational pull inched toward a jurisprudence that rejected the right to an abortion and other unenumerated fundamental-rights claims that offended social conservatives. The pivot away from *Roe v. Wade* coincided with the rise of Ronald Reagan. In 1980, the Supreme Court upheld a rider to congressional appropriations known as the Hyde Amendment, which prevented spending federal funds for abortions unless the procedure was necessary to save the life of the pregnant woman, or the patient was a victim of rape or incest. Consequently, women living below the poverty line who relied on federally funded medical care could not avail themselves of the full range of reproductive healthcare available to women with private health insurance. In *Harris v. McRae*, the Supreme Court held in a 5–4 decision that the federal government's decision not to expend government funds to support elective abortions did not run afoul of equal protection guarantees because the right to an abortion was a negative right, not a positive, substantive right that imposed an affirmative obligation on the government—nor was there a special duty on the part of the government to ensure abortion access to women based on socioeconomic status.[83]

The Court's first opportunity to overturn *Roe v. Wade* fell short of conservatives' aspirations, but the justices pulled back the abortion right. Between 1981 and 1991, five members of the Court that helped form the 7–2 majority in *Roe*, Potter Stewart, Warren Burger, Lewis Powell, William Brennan, and Thurgood Marshall, retired, allowing Ronald Reagan and George H. W. Bush to fashion the Court in the Republican Party's image. Reagan appointed Sandra Day O'Connor, Antonin Scalia, and Anthony Kennedy to fill vacancies, and Bush appointed David Souter and Clarence Thomas. While the Republican Party faithful become more antiabortion, public opinion tepidly favored abortion rights; still, Americans supported certain restrictions—

perhaps aligning them with Bill Clinton, who championed a cautious idea that abortion should be "safe, legal, and rare" in his victorious 1992 presidential campaign. Despite reaffirming the essential holding of *Roe*, in a lead opinion joined by O'Connor, Kennedy, and Souter, the Court allowed states to impose new restrictions on the abortion right. States could only ban abortions once fetuses were viable outside the womb (around 23 or 24 weeks). However, the state could regulate abortions much earlier in a pregnancy provided the regulation did not pose a substantial obstacle in the way of a woman. In reaffirming the core of *Roe* while opening the door to a spate of new state-level restrictions, the new conservative Rehnquist Court breathed life into the antiabortion movement and destabilized the right at the edges.

The antiabortion movement finally captured the Court after appointments made by Donald Trump between 2017 and 2020 entrenched a 6–3 right-wing majority by replacing Anthony Kennedy and Ruth Bader Ginsburg with hyperconservative justices. In *Dobbs v. Jackson Women's Health*, the Court overturned *Roe v. Wade* in a 5–4 decision, arguing that the right to abortion was unsupported by history and tradition or constitutional text.[84] Unlike nearly every decision explored in this book, *Dobbs* reflects raw countermajoritarian partisan capture of the judiciary rather than a new string of jurisprudence following a majoritarian realignment. Public opposition to *Dobbs* was evidenced not only in polling showing majority opposition to the ruling but also in sweeping Democratic victories in the 2022 midterm election, which gave Joe Biden and Democrats the best midterm performance for an incumbent president's party since FDR.

Long before the Republican-installed supermajority undid the protections established in *Roe*, conservative thinkers laid the groundwork for unwinding abortion rights, rejecting the expansion of unenumerated fundamental rights, particularly concerning existential questions of life and death. Over three decades before the *Dobbs* decision, the Court rejected a claim that Missouri violated a fundamental right when it required a patient surrogate seeking to end life-sustaining health care on behalf of an incapacitated patient with no prognosis for recovery to meet a high standard of evidence by showing that the decision was consistent with the patient's wishes.[85] Seven years later, the Court rejected a claim that persons unable to end their lives had a fundamental right to physician-assisted suicide.[86]

The Republican stoking of the culture wars reached a fever pitch in 1992 as President George H. W. Bush, heir of the Reagan revolution,

fought off an eventually successful challenge from his Democratic oppo-
nent, Governor Bill Clinton. Notably at the 1992 GOP Convention, Pat
Buchanan, Reagan's communication adviser, who also challenged Bush for
the nomination, delivered an address that blasted soon-to-be president Bill
and future first lady Hillary Clinton's positions on a host of social matters:

> The agenda Clinton & Clinton would impose on America—abortion on
> demand, a litmus test for the Supreme Court, homosexual rights, discrimina-
> tion against religious schools, women in combat units—that's change, all
> right. But it is not the kind of change America needs. It is not the kind of
> change America wants. And it is not the kind of change we can abide in a
> nation we still call God's country.[87]

Buchanan's rhetoric mirrored the sharp rightward turn in the party
platform that previously gestured to antigay politics through the veiled
language of "family values" but, in 1992, embraced a more hostile position. The party adopted a platform plank for the first time that expressly
opposed same-sex family formation and recognition. The Republicans
also endorsed a strong associative right to keep sexual minorities out of
civic organizations. They rejected calls for adding sexual orientation as
a protected trait under civil rights laws:

> We also stand united with those private organizations, such as the Boy Scouts
> of America, who are defending decency in fulfillment of their own moral
> responsibilities. We reject the irresponsible position of those corporations
> that have cut off contributions to such organizations because of their coura-
> geous stand for family values. Moreover, we oppose efforts by the Democrat
> Party to include sexual preference as a protected minority receiving preferen-
> tial status under civil rights statutes at the federal, State, and local level.[88]

The Supreme Court's sexual-orientation rights jurisprudence followed the GOP position in meaningful ways. Still, it diverged from the
staunchly antigay positions held by social conservatives into the 2000s
as the public warmed to decriminalizing same-sex sexual conduct and
recognizing same-sex marriages. The success of the LGBT community's
social movement for greater acceptance and subsequent litigation campaign relied on the politics of respectability and access to traditional
institutions in ways that were well suited for a conservative era and
essential for securing wins in federal court. In 1986, at a period when
Americans favored criminalizing same-sex relationships at a rate of
nearly two to one and broke even over whether nonheterosexuals
should enjoy equal job opportunities, the Supreme Court, 5–4, gave
their blessing to state laws banning sodomy in *Bowers v. Hardwick*.[89]

Just seventeen years later, the Supreme Court reversed course and overturned *Bowers*. In a 6–3 decision, the Court held in *Lawrence v. Texas* that states could no longer prosecute individuals for having intimate sexual relationships with persons of the same sex. The justices' ruling came on the heels of the AIDS crisis; an energized gay rights movement that encouraged activists to engage in the political process; gay, lesbian, and bisexual Americans becoming more open about their sexual orientation; and the softening of public opposition toward gay rights. The nation's sodomy laws reflected this as well. After *Bowers*, twelve state sodomy bans were either repealed legislatively or struck down by state courts,[90] leaving fourteen outlier states with antisodomy laws on the books. The bottom line in *Lawrence* was consistent with the nation's evolving mores: while Americans continued to believe homosexuality was immoral and opposed relationship recognition on par with marriage, large swaths of the public disfavored criminalizing sexually intimate relationships between same-sex couples. In tension with *Lawrence* and the lead-up to it was the pulse of Reaganism's antistatism and the core constituency social conservatives played in the development of American politics. Aligned with the views of the public increasingly sympathetic to the cause of gay rights, skepticism of government won out perhaps, in part, because antigay politics were more at the periphery of the Reagan revolution than the politics of government regulation, abortion, and racial grievance and were also in greater flux during Reaganism's formative years because of the intervening HIV/AIDS crisis.

A similar pattern emerged with the social movement in support of marriage rights for same-sex couples. Beginning in the early 1990s, same-sex marriage advocates attempted to use litigation as a breakthrough strategy to secure marriage recognition in the courts against widespread opposition. The first of these came in a 1990 challenge to the District of Columbia's marriage laws,[91] followed by a state constitutional challenge to Hawaii's same-sex marriage ban in 1991.[92] Polling data around this period is sparse, but a 1996 national poll registered only 27 percent of Americans supported same-sex marriage. State-level responses to the prospect of same-sex marriage were muted at first. Only Alaska and Hawaii amended their state constitutions to thwart equal marriage before 2000 in direct response to litigation gaining steam in state courts.[93]

After the Vermont Supreme Court required relationship recognition (though not necessarily marriage) for same-sex couples under the Vermont

Constitution and the Supreme Judicial Court of Massachusetts ruled in 2003 for unadulterated equal marriage rights in *Goodridge v. Department of Public Health* under the Massachusetts Constitution,[94] same-sex couples scored major victories, which nationalized the question. At the time, *Gallup* recorded just over 40 percent support for same-sex marriage nationally. Angry electorates—used by Republicans in 2004 to turn out voters in the presidential election in favor of George W. Bush—responded by adopting anti–gay marriage bans in twenty-three states between 2004 and 2006. Meanwhile, the stiff opposition to same-sex marriage eased as Americans endorsed relationship recognition like domestic partnerships and civil unions.[95]

The organized resistance to same-sex marriage from social conservatives and influential Republicans like President George W. Bush and Senator John McCain and the headwinds that caused liberals like President Barack Obama to offer tepid support for relationship recognition—but not marriage rights—were formidable. Nonetheless, ten years after the contentious political environment between 2004 and 2006 that appeared to doom marriage rights expansion, most Americans accepted and supported marriage equality. The cake was baked when the Supreme Court squarely addressed whether the United States Constitution required states to afford same-sex couples equal access to marriage. The success of the social movement made the Court's extension of the freedom to marry an easier lift in *Obergefell v. Hodges*. The close 5–4 decision, authored by Reagan appointee Anthony Kennedy, was a blow to social conservatives but was simultaneously rooted in a conservative theme of traditional heteronormative values. Kennedy's opinion raised the institution of marriage on a pedestal, validating its primacy in society while also tethering the marriage rights of same-sex couples to raising children. Kennedy characterized the well-being of children in same-sex-coupled households as a weighty factor in constitutionalizing these marriage rights.[96]

The *Obergefell* opinion concluded with a judicial sermon on the virtues of marriage:

> No union is more profound than marriage, for it embodies the highest ideals of love, fidelity, devotion, sacrifice, and family. In forming a marital union, two people become something greater than once they were. As some of the petitioners in these cases demonstrate, marriage embodies a love that may endure even past death. It would misunderstand these men and women to say they disrespect the idea of marriage. Their plea is that they do respect it, respect it so deeply that they seek to find its fulfillment for themselves. Their

hope is not to be condemned to live in loneliness, excluded from one of civilization's oldest institutions. They ask for equal dignity in the eyes of the law. The Constitution grants them that right.[97]

Regarding *Obergefell*, Allison Tait astutely observed that the politics of respectability and profoundly conventional notions of family formation were at the heart of a decision expanding access to the institution of marriage: "With the decision in *Obergefell*, not only did the notion of love win, the institution of marriage also won. And through it all, a particularly conventional iteration of marriage predominated. In Kennedy's idealistic and idealizing concept of marriage, the relationship is important because it models good governance, social stability, and enduring commitment."[98] Rather than calling for the abolition of marriage rights altogether in favor of universal civil partnerships or reducing state marriage recognition to a simple contract, same-sex marriage advocates and judges leaned into marriage as a civic ideal. Thus, on the one hand, the safeguarding of equal rights for same-sex couples was out of step with the political right's social conservative vision since it gave gay, lesbian, and bisexual Americans equal footing. On the other hand, however, the successful social movement paving the way to *Obergefell* was not one of radical liberation but a call for acceptance into roles embraced by social conservatives as essential for social stability and traditional values. Unmistakably conservative in its flavor, *Obergefell* was a gay rights decision made for the era Reagan built.

But lest the cause of gay rights in the courts suggests a radical position on sexual equality against traditional values, associative and religious objections to sexual minorities' civil rights trumped sexual minority equality. The Court's treatment of LGBT civil rights outside relationship decriminalization and recognition was significantly less protective of sexual minorities than it was of social conservatives. In 1984, the Supreme Court held that the United States Junior Chamber, known as the Jaycees, an all-male group dedicated to building business-minded leadership skills among its members, who were under thirty-five-years-old, could be compelled to admit women under Minnesota's anti–sex discrimination public accommodations law, reasoning that the core mission of the group was not undermined by female membership.[99] The Supreme Court did not extend similar deference to New Jersey's nondiscrimination statute, which the New Jersey Supreme Court ruled applied to the Boys Scouts of America, requiring them to allow scout leaders on an equal basis regardless of sexual orientation. Like in the Jaycees case, the New Jersey Supreme Court rejected the Boy Scouts' claim that the Law Against Discrimination vio-lated the organization's First Amendment right of intimate association given the Boy Scouts' "large size, nonselectivity, inclusive rather than exclusive purpose, and practice of inviting or allowing nonmembers to attend meetings" and evidence that the Boys Scouts' wish to exclude openly gay or bisexual persons from their ranks was born out of nothing more than prejudice.[100] The Supreme Court reversed the lower court finding—without a substantial record of evidence—concluding that oppo-sition to homosexuality was core to the Boy Scouts' identity and that the state's interest in equal opportunity could not override the Boy Scouts' desire to exclude gay and bisexual men.[101] While in *Lawrence* and later in the marriage cases, the Court sided against the use of state power to dis-criminate against LGBTQ persons, it eagerly endorsed constitutional limi-tations on the power of the state to combat private discrimination against sexual minorities justified by broad secular morals or religious beliefs.

In cases following *Obergefell*, the Court hamstrung state and local officials enforcing antidiscrimination where there was evidence that a member of a state's civil-rights-enforcement agency expressed hostility to a religiously motivated denial of service to a same-sex couple.[102] In a later decision from 2021, the Court voided a policy adopted by Phila-delphia that required religiously affiliated city contractors providing foster care services to place children with same-sex couples as a viola-tion of the free exercise clause of the First Amendment. While the Court acknowledged the overriding interest governments have in mandating nondiscrimination policies for government contractors and those apply-ing to use government funds, the fact that Philadelphia's policy also provided for discretionary exemptions to the nondiscrimination rule rendered the rule constitutionally deficient because the city could not justify denying an exception.[103] Beyond sexual-minority civil rights, in 2012 and 2020, the Roberts Court issued sweeping rulings stipulating that federal civil rights laws could not be brought by employees of reli-gious institutions who were responsible in their position for carrying out any religious function, broadly defined.[104]

With social conservatives and Christian Evangelicals forming a key constituency for the Reagan coalition, the Supreme Court's free-exercise-clause and establishment-clause doctrine reflected a kind of Christian religious supremacy as movement conservatives gained more power over the Court. Regarding establishment-clause jurisprudence, the Court's conservatives snubbed the idea of "separation of church and state," ced-ing significant latitude to government actors to entangle the work of the state with religion outside the sphere of public schools.[105] During the period that Burger, Rehnquist, and Roberts led the Supreme Court, proponents of a return to mixing government and religion—especially Christianity—had a relatively free hand in granting to the Christian tradition a privileged station in the American public square. In this spirit, religious conservatives sought to diminish the constitutional right utilized by religious minorities under the free exercise clause to apply for judicial exemptions from laws when compliance would conflict with their sincerely held religious practices as a way to uniformly impose legal restrictions on the public without granting special dispensations for nonmainstream Christian practices or non-Christian religious practices.

Consistent with heightened sensitivity to civil liberties and the rights of powerless minority groups, the Warren and Burger Court held that when a governmental mandate collided with a person's sincerely held religious belief, the believer was entitled to an exemption as a matter of constitutional right unless the government could demonstrate it had a compelling interest in adopting the policy and unless there was no other manner that would have a lesser burden on the religious practice in which to achieve the government's goal. Under this exacting judicial review, which was established in *Sherbert v. Verner* and *Yoder v. Wisconsin*, religious minorities could secure judicially crafted carveouts from generally applicable laws. The Sherbert-Yoder-exemption regime undermined the supremacy of traditionally dominant faith traditions, which otherwise would have the legislative capacity to require conformity with religious majoritarian rules. For the Reagan administration, court-created constitutional exemptions also represented the kind of judicial intervention conservatives railed against as "activist judging."[106]

In two major free exercise cases before the Supreme Court, the Reagan administration advocated for inserting a cost-benefit framework into free-exercise-clause analysis that would have made a wide swath of religious exemption claims dead on arrival; in a third case, the administration argued against accommodating religious apparel in Air Force dress codes as disruptive to military operations.[107] As Douglas Laycock observed in 1986, conservative lawyering rejected the New Deal order's construction of the First Amendment:

> [The Reagan Administration] has been quite vocal in its minimalist view of the establishment clause. But in these cases it took an equally minimalist view of the free exercise clause. Its position in these briefs is not proreligion, but simply statist. The Administration does not believe that minorities should have many rights that are judicially enforceable against majorities.[108]

Conservatives' assault on the constitutional exemption system for religious objectors succeeded at the Supreme Court in 1990 when a coalition of five justices adopted a new rule that shunned *Sherbert* and *Yoder* in favor of a principle of neutrality. In *Employment Division v. Smith*, generally applicable laws that were neutral toward religious practice met constitutional muster, leaving members of new or minority faith traditions seeking statutory exemptions at the mercy of the legislative process. So long as disfavored religious groups were shown indifference by state and federal legislators, lawmakers had a relatively free hand to regulate conduct. Writing for the majority, the archconservative Justice Antonin Scalia suggested that continuing the old doctrine "would be courting anarchy," which was acutely worrisome for an increasingly diverse nation like the United States because "the danger [of anarchy] increases in direct proportion to the society's diversity of religious beliefs, and its determination to coerce or suppress none of them."[109] And while three of the Court's liberals joined by Sandra Day O'Connor warned that the new rule would harm religious minorities, the majority opinion dismissed their complaint with a collective shrug:

> It may fairly be said that leaving accommodation to the political process will place at a relative disadvantage those religious practices that are not widely engaged in; but that unavoidable consequence of democratic government must be preferred to a system in which each conscience is a law unto itself or in which judges weigh the social importance of all laws against the centrality of all religious beliefs.[110]

In 1993, Congress enacted the Religious Freedom Restoration Act (RFRA), which reinstated the old test for federal laws and regulations, but federal courts remained long-shot venues to challenge state and local laws under the free exercise clause. Perhaps what Scalia and other conservatives did not foresee was that cultural inversion threatened to place religious conservatives on the outside looking in as the nation's religiosity declined and public support for things like civil rights laws protecting gay, lesbian, bisexual, and transgender Americans; contraception access; and liberal abortion laws would grow. As the *Smith* rule threatened the conservative regime, the value of reinstating a version of the old constitutional exemption scheme as a tool to reinforce the dominant coalition rose.

After a decision by the Supreme Court that sided with closely held corporations (corporations with few shareholders, often members of one family) suing to avoid providing free contraception to their employees by stating a religious objection under the Religious Freedom Restoration Act and in anticipation of the expansion of marriage to same-sex couples in *Obergefell*,[111] religious conservatives flocked to state legislatures to pass state-level RFRAs. In doing so, they turned the RFRA, which had been a way to protect unpopular and politically weak religious minorities, into a weapon to reassert their claim to power. In 2015, state legislators in seventeen states proposed bills to empower religious objectors—though only Indiana and Arkansas succeeded, and Indiana's law caused a nationwide backlash with major corporations lining up against it, forcing then governor Mike Pence to sign an amendment protecting civil rights laws from challenges lodged by religious objectors. Hoping to avoid the national boycotts and widespread opposition that Indiana suffered, in 2016, Governor Nathan Deal vetoed RFRA legislation in Georgia.

The undercurrents in social conservative circles, which called for the revival of judicial oversight to craft religious exemptions, were at odds with two sitting conservative justices, Antonin Scalia and Anthony Kennedy, who voted with the majority in *Smith*. With the deaths of Scalia and liberal Ruth Bader Ginsburg and Kennedy's retirement, the three Trump appointees to the Court, Neil Gorsuch, Brett Kavanaugh, and Amy Coney Barrett, could now reshape religious liberty doctrine to reinvent religious conservatives' power against the tides of a changing nation. The COVID-19 pandemic that began in 2020 presented the first vehicle for the new cadre of conservatives on the bench to reorient *Smith* to be more favorable to people of faith.

One group took to the emergency docket asking the Court to enjoin the enforcement of a California pandemic quarantine policy that, in order to prevent the transmission of the virus, limited the number of households that could intermingle in private settings. This policy thus limited at-home prayer services and Bible studies, while allowing public activities that provided essential services, like transportation hubs, grocery stores, medical facilities, or manufacturers of critical goods, to continue to operate. In a 5–4 per curiam opinion, the Supreme Court's conservatives granted injunctive relief against California officials because the state's regulations were not neutral toward religion since officials treated some secular gatherings more favorably than religious gatherings.[112] The justices signaled that a shift in free exercise jurisprudence was on the horizon by granting religious practitioners "most favored nation" status so that any exemptions extended to comparable secular conduct would trigger more exacting judicial review and a presumptive right to accommodation as a matter of constitutional right.

Congress stalled the rights retrenchment for religious minorities, but the Court constitutionalized the politics of racial grievance and pulled back on racial justice. Civil rights resentment and the politics of racial grievance were some of the most potent weapons used by movement conservatives to bind a conservative coalition. Reagan tapped into white identity politics at Philadelphia, Mississippi. George H. W. Bush's campaign manager exploited it in 1988. The election of the nation's first Black president, Barack Obama, spawned a racial backlash in the Tea Party Movement and boosted the election of Donald J. Trump. And it was ethnocentric skepticism that fomented a conspiracy-theory backlash to the election—which had been made possible by a multiracial coalition—of Joseph Biden as president in 2020. The backlash disrupted the peaceful transfer of power, with an insurrection at the United States Capitol on January 6, 2021, and restrictions on access to the ballot box. While less virulent in overt racism than episodes of the late twentieth and early twenty-first centuries, the law of equal protection was unfriendly to social equity. On the voting rights front, the Court undermined efforts to enhance Black political power and gut safeguards against racially discriminatory election laws. Conservatives would similarly roll back policies that imposed affirmative obligations on governmental entities and recipients of government funding to address inequalities in education and employment. With time, the constitutional canon reflected the Reagan revolution's idea of a "colorblind constitution."

When Congress passed the Voting Rights Act of 1965, Section 5 of the Act prohibited certain jurisdictions with a history of discriminatory voting laws from changing any "standard, practice, or procedure with respect to voting" without prior approval from the Department of Justice. Pursuant to the preclearance requirements, North Carolina submitted a new congressional map after the decennial census that included one majority-Black congressional district in 1991. The federal government rejected the state's plan because the state failed to create an additional Black majority district, notwithstanding the fact that North Carolina's population could support two. North Carolina created a new district to comply with the Department of Justice's demands, but it was unusually shaped and was held together by the length of an interstate highway approximately 160 miles long, with much of this connecting area no wider than the highway itself. Several North Carolina residents challenged the new majority-Black district, arguing that it was drawn solely to enhance a racial minority group's power: state officials made no effort to make the district compact or contiguous, nor did state officials fashion the district boundaries around geographical features or political subdivisions.

The Supreme Court in *Shaw v. Reno* invalidated the North Carolina map because it was solely created using race-based criteria. Calling it a form of "racial apartheid," the majority reasoned that placing a racial minority in a legislative district with a wide wingspan with few common characteristics other than race to bind it "reinforces the perception that members of the same racial group—regardless of their age, education, economic status, or the community in which they live—think alike, share the same political interests, and will prefer the same candidates at the polls."[113] With regard to the equal protection clause, the Court embraced an anticlassification view of racial discrimination over an antisubordination view: the state could never use race as a factor in policymaking without meeting heavy judicial resistance even when the state's use of race was for noninvidious purposes intended to benefit a minority group. The Court's antagonism against the government putting a thumb on the scales in favor of racial minorities was consistent with Reaganism's resistance to the New Deal's rights revolution. Justice John Paul Stevens's dissent pointed out that conservatives' understanding of equal protection meant that, even though the Fourteenth Amendment was brought about to ensure racial equality, the Court was denying Black Americans the influence required to secure that equality. Moreover, the ruling would have the effect of granting an outsized influence to other groups instead:

> If it is permissible to draw boundaries to provide adequate representation for rural voters, for union members, for Hasidic Jews, for Polish Americans, or for Republicans, it necessarily follows that it is permissible to do the same thing for members of the very minority group whose history in the United States gave birth to the Equal Protection Clause. A contrary conclusion could only be described as perverse.[114]

In the mid-1990s, the Court struck down two more legislative maps as impermissibly taking race into account in ways akin to North Carolina in *Shaw v. Reno*.[115] But Section 5 of the Voting Rights Act, which required jurisdictions with a history of discrimination and limiting voting rights to obtain the federal government's approval of any voting policy changes, came under attack by conservative justices in 2013. The coverage formula and preclearance requirement had a sunset provision of five years when the initial law came into effect. Subsequently, the law was reauthorized in 1970, 1975, 1982, and 2006. In 2006, Congress extended the Voting Rights Act for another twenty-five years. However, the coverage formula remained unchanged for years and continued to center on voter registration and turnout data from the 1960s and 1970s. Consequently, Southern states that historically adopted Jim Crow laws and employed discriminatory tactics like poll taxes and literacy exams to deter Black voter registration remained subject to preclearance forty years after the breakdown of segregation.

In *Shelby County v. Holder*, the Court invalidated Congress's formula that determined which jurisdictions were subject to Section 5 preclearance. When the constitutionality of the Voting Rights Act was initially confirmed in *South Carolina v. Katzenbach*, the Warren Court took the position that Congress's authority to adopt voting rights laws was subject to considerable deference. In *Shelby County*, the Court sidestepped that precedent and created a new principle of law that echoed Reagan's Neshoba County Fair speech, decimating one of the New Deal era's pinnacle legislative achievements under the guise of states' rights. Citing a "tradition of equal sovereignty," the Roberts Court determined that because Congress failed to recalibrate how jurisdictions were subject to federal oversight by taking into account progress made (particularly in the Deep South),[116] the reauthorization of the Voting Rights Act coverage formula was constitutionally deficient.[117]

The opinion written by Chief Justice John Roberts waxed poetic about principles of equal sovereignty as a constitutional tradition. Far from offering something new, the opinion's hostility toward the Voting Rights Act was the child of Reagan, who described the Act as "vindictive" and "humiliating to the South."[118] Reagan asked Attorney General William French to review the continued necessity of the Voting Rights Act in 1981, offering his skepticism: it "impose[d] burdens unequally upon different parts of the nation."[119] But it was perhaps Justice Antonin Scalia who most bluntly tapped into the Reagan revolution's politics of grievance by pronouncing during the *Shelby County* oral arguments that Congress's enthusiastic and near-unanimous support for the 2006 extension of the Voting Rights Act was perhaps less evidence of the law's importance than it was evidence that the Act was a "perpetuation of racial entitlement."[120] Scalia's characterization of longstanding support for voting rights legislation was repudiated by civil rights advocates and liberals, but it was unsurprising given that his remark was consistent with his view that any benign governmental intervention to assist racial minorities constituted an unearned handout. Indeed, in 1979 Scalia cast affirmative action in these very same terms, writing that race-conscious programs were "racist" because they were "based upon concepts of racial indebtedness and racial entitlement rather than individual worth and individual need."[121]

As the Reagan coalition turned on the kinds of government benefits that had helped lower-class white Americans out of poverty, middle-class Americans who were willing to pull the ladder up from behind them accepted Scalia's view: government policies that considered race in order to enhance minority opportunities in government contracting, employment, and education were not only an unearned entitlement but were racist and deserving of the moniker "reverse discrimination."[122] Policies like "affirmative action," which were designed to address racial inequality in government, schools, and the workplace, were understood as a zero-sum game whereby any race-conscious decision necessarily came at the expense of white Americans who bore no responsibility for past episodes of racial discrimination. The zero-sum-game framework was a natural fit for conservatives given that one of the Reagan revolution's key coalitional building blocks was white suburbia where, as one scholar described, a "color-blind ideology shaped by an identity politics of suburban innocence" resonated.[123] Ironically, however, the success of the Voting Rights Act's mission to enhance minority political power and the drawing of majority-minority districts also made many districts in suburban areas more white and, consequently, more Republican. Accordingly, by the mid-1990s, the Republicans incentive to soften the politics of racial grievance faded. The GOP continued to lean into Reagan's message of white racial and economic anxiety, which, coupled with religious conservatives' fears over the role of sex and religion in society, agitated Southern voters and brought them into the GOP fold, creating a coalition to take the House and solidify realignment in 1994.

The Reagan administration forcefully opposed affirmative action policies. It went as far as attempting to rescind federal policies meant to ensure that government contracts took positive steps towards including underrepresented racial minorities in the workforce on a nondiscriminatory basis. While, during George H.W. Bush's presidency (1989–1993), the executive branch attempted to distance itself from the Reagan administration's hard line on affirmative action, other members of the GOP, like North Carolina senator Jesse Helms, leaned into racist campaigns by using affirmative action as a wedge issue in 1990. The coalition's opposition intensified throughout the 1990s. Senator Phil Gramm of Texas and Senate Majority Leader Bob Dole, leading contenders for the 1996 Republican presidential nomination, jockeyed for the more aggressive stance on ending federal affirmative action in the run-up to the GOP nomination. In subsequent years, beginning with an amendment to the California Constitution prohibiting the government from adopting affirmative action politics in 1996, opponents of race-conscious programs in multiple states made headway securing statutory and state-constitutional affirmative action bans. Calls to curb or end race-conscious programs continued through George W. Bush's presidency and proceeded to escalate. When Donald Trump occupied the White House, the Department of Justice moved from more passive forms of opposition to affirmative action programs to directing resources and lodging direct attacks against diversity programming in public and federally funded colleges and universities.

The Court's turn against affirmative action began in the 1980s when it held unconstitutional a school board's layoff policy, which required the disproportionate termination of white teachers with the most seniority and the retention of junior nonwhite teachers at a higher rate to ensure racial diversity in schools. Tapping into the narrative of white innocence and colorblind equal protection, the 1986 opinion authored by Justice Lewis Powell in *Wygant v. Jackson Board of Education* made clear the direction racial justice would take as movement conservatives gained power: "No one doubts that there has been serious racial discrimination in this country. But as the basis for imposing discriminatory *legal* remedies that work against innocent people, societal discrimination is insufficient and over expansive."[124] Three years later, a 6–3 majority invalidated a Richmond, Virginia, policy that guaranteed city construction contracts on the condition that 30 percent of the funds flow to minority-owned business subtractors, which city officials adopted to remedy racial inequality in the construction industry. Richmond officials had not, however, identified any past discrimination by the city in Richmond's contracting practices. In *City of Richmond v. J. A. Croson Co.*, the Court reasoned that only Congress—not state and local governments even in the heart of the former Confederacy—could make broad findings of discrimination and subsequently legislate to remedy past discrimination under the Fourteenth Amendment.[125] Whatever cold comfort the *Croson* ruling might have provided advocates for economic justice at the federal level, it was short-lived. The Rehnquist Court undercut the federal government's capacity to remedy racial inequality through contracting rules, holding that a policy that offered financial incentives to government contractors to hire racial minority businesses to work on federally funded projects was presumptively unconstitutional.[126] Again,

the justices tried to hedge against criticism that all race-conscious policies were unconstitutional at the same time that Antonin Scalia blasted
financial benefits to ease racial wealth and opportunity gaps as wrongly
establishing "a creditor or a debtor race" and that Justice Thomas
lamented that federal intervention was "paternalistic."[127] The equal protection jurisprudence of the 1980s and 1990s took a hard turn right,
leaning into ethnocentric skepticism and white grievance, which was
foundational to the message that buoyed the New Right and resonated
with a core constituency within the Republican Party.

The march against race-conscious educational policies in college
admissions and primary education was more protracted than the judiciary's work to dismantle public employment and contracting policies. A
1978 opinion authored by Lewis Powell in *Bakke* governed institutions
of higher education for decades, allowing admissions offices to consider
racial demographics as a plus factor in a holistic, individualized consideration of an applicant's file. Schools had a compelling interest to assem-
ble a diverse class for the pedagogical and intellectual benefits racial
diversity provided, consistent with the values of academic freedom. That
approach was ratified in two cases handed down in 2003, *Gratz v. Bollinger* and *Grutter v. Bollinger*.[128] The Court struck down an undergraduate admissions system that assigned points based on racial identity
to rank candidates but blessed the Law School's admissions approach,
which used race as one of many factors admissions officers considered in
a comprehensive, individualized assessment. But notwithstanding the
reaffirming of *Bakke*, the *Grutter* opinion proposed a sunset for diversity programming of twenty-five years, a timetable that might have made
sense for remedial actions to address past discrimination but less so for
the asserted interests of educational institutions like the University of
Michigan that wanted to compose diverse student bodies to enhance
students' experiences and enrich intellectual discourse on campus.[129]

The twin decisions in *Gratz* and *Grutter* ratified a status quo that
permitted the flexible use of race in higher education. However, they
simultaneously placed diversity, equity, and inclusion in higher education admissions in long-term jeopardy. It was not a long time, however,
until the Court struck another blow to diversity goals in education. Just
four short years later, after John Roberts and Samuel Alito replaced
vacancies left by William Rehnquist and Sandra Day O'Connor, a 5–4
divided court excepted primary and secondary schools from the rules
governing higher education. Reasoning that racial diversity has no bearing on schools' missions to educate in the basics of reading, writing, and

math and sidestepping the idea that diversity in schools serves a demo-cratic function to prepare students to live in a pluralistic society, con-servatives panned voluntary diversity plans in American school districts. Democratically accountable school districts were powerless to combat de facto housing segregation, protect students from feelings of isolation, or build a school community that reflected the heterogeneity of the real world. Embracing the idea of a colorblind constitution, the lead opinion authored by Chief Justice John Roberts proclaimed, "The way to stop discrimination on the basis of race is to stop discriminating on the basis of race."[130]

In 2023, Roberts finally capped the decades-long conservative drive to end affirmative action in two companion cases against Harvard Uni-versity and the University of North Carolina at Chapel Hill in *Students for Fair Admissions v. President and Fellows of Harvard College*,[131] rul-ing that race-conscious admissions programs designed to improve insti-tutional diversity violated the Fourteenth Amendment and the Civil Rights Act of 1964. Reaganism's colorblind constitution at long last prevailed unconditionally.

CONCLUSION

Between 1980 and 2022, American constitutionalism embraced the Rea-gan revolution's hostility toward a powerful federal government, distaste for the sprawling federal administrative state, resentment of the civil rights movement, and a fondness for the language of states' rights to unravel the social welfare state Franklin Roosevelt and his successors made. What might make this era especially remarkable is how many justices who had deep ties to the Reagan administration served alongside one another: Kennedy and Scalia were both Reagan appointees, while the formative years of John Roberts, Clarence Thomas, and Samuel Alito's legal careers trace back to service in the Reagan administration— these four men served together on the court for a decade. Even Neil Gorsuch, who was confirmed to fill Scalia's seat, had a close connection to the Reagan administration. Gorsuch's mother, Anne Gorsuch, was the administrator of the Environmental Protection Agency assigned with the mission of disabling the agency by slashing its budget, stymieing enforce-ment actions against polluters, and inviting states to take greater respon-sibility for matters that had been under its purview in administrations past. Though liberals had occasional success (until 2022) at keeping pro-tections for abortion and the bar on public school prayer in the constitutional canon, as well as expanding constitutional protections for sexual minorities, the jurisprudence of the Rehnquist and Roberts Courts was Reagan's governing philosophy. In some ways, American law echoed Reagan's famous 1986 reelection television advertisement, which proudly proclaimed that the nation was rescued from the clutches of New Dealers: "It's morning in America again." The ad emphasized the virtue of hard work and traditional family values by showcasing suburban lifestyles and displays of patriotism—a blend of antistatism, individualism, and moral hegemony.

CHAPTER 6

Of Wax and Time

A recurring error in approaches to understanding or describing American constitutional law is the propensity to see juricentric drift. The presupposition that courts are disproportionately, if not singularly, responsible for safeguarding the public's civil rights and civil liberties by arbitrating the rules that control whether and how government can act and by dispensing justice consistent with indissoluble, neutral constitutional principles looms large in debates about how constitutionalism works in the United States. But the Constitution is a thing of wax, which generations of Americans have molded, broken, melted, and reshaped in different ways through the multiple political regimes that the nation has cycled through over time. The origins of constitutional inertia and change lie in polling locations, in Congress, in the executive, in state legislatures, in small town meetings, in city streets, and in state *and* federal courts.

The essential question is not whether law and politics are severable but what the relationship is between the two. In constitutional law, jurisprudence tends to reflect the ideological commitments of the contemporaneous regime in both outcome and tone. Thus, the key to understanding constitutional law and the work of the Supreme Court as an institution is to identify these things: the reconstructive moments in electoral politics that reset the terms and conditions of the constitutional order, the ideological underpinnings that informed long-term political change, and the critical junctures in American history that forged and hardened pathways of political development.

The elections of 1800, 1828, 1860, 1932, and 1980 all profoundly shaped American life. The outcomes established governing principles that cast a shadow over politics for decades. The ideological commitments of these regimes laid the foundation for years of the constitutional law that was to come. Jacksonians built a constitutional order on white supremacy and limited federal power. Mid-nineteenth-century Republicans ushered in an era of constitutionalism hyperfocused on the freedom to work and the fear of socialism. New Dealers brought an egalitarian vision for America, which valued pragmatism and pluralism, to the fore. The Reagan revolution called for a constitutional system that limited the national state's reach while affirming the primacy of a white, suburban, Christian moral worldview.

These reconstructive stages alone fail to tell the entire story. Amid the duration of these regimes, watershed events, often in the form of policies producing politics, generated pathways of political development that steered the course of American politics and foreshadowed significant developments in constitutional jurisprudence. The three most consequential junctures for constitutional law occurred in 1848, 1871, and 1935. The Treaty of Guadalupe Hidalgo, which ended the Mexican-American War in 1848, vastly enlarged the territorial reach of the United States. The marriage of westward expansion and Jacksonian ideals augured the jurisprudence of the Taney Court and helped to foment a civil war. The Republican Party's close constituent relationship with industrialists and financiers during the 1860s, coupled with the fears of socialism sparked by events unfolding in Europe in 1871, catalyzed the downfall of Reconstruction and ignited a constitutional spark for legal doctrines that valued business over people and contractual relationships over social equality. Finally, in 1935, the Second New Deal and the beginning of a federal social safety net created reliance interests that made the commerce-clause doctrine of the era too sticky for movement conservatives and the Reagan revolution to undo. Reducing the federal government's footprint proved elusive, but Reaganites successfully imposed stricter limitations on federal power. Another critical development central to understanding the evolution of American constitutional law was the Great Migration and the subsequent shift in the 1930s in the party identification of Black voters in the North from the Republican Party to the Democratic Party. This turn influenced how the New Deal coalition—and the Supreme Court through the 1940s and 1950s—fostered a budding commitment to racial equality. Moreover, it was that growing attentiveness to racial justice and the diversifying of America, along with the success of liberals' economic policies, that intensified feelings of racial grievance, calls for small government, and aspirations for a return to older American values. In that stew, movement conservatives cooked up a theory of law in originalism and championed the idea of a colorblind constitution.

What, then, is the role of courts and the nature of constitutional decision-making in America's political system? American constitutional development has been a product of majoritarian thought and regime-building exercises. The Supreme Court has not historically been a countermajoritarian institution. The origin of the academic critique against the Supreme Court as a countermajoritarian institution is traceable to Alexander Bickel's influential book, *The Least Dangerous Branch: The Supreme Court at the Bar of Politics*. In that seminal publication, Bickel argued that judicial review was a "deviant institution in a democratic society"[1] because "when the Supreme Court declares a law unconstitutional, it thwarts the will of the representatives of the people of the here and now."[2] For Bickel, the Court's need to enforce federal statutory law against states was one thing, but constitutionalizing questions and constraining state policy choices was worthy of heightened skepticism. On this point, he wrote, "The need to effectuate the superiority of federal law over state law is not a sufficient justification of judicial review of state actions in those instances in which the federal law in question is constitutional and hence judge-made."[3]

One problem with describing the federal judiciary's constitutional role as countermajoritarian lies with the definition of the term. Suppose a court strikes a legislative act when a significant portion of the population is disenfranchised. In that instance, judicial review is hardly undemocratic—especially if the voided law subordinated the unrepresented group. Similar questions arise when a legislative body is gerrymandered or malapportioned. Is overturning a law enacted by an unrepresentative body deviant? If public sentiment is the appropriate metric, who counts? One metric for assessing countermajoritarian acts could be national public opinion. Similarly, in the case of state laws, it could be weighed against the prevailing mood of the public subject to the law in question. None of these constructions of what is meant by countermajoritarian are perfectly satisfying. The best definition of countermajoritarian judicial decision-making is outcomes that are inconsistent with popular, dominant regime principles—which are exceptions to the general rule. The mistaken belief that a countermajoritarian difficulty exists is no doubt a consequence of juricentric analysis.

The problem with the countermajoritarian debate is that it has been perpetually stuck in the political dynamics of the 1960s. The Warren Court's civil rights, civil liberties, and criminal procedure liberalism defined the terms of the discussion. In the eye of liberals, countermajoritarian courts advanced an egalitarian constitutional order against prejudice and economic power imbalances. This is a romanticized countermajoritarian judiciary. In the eye of conservatives, countermajoritarian courts corroded democracy through unprincipled judicial activism that embodied the excesses of the New Deal. The common mistake made by people who celebrate countermajoritarian courts as properly functioning institutions or who decry countermajoritarian courts as improperly functioning institutions is not understanding the paths political party development and social movements made to clear the way for constitutional change through judicial review. Those who desire *truly* countermajoritarian courts or more constrained courts are generally people who have failed to win control of national institutions at the ballot box and, consequently, have failed to win control of the courts. The source of complaints about countermajoritarian courts or judicial activism all depends on whose ox is being gored.

Historically, the federal judiciary has been a decidedly majoritarian institution that reflects the values of dominant national political coalitions, which shape it through judicial appointments, institutional changes, and procedural limits. In truth, constitutional law is the application of politics—the interactive effect of political party development, elections, and institutional design. This is not meant to suggest that courts are ceaselessly free-wheeling or that precedent *never* matters. Unwinding well-established constitutional principles cannot always be done by sheer political force when reliance interests or public sentiment is too great to overcome. In this sense, constitutional decision-making is raw political power tempered by path dependency and reason.

The judiciary's majoritarian function furthers its role in state building. Too often federal courts are considered distant actors occupying a different plane from that of the rest of the national government's players rather than actors maneuvering in concert with them. Courts are state-building partners. Judges articulate the dominant coalition's values—the big ideas—and redraw constitutional lines to accommodate those core ideological commitments while bringing outliers into the fold. This is the disciplinarian role of America's national courts. When courts of an old order frustrate an emerging coalition's work to mold the state in the new coalition's ideological image, judges are likely to find themselves on

the receiving end of blunt political measures that undercut their authority. This is the lesson of John Marshall's early tenure in which the
Supreme Court caved to Jefferson and his co-partisans in the wake of the
Election of 1800. This was the lesson from the 1860s when Radical
Republicans stripped the Supreme Court of jurisdiction and reduced the
size of the Supreme Court to prevent Andrew Johnson from nominating
justices. And it was the lesson of the Hughes Court, which under
immense pressure in the wake of multiple New Dealer electoral victories, capitulated by abandoning its pattern of hostility against major acts
of Congress.

In a well-functioning system, constitutional jurisprudence and
national policy are bound together in political time. A model of the
courts as coalitional, state-building partners assumes that judicial turnover is steady and that the institutions that produce judges mirror repre-
sentations of popular will. Democratic decay in the political branches or
antidemocratic decisions within the judiciary can foment a crisis of legitimacy for the Supreme Court of a different magnitude. This may well
describe the state of the judiciary for the foreseeable future. Compared to
earlier periods of American history, judges live longer than their prede-
cessors and benefit from a social safety net. These differences permit
judges to retire at a time that guarantees a successor of ideological kin. A
system in which judges treat their seats as a form of bequeathable property is anathema to healthy democratic norms and a practice that can
create zombie courts that outlive their timely welcome. Moreover, and
perhaps even more destabilizing, countermajoritarian institutions like
the malapportioned United States Senate and the Electoral College permit the installation of judges nominated by a president who lost a
national popular vote and was confirmed by a group of senators who
represent a minority of the American public. Decades long entrenchment
of minoritarian-on-minoritarian rule might provoke a crisis of legitimacy
should that minority coalition produce courts that disrupt the natural
flow of constitutional law in political time. Under a set of conditions
where coalitions are starkly divided along urban and rural lines and the
political strength of geography vastly outweighs the voting strength of
the people, the structure of the Constitution poses the gravest countermajoritarian problem.

The Supreme Court is not exempt from the forces of political time,
and constitutional doctrine tracks the commitments of the ideological
regimes that shape it. Far from an institution historically out of step
with society's prevailing attitudes, the Court is far more apt to synthe-

size the majority's values than to buck them. Constitutional law is most disrupted in the lurch of radical political moments that demand revisions to the constitutional order. In the long run, the Constitution and its explication will only be as virtuous as the enfranchised public is good.

Notes

CHAPTER 1. JUDICIAL REVIEW IN THE
PUZZLE OF AMERICAN CONSTITUTIONALISM

1. Robert J. Reinstein and Mark C. Radhert, "Reconstructing Marbury,"
Arkansas Law Review 57 (2005): 740–41.

2. Marbury v. Madison, 5 U.S. 137, 155 (1803).

3. Ibid. at 173.

4. Ibid. at 174–76.

5. Stuart v. Laird, 5 U.S. 299 (1803).

6. Act of March 8, 1802, Ch. 8, 2 Stat. 132; Act of April 29, 1802, Ch. 31,
2 Stat. 156.

7. A number of academics, including Ronald Formisano, John Gerring, and
Joel Silbey, have made this important point. While the time between 1800 and
1828 was one in which stable partisan coalitions formed and Jeffersonian
Republicans dominated, the kind of institutional structure and ideological
cohesion that is a hallmark of modern political parties only started to develop
after the War of 1812 and was cemented by the 1830s.

8. Some scholars, however, question whether electoral realignments in American politics are punctuated equilibriums and see realignment as a gradual process instead. See David R. Mayhew, *Electoral Realignments: A Critique of an
American Genre* (New Haven: Yale University Press, 2002).

9. Paul Pierson and Theda Skocpol, "American Politics in the Long Run," in
*The Transformation of American Politics: Activist Government and the Rise of
Conservativism*, ed. Theda Skocpol and Paul Pierson (Princeton: Princeton Uni-
versity Press, 2007), 3, 6.

10. Civil Rights Cases, 109 U.S. 3 (1883).

11. Yick Wo. v. Hopkins, 118 U.S. 356 (1886).

12. Lochner v. New York, 198 U.S. 45 (1905).

13. Jacobson v. Massachusetts, 197 U.S. 11 (1905).

14. Lieberman v. Van de Carr, 199 U.S. 552 (1905).

15. Paul Pierson, "When Effect Becomes Cause: Policy Feedback and Political Change," *World Politics* 45 (1993): 595.

16. William G. Mayer, "The Cycles of Constitutional Time: Some Skeptical Questions," *Northeastern University Law Review* 13 (2021): 657. For another major work on the institutional development of the American judiciary, see Justin Crowe, *Building the Judiciary: Law, Courts, and the Politics of Institutional Development* (Princeton: Princeton University Press, 2012).

17. Robert A. Dahl, "Decision-Making in a Democracy: The Supreme Court as a National Policymaker," *Journal of Public Law* 6 (1957): 285.

18. Ibid. at 291.

19. Jeffrey Rosen, *The Most Democratic Branch: How the Courts Serve America* (Oxford: Oxford University Press, 2006), 185.

20. Michael J. Klarman, "Rethinking the Civil Rights and Civil Liberties Revolutions," *Virginia Law Review* 82 (February 1996): 14.

21. Barry Friedman, *The Will of the People: How Public Opinion Has Influenced the Supreme Court and Shaped the Meaning of the Constitution* (New York: Farrar, Straus and Giroux, 2010).

22. Gerald N. Rosenberg, *The Hollow Hope: Can Courts Bring About Social Change*, 2nd ed. (Chicago: University of Chicago Press, 2008).

CHAPTER 2. JACKSONIANISM AND THE CONSTITUTION OF WHITE PREROGATIVE

1. "Kansas-Nebraska Act: Primary Documents in American History; Introduction," Research Guides, Library of Congress.

2. "The Fugitive Slave Act: Primary Documents in American History; Introduction," Research Guides, Library of Congress.

3. John William Burgess, *The Middle Period* (New York: Scribner's, 1897), 164.

4. Rogers M. Smith, *Civic Ideals* (New Haven: Yale University Press, 1997), 215.

5. Richard Hofstadter, *The American Political Tradition and the Men Who Made It* (New York: Knopf, 1948), 50.

6. Joseph Fishkin and William E. Forbath, *The Anti-Oligarchy Constitution: Reconstructing the Economic Foundations of American Democracy* (Cambridge, MA: Harvard University Press, 2022), 73.

7. Stephen Skowronek, *The Politics Presidents Make: Leadership from John Adams to George Bush* (Cambridge, MA: Belknap Press, 1997), 111.

8. Hofstadter, *The American Political Tradition and the Men Who Made It*, 53.

9. Harry L. Watson, *Liberty and Power: The Politics of Jacksonian America* (New York: Hill and Wang, 1990), 93.

10. Daniel Walker Howe, *What Hath God Wrought: The Transformation of America, 1815–1848* (New York: Oxford University Press, 2007), 276.

11. Andrew Jackson, "Letter from Andrew Jackson to James Hamilton Jr.," June 29, 1828, Library of Congress.

12. Desmond S. King and Rogers M. Smith, "Racial Orders in American Political Development," *American Political Science Review* 99, no. 1 (2005): 80.

13. John Gerring, *Party Ideologies in America, 1828–1996* (Cambridge: Cambridge University Press, 2001), 166.

14. Andrew Jackson, "First Annual Message to Congress," December 8, 1829, University of Virginia Miller Center.

15. Andrew Jackson, "Farewell Address," March 4, 1837, University of Virginia Miller Center.

16. *Congressional Globe*, 21st Congress, 1st Session, 332 (Apr. 28, 1830).

17. Andrew Jackson, "Maysville Road Veto Message," May 27,1830, University of Virginia Miller Center.

18. Andrew Jackson, "Bank Veto Message," July 10, 1832, National Constitution Center.

19. Mark A. Graber, "Federalist or Friends of Adams: The Marshall Court and Party Politics," *Studies in American Political Development* 12, no. 2 (1998): 264.

20. Jackson, "Bank Veto Message," July 10, 1832.

21. Crowe, *Building the Judiciary*, 111. Between 1829 and 1833, the Supreme Court issued three opinions embracing Jackson's preferences: first, allowing states to regulate commercial activity in the absence of federal preemption in Willson v. Blackbird Creek Marsh Company, 27 U.S. 245 (1829); second, allowing the taxation of banks by states in Providence Bank v. Billings, 27 U.S. 514 (1830); and third, limiting the application of the Bill of Rights to the federal government in Barron v. Baltimore, 32 U.S. 243 (1833).

22. The Court also upheld state banking as a constitutional exercise that did not violate the bills of credit provision of the contract clause in Article I, Section 10, which disallows a state to "coin Money; emit Bills of Credit; make any Thing but gold and silver Coin a Tender in Payment of Debts." Briscoe v. Bank of Kentucky, 36 U.S. (11 Pet.) 257 (1837).

23. Proprietors of Charles River Bridge v. Proprietors of Warren Bridge, 36 U.S. 420, 553, (1837).

24. While the major decisions from Taney Court on this question centered around the commerce clause and slavery, another decision that captured the Court's caution against federal power generally was an 1849 case that challenged Rhode Island's undemocratic state government, which limited suffrage to well-to-do landowning elites. While the challengers to Rhode Island's oligarchy were more friendly to Taney and Jacksonians, their claim that the federal courts could second-guess the form of state governments under the Constitution's guarantee clause, which, in Article IV, Section 4, provides that each state shall have a republican form of government, threatened states' sovereign rights. Unsurprisingly, the Supreme Court declined the invitation to decide whether Rhode Island was sufficiently democratic. The Court held these questions were political and unsuitable for judicial resolution, thus limiting the federal judiciary's power to question the legitimacy of undemocratic institutional rearrangements in states. Luther v. Borden, 48 U.S. 1 (1849).

25. Mayor, Aldermen & Commonalty of City of New York v. Miln, 36 U.S. 102, 111 (1837).

26. Ibid. at 136–37.

27. Ibid. at 142–43.

28. See Joel H. Silbey, "The Political World of Antebellum Presidents," in *A Companion to the Antebellum Presidents, 1837–1861*, ed. Joel H. Silbey (Chichester: John Wiley & Sons, 2014), 17–18.

29. Tim Verhoeven, "The Case for Sunday Mails: Sabbath Laws and the Separation of Church and State in Jacksonian America," *Journal of Church and State* 55, no. 1 (2013): 71–91.

30. "Transportation of the Mail on the Sabbath," January 19, 1829, Library of Congress.

31. Ibid.

32. Ibid.

33. Bertram Wyatt-Brown, "Prelude to Abolitionism: Sabbatarian Politics and the Rise of the Second Party System," *Journal of American History* 58, no. 2 (1971): 334.

34. Andrew Jackson, "Letter from Andrew Jackson to Amos Kendall," August 9, 1835, Library of Congress.

35. Joseph Gales and William Winston Seaton, Register of Debates in Congress, 21st Congress, 1st session, pt. 1. Dec. 7, 1829 to Mar. 24, 1830, 1020.

36. Andrew Jackson, "Letter from Andrew Jackson to John Freeman Schermerhorn," June 12, 1832, Library of Congress.

37. Howe, *What Hath God Wrought*, 345.

38. Edward Everett, "Speech on the Bill for Removing the Indians from the East to the West Side of the Mississippi, Delivered in the House of Representatives," Washington, DC, May 19, 1830, Library of Congress.

39. Jackson, "First Annual Message to Congress," December 8, 1829.

40. Andrew Jackson, "Second Annual Message to Congress," December 6, 1830, University of Virginia Miller Center.

41. State v. Forman, 16 Tenn. 256, 270–71, 1835 WL 945 (Tenn.), 8.

42. Maggie Blackhawk, "Federal Indian Law as Paradigm within Public Law," *Harvard Law Review* 132 (2019): 1822.

43. Charles Warren, *The Supreme Court in United States History* (Boston: Little, Brown, and Company, 1926), 759.

44. Keith E. Whittington, *Political Foundations of Judicial Supremacy: The Presidency, the Supreme Court, and Constitutional Leadership in U.S. History* (Princeton: Princeton University Press, 2007), 34, 59.

45. Bethany R. Berger, "Power over This Unfortunate Race: Race, Politics and Indian Law in United States v. Rogers," *William & Mary Law Review* 45 (2004), 1959.

46. United States v. Rogers, 45 U.S. 567, 572, 11 L. Ed. 1105 (1846).

47. Ralph Waldo Emerson, *Emerson in His Journals*, ed. Joel Porte (Cambridge, MA: Harvard University Press, 1982), 358.

48. Free Soil Party, "Free Soil Party Platform of 1848," June 22, 1848, The American Presidency Project, University of California, Santa Barbara.

49. *Congressional Globe*, 31st Congress, 1st Session, 455. (Mar. 4, 1850).

50. Justin Crowe, "Westward Expansion, Preappointment Politics, and the Making of the Southern Slaveholding Supreme Court," *Studies in American Political Development* 24, no.1 (2010): 95–96.

51. Andrew Jackson, "Farewell Address," March 4, 1837, University of Virginia Miller Center.

52. Democratic Party, "1848 Democratic Party Platform," May 22, 1848, The American Presidency Project, University of California, Santa Barbara.

53. "An Act to Organize the Territories of Nebraska and Kansas," 10 Stat. 277 (1854).

54. Prigg v. Com. of Pennsylvania, 41 U.S. 539 (1842).

55. Prigg v. Com. of Pennsylvania, 41 U.S. 539, 622 (1842).

56. Jones v. Van Zandt, 46 U.S. 215 (1847).

57. Jones v. Van Zandt, 46 U.S. 215, 227 (1847).

58. Scott v. Emerson, 15 Mo. 576, 582 (1852).

59. Scott v. Emerson, 15 Mo. 576, 590 (1852) (internal citations omitted).

60. Scott v. Emerson, 15 Mo. 576, 585 (1852).

61. Scott v. Emerson, 15 Mo. 576, 586–87 (1852).

62. Dred Scott v. Sandford, 60 U.S. 393, 407 (1857), superseded (1868).

63. Dred Scott v. Sandford, 60 U.S. 393, 452 (1857), superseded (1868).

64. Dred Scott v. Sandford, 60 U.S. 393, 452 (1857), superseded (1868).

65. Frederick Douglass, *Two Speeches* (Rochester: C. P. Dewey, 1857), 31.

66. "A New Federal Constitution," *Chicago Tribune*, March 13, 1857, 2.

67. "The Political Judges and their Belongings," *New York Tribune*, March 17, 1857, 5.

68. Editorial, *New York Tribune*, March 12, 1857, 4.

69. Democratic Party, "1856 Democratic Party Platform," June 2, 1856, The American Presidency Project, University of California, Santa Barbara.

70. Ibid.

71. R. G. Horton, *The Life and Public Services of James Buchanan* (New York: Derby & Jackson, 1856), 427.

72. Stephen A. Douglas, "The Lincoln-Douglas Debates: Sixth Debate," (Quincy, Illinois, October 13, 1858), Northern Illinois University Library.

73. Stephen A. Douglas, "The Lincoln-Douglas Debates: Third Debate," (Jonesboro, Illinois, September 15, 1858), Northern Illinois University Library.

74. Opinion of the Supreme Judicial Court, 44 Me. 507, 515–16 (1857).

75. "The Dred Scott Decision in the Pennsylvania Legislature," *New York Times*, April 27, 1857, 8.

76. "Majority Report of the Select Committee of the Senate of Pennsylvania, upon the decision in the case of Dred Scott vs. John F. A. Sanford," *The Bedford Inquirer and Chronicle*, May 15, 1857.

77. "The Dred Scott Decision," *New York Times*, April 11, 1857, 11.

78. "The Dred Scott Decision in the Ohio Legislature," *New York Times*, April 11, 1857, 11.

79. "Constitution of the State of Kansas (Topeka Constitution)," October 23, 1855, Records of the US Senate, National Archives.

80. James Buchanan, "Message to Congress Transmitting the Constitution of Kansas," February 2, 1858, University of Virginia Miller Center.

81. Ibid.

82. William W. Freehling, *The Road to Disunion: Secessionists Triumphant, 1854–1861* (New York: Oxford University Press, 2007), 138.

83. James Buchanan, "Fourth Annual Message to Congress on the State of the Union," December 3, 1860, University of Virginia Miller Center.

84. Ibid.

CHAPTER 3. CIVIL WAR, CONSTITUTIONAL REFORMATION, AND FREE LABOR

1. James Buchanan, "Inaugural Address," United States Capitol, Washington, DC, March 4, 1875, University of Virginia Miller Center.

2. Dred Scott v. Sandford, 60 U.S. 393 (1857).

3. Abraham Lincoln, *The Collected Works of Abraham Lincoln: The Abraham Lincoln Association, Springfield, Illinois,* ed. Roy P. Basler, vol. 3 (New Brunswick: Rutgers University Press, 1953 [Ann Arbor: University of Michigan Digital Library Production Services, 2001]), 387–88.

4. John Hope Franklin, *Reconstruction after the Civil War* (Chicago: University of Chicago Press, 2013), 12.

5. Legal Tender Act, Ch. 142, 12 Stat. 532 (1862).

6. The Homestead Act of 1862, Ch. 75, 12 Stat. 392, repealed by Pub. L. No. 94-579, tit. VII, § 702, 90 Stat. 2787 (1976); Morrill Act of 1862, Act of July 2, 1862, Ch. 130, § 1, 12 Stat. 503.

7. An Act to Establish a Department of Agriculture, 12 Stat. 387–88 (1862).

8. Pacific Railway Act, 37th Cong., Ch. 120, 12 Stat. 489 (1862).

9. National Banking Act of 1863, Ch. 58, 12 Stat. 665.

10. An Act to Establish a Bureau for the Relief of Freedmen and Refugees, Ch. 90, 13 Stat. 507 (1865).

11. Skowronek, *The Politics Presidents Make,* 217.

12. Eric Foner, *Reconstruction: America's Unfinished Revolution, 1863–1877* (New York: Harper & Row, 1988), 191.

13. An Act to make it a misdemeanor to hunt with fire arms or a dog or dogs, on the Sabbath day, in certain counties in this State therein named, 1866 Ga. Laws 154.

14. An Act to define certain acts of Trespass, and make the same penal, 1866 Ga. Laws 248.

15. Madison J. Wells, "Letter from J. Madison Wells, Governor of Louisiana, to Andrew Johnson, President of the United States," July 29, 1865, reprinted in Paul H. Bergeron, *The Papers of Andrew Johnson* (Knoxville: University of Tennessee Press, 1989), 503.

16. Carl Schurz, *Report of Carl Schurz on the States of South Carolina, Georgia, Alabama, Mississippi, and Louisiana, Executive Documents of the Senate of the United States for the First Session Thirty-Ninth Congress, 1865–1866* 1, no. 2 (1866), 32.

17. Carl Schurz, "Letter from Carl Schurz to Andrew Johnson," August 13, 1865, in *Advice after Appomattox: Letters to Andrew Johnson, 1865–1866*, ed. Brooks D. Simpson, LeRoy P. Graf, and John Muldowny (Knoxville: University of Tennessee Press, 1987), 85.

18. Carl Schurz, *Report on the Condition of the South: Views Expressed by Major General Steedman in Conversation with Carl Schurz* (Washington, DC: US Congress, Senate, 1865).

19. J. L. Gaynes, "Letter from J. L. Gaynes, Colonel First Texas Calvary to Captain B. F. Morey, Assistant Adjutant General," July 8, 1865, Smithsonian Institute.

20. Peter Joseph Osterhaus, "Statement from Peter Joseph Osterhaus, Major General United States Volunteers to Carl Schurz," August 27, 1865, in *Report of Carl Schurz on the States of South Carolina, Georgia, Alabama, Mississippi, and Louisiana, Executive Documents of the Senate of the United States for the First Session Thirty-Ninth Congress, 1865–1866* 1, no. 2 (1866), 60.

21. Knote v. United States, 95 U.S. 149.

22. Civil Rights Act of 1866, Ch. 31, 14 Stat. 27 (1866).

23. Ibid.

24. Civil Rights Act of 1866 (codified at 42 U.S.C. § 1981).

25. Ibid.

26. Civil Rights Act of 1866 (codified at 42 U.S.C. § 1982).

27. "Governor Warmoth's Veto," *New Orleans Crescent*, September 29, 1868.

28. Journal of the Senate of the State of Mississippi (1870), Appendix A 3.

29. Foner, *Reconstruction*, 369.

30. Heather Cox Richardson, *The Death of Reconstruction: Race, Labor, and Politics in the Post-Civil War North, 1865-1901* (Cambridge: Harvard University Press, 2001), 89.

31. Cummings v. Missouri, 71 U.S. (4 Wall.) 277 (1867); Ex Parte Garland, 71 U.S. 333 (1866).

32. Ex Parte Milligan, 71 U.S. 2 (1866).

33. Georgia v. Stanton, 73 U.S. 50 (1868).

34. Texas v. White 74 U.S. 700, 726 (1869).

35. Ex parte McCardle, 74 U.S. 506 (1868).

36. Judicial Circuits Act of 1866, Ch. 210, § 1, 14 Stat. 209, 209.

37. G. Edward White, *Law in American History: From Reconstruction through the 1920s* (New York: Oxford University Press, 2012), 203.

38. Hepburn v. Griswold, 75 U.S. (8 Wall.) 603 (1870).

39. Legal Tender Cases, 79 U.S. 457, 572 (1870).

40. In Wabash, St. Louis & Pacific Railway Company v. Illinois, 118 U.S. 557 (1886).

41. An Act to Provide for the Appointment of a Land Commissioner, and to Define His Powers and Duties, 186, 1868.

42. The Proceedings of the 1868 Constitutional Convention of South Carolina, 84, University of Michigan Digital Archives.

43. The Proceedings of the 1868 Constitutional Convention of South Carolina, 138.

44. S.C. Const. Art. I § 10 (Adopted 1868).

45. S.C. Const. Art. I § 12 (Adopted 1868).

46. S.C. Const. Art. I § 29 (Adopted 1868).

47. The Proceedings of the 1868 Constitutional Convention of South Carolina, 353.

48. S.C. Const. Art. XI § 1 (Adopted 1868).

49. S.C. Const. Art. X § 8 (Adopted 1868).

50. 1870, Act 261, An Act to Provide for the Care of the Poor.

51. 1870, Joint Resolution to Provide Medical Aid for the Indigent Sick in the Respective Counties in the State, Mar. 1, 1870.

52. 1872, Act 161, An Act for the Relief of the Widows and Orphans of Persons Killed Because of Their Political Opinions. See Ku Klux Klan Act of 1871, Ch. 22, § 4, 17 Stat. 13, 14–15; Proclamation No. 4 of 1871, reprinted in 17 Stat. 951, 951–52 (1871).

53. 1872, Act 165, An Act to Provide for the Establishment of a School in the State Penitentiary.

54. 1873, Act 413, An Act to Provide for the Establishment of a House of Refuge and Industrial School in the Cities of Charleston and Columbia.

55. S.C. Const. Art. X § 3 (Adopted 1868).

56. S.C. Const. Art. X § 10 (Adopted 1868).

57. 1874, Act 462, An Act to Establish Certain State Scholarships in the University of South Carolina.

58. S.C. Const. Art. I § 36 (Adopted 1868).

59. The Proceedings of the 1868 Constitutional Convention of South Carolina, 707.

60. *Congressional Globe*, 39th Congress, 2nd Session. 15. (December 5, 1866).

61. 1872, Act 63, An Act to Authorize Aliens to Hold Property.

62. 1870, Act 233, An Act to Secure Equal Civil Rights and the Provide for the Enjoyment of All Remedies in Law by All Persons Regardless of Race or Color.

63. S.C. Const. Art. VIII Sec. 8 (Adopted 1868) ("The General Assembly shall never pass any law that will deprive of any of the citizens of this State of the right of suffrage except for treason, murder, robbery, or duelling, whereof the persons shall have been duly tried and convicted.").

64. Art. IV, Sec. 34.

65. The Proceedings of the 1868 Constitutional Convention of South Carolina, 218.

66. Calhoun v. Calhoun, 2 S.C. 283 (1870).

67. The Proceedings of the 1868 Constitutional Convention of South Carolina, 227.

68. The Proceedings of the 1868 Constitutional Convention of South Carolina, 231.

69. Osborn v. Nicholson, 80 U.S. 654, 663 (1871).

70. Hall v. United States, 92 U.S. 27, 30 (1875).

71. Act No. 147, An Act to Prohibit Laborers and Persons Working Under Contract on Shares of Crops 1869.

72. 1872, Act 33, An Act to Regulate the Labor of Persons Confined in the Penitentiary of the State of South Carolina; 1872, Act 169, An Act to Regulate the Issuing of Checks to Laborers Upon Plantations or Elsewhere.

73. Foner, *Reconstruction*, 377.

74. "A New Democratic Grievance," *New York Times*, March 28, 1871.

75. "The Negro Declaration of War!" *Charleston Daily News*, November 7, 1870, 2.

76. Philip M. Katz, *From Appomattox to Montmartre: Americans and the Paris Commune* (Cambridge, MA: Harvard University Press, 1998), 1–2.

77. Howard Jay Graham, "Justice Field and the Fourteenth Amendment," *Yale Law Journal* 52, no. 4 (1943): 851, 868.

78. "The Woes of South Carolina," *New York Daily Herald*, May 10, 1871.

79. Robert Somers, *The Southern States Since the War, 1870–1* (London: Macmillan, 1871), 41.

80. *Proceedings of the Tax-Payers' Convention of South Carolina* (Charleston: Tax-Payers' Convention of South Carolina, 1871), 20.

81. *Proceedings of the Tax-Payers' Convention of South Carolina*, 38.

82. *Congressional Globe*, 42nd Congress, 2nd Session. 3585. (May 18, 1872).

83. "South Carolina," *New York Times*, June 8, 1874.

84. *Proceedings of the Tax-Payers' Convention of South Carolina* (Charleston: Tax-Payers' Convention of South Carolina, 1874), 14.

85. "Negro Rule in South Carolina," *New York Times*, February 17, 1874.

86. Ibid.

87. Fred Rodell, *Nine Men: A Political History of the Supreme Court from 1790 to 1955* (New York: Vintage Books, 1955), 173.

88. Pollock v. Farmers' Loan & Tr. Co., 158 U.S. 601, 695 (1895).

89. Joseph P. Bradley, "Letter from Joseph P. Bradley to Carry Bradley," April 30, 1867, MG 26, box 3, Joseph P. Bradley Papers, New Jersey Historical Society, Newark. Quoted in James Gray Pope, "Snubbed Landmark: Why United States v. Cruikshank (1876) Belongs at the Heart of the American Constitutional Canon," *Harvard Civil Rights—Civil Liberties Law Review* 49 (2014): 419.

90. Quoted in Brian Kelly, "Black Laborers, the Republican Party, and the Crisis of Reconstruction in Lowcountry South Carolina," *International Review of Social History* 51, no. 3 (2006): 382.

91. "What Has Become of the Southern Negro?" *New York Times*, March 7, 1871.

92. Kelly, "Black Laborers, the Republican Party, and the Crisis of Reconstruction in Lowcountry South Carolina," 397.

93. Ibid. at 382.

94. "The Rulers of the South," *New York Times*, March 8, 1875.

95. Eric Foner, *Nothing but Freedom: Emancipation and Its Legacy* (Baton Rouge: Louisiana State University Press, 1983), 92.

96. Foner, *Nothing but Freedom*, 101.

97. "Slavery in Colleton," *Charleston News & Courier*, May 29, 1876.

98. "The Result in South Carolina," *The Atlantic*, January 1878.

99. Slaughterhouse Cases, 83 U.S. 36 (1872).

100. Homer H. Moore, *An Anatomy of Atheism: As Demonstrated in the Light of the Constitution and Laws of Nature* (Cincinnati: Cranston and Stowe, 1890), 324.

101. James Parton, *General Butler in New Orleans: History of the Administration of the Department of the Gulf in the Year 1862* (New York: Mason Brothers, 1864), 309.

102. Lawrence Powell, "Centralization and Its Discontents in Reconstruction Louisiana," *Studies in American Political Development* 20, no. 2 (2006): 121.

103. Slaughterhouse Cases, 83 U.S. at 84.

104. Ibid.

105. Stephen Ross, "Justice Miller's Reconstruction: The Slaughter-House Cases, Health Codes, and Civil Rights in New Orleans, 1861–1873," *Journal of Southern History* 64, no. 4 (1998): 667.

106. Slaughterhouse Cases at 79.

107. Strauder v. State of W. Virginia, 100 U.S. 303, 308 (1879).

108. Buchanan v. Warley, 245 U.S. 60, 81 (1917).

109. Corrigan v. Buckley, 271 U.S. 323 (1926).

110. The Supreme Court also struck down grandfather clauses—exceptions to rules requiring stringent literacy tests to qualify as an elector if a person was a descendant of a pre-Reconstruction eligible voter, which empowered white voters—as a violation of the Fifteenth Amendment. Guinn v. United States, 238 U.S. 347 (1915).

111. C. Vann Woodward, *Origins of the New South, 1877–1913: A History of the South* (Baton Rouge: Louisiana State University Press, 1995), 20.

112. "That all persons within the jurisdiction of the United States shall be entitled to the full and equal enjoyment of the accommodations, advantages, facilities, and privileges of inns, public conveyances on land or water, theaters, and other places of public amusement; subject only to the conditions and limitations established by law, and applicable alike to citizens of every race and color, regardless of any previous condition of servitude." Civil Rights Act of 1875, Ch. 114, 18 Stat. 335 (1875).

113. Henry Jones, *An Abridgment of the Debates of Congress* (New York: Henry Holt and Company, 1875), 696.

114. "The Civil-Wrongs Bill," *Chicago Tribune*, May 31, 1874, 8.

115. John Hope Franklin, "The Enforcement of the Civil Rights Act of 1875," *Prologue Magazine*, Winter 1974, 215.

116. *Daily Memphis Avalanche*, March 30, 1875, 2.

117. "Law and Partisanship," *Detroit Free Press*, March 25, 1875, 2.

118. United States v. Cruikshank, 92 U.S. 542, 554 (1875). This principle was applied to the Fifteenth Amendment in James v. Bowman, 190 U.S. 127 (1903).

119. The Civil Rights Cases, 109 U.S. at 14.

120. United States v. Stanley, 109 U.S. 3, 14 (1883).

121. Civil Rights Cases, 109 U.S. 3, 25 (1883).

122. Plessy v. Ferguson, 163 U.S. 537, 545 (1896), overruled by Brown v. Bd. of Ed. of Topeka, Shawnee Cty., Kan., 347 U.S. 483 (1954).

123. Ibid. at 551.

124. Ibid. at 550.

125. Yick v. Hopkins, 118 U.S. 356, 373–74 (1886).

126. Sav. & Loan Ass'n v. City of Topeka, 87 U.S. 655 (1874).

127. Ibid. at 662.

128. Peter Karsten, "Supervising the 'Spoiled Children of Legislation': Judicial Judgments Involving Quasi-Public Corporations in the Nineteenth Century U.S.," *American Journal of Legal History* 41, no. 3 (1997): 319.

129. Ibid.

130. Sav. & Loan Ass'n., 87 U.S. at 663.

131. Ibid. at 669 (Clifford, J., dissenting).

132. Munn v. Illinois, 94 U.S. 113 (1876).

133. In Charles Wolff Packing Co. v. Ct. of Indus. Rels. of State of Kansas, 262 U.S. 522, 535 (1923), the Court explained that the government had a freer hand to regulate businesses created by a public charter, common carriers, and businesses that owed their existence to government regulation under the public affectation test.

134. Munn v. Illinois, 94 U.S. 113 at 125.

135. Stone v. Farmers' Loan & Tr. Co., 116 U.S. 307, 331 (1886).

136. Civil Rights Cases, 109 U.S. 3 (1883).

137. Allgeyer v. Louisiana, 165 U.S. 578 (1897).

138. Ibid. at 589.

139. Lochner v. New York, 198 U.S. 45, 45 (1905), abrogated by W. Coast Hotel Co. v. Parrish, 300 U.S. 379 (1937).

140. Ibid. at 56.

141. Ibid. at 57.

142. Ibid. at 68.

143. Ibid. at 64.

144. Ibid.

145. Robin West, *Progressive Constitutionalism: Reconstructing the Fourteenth Amendment* (Durham: Duke University Press, 1994), 339.

CHAPTER 4. NEW DEAL CONSTITUTIONALISM

1. Franklin D. Roosevelt, "Address Accepting the Presidential Nomination," Democratic National Convention, Chicago, July 2, 1932, The American Presidency Project, University of California, Santa Barbara.

2. "Text of Governor Roosevelt's Speech at Commonwealth Club, San Francisco," *New York Times*, September 24, 1932, 6.

3. Ibid.

4. Franklin D. Roosevelt, "First Inaugural Address of Franklin D. Roosevelt," March 4, 1933, The Avalon Project, Yale Law School. Roosevelt's message was one of reassurance that fearmongering and demagoguery were counterproductive to advancing the national interest and that "public policy could overcome fear" in an age when other nations turned away from liberal democratic principles. Ira Katznelson, *Fear Itself: The New Deal and the Origins of Our Time* (New York: W. W. Norton & Company, 2013), 35.

5. Home Bldg. & Loan Ass'n v. Blaisdell, 290 U.S. 398, 425 (1934).

6. Ibid. at 442.

7. Nebbia v. New York, 291 U.S. 502.

8. Mayflower Farms v. Ten Eyck, 297 U.S. 266, 274 (1936).

9. Morehead v. People of State of New York ex rel. Tipaldo, 298 U.S. 587, 610 (1936), overruled in part by Olsen v. Nebraska ex rel. W. Reference & Bond Ass'n, 313 U.S. 236 (1941).

10. United States v. Butler, 297 U.S. 1 (1936).

11. Ibid. at 66.

12. Ibid. at 75–76.

13. Panama Refining Co. v. Ryan, 293 U.S. 388 (1935).

14. Ibid. at 430.

15. Carter v. Carter Coal Co., 298 U.S. 238, 303 (1936) ("Production is not commerce; but a step in preparation for commerce."); A. L. A. Schechter Poultry Corp. v. United States, 295 U.S. 495, 543 1570 (1935).

16. United States v. E. C. Knight Co., 156 U.S. 1, 12 (1895) (holding that the federal government could not regulate manufacturing monopolies because "[c]ommerce succeeds to manufacture, and is not a part of it"); Hammer v. Dagenhart, 247 U.S. 251, 272 (1918) (invalidating a federal law regulating child labor–made products because production and attendant work conditions were complete before shipping and thus distinct from interstate commerce).

17. Railroad Retirement Board v. Alton Railroad Co., 295 U.S. 330 (1935).

18. Ashton v. Cameron County Dist, 298 U.S. 513 (1936).

19. NLRB v. Jones & Laughlin Steel Corp., 301 U.S. 1 (1937) (affirming the constitutionality of the Wagner Act under the Commerce Clause).

20. Steward Machine Company v. Davis, 301 U.S. 548 (1937) (upholding unemployment insurance under the federal taxing power). The Court upheld the Social Security Act's old-age insurance, 7–2, in Helvering v. Davis, 301 U.S. 619 (1937), under the federal government's spending power.

21. United States v. Darby Lumber Co., 312 U.S. 100 (1941) (rejecting the argument the commerce clause power could not reach employment relationships and working conditions).

22. Wickard v. Fillburn, 317 U.S. 111 (1942); Katzenbach v. McClung, 379 U.S. 294 (1964); and Daniel v. Paul, 395 U.S. 298 (1969).

23. See Drexel Furniture Co., 259 U.S. 20 (1922) (striking down a federal tax on businesses employing child labor as an unconstitutional attempt to regulate labor conditions and not a legitimate revenue-generating measure).

24. Sonzinsky v. United States, 300 U.S. 506 (1937) (upholding then National Firearms Act of 1934's annual excise tax on firearms dealers).

25. Norris-LaGuardia Act of 1932, 29 U.S.C. § 102. The Norris-LaGuardia Act banned yellow dog contracts, which required workers to pledge not to unionize as a condition of employment and limited federal courts from issuing injunctive relief against strikes.

26. National Industrial Recovery Act, Pub. L. 73–67, 48 Stat. 195, enacted June 16, 1933.

27. Ibid.

28. Labor Management Reporting and Disclosure Act of 1959, Pub. L. 86–257, 73 Stat. 519 (1959). The Supreme Court said the law's goal was "to insure 'free and democratic' elections." Wirtz v. Loc. 153, Glass Bottle Blowers Ass'n, 389 U.S. 463, 470 (1968).

29. De Jonge v. State of Oregon, 299 U.S. 353, 365 (1937).

30. Thomas v. Collins, 323 U.S. 516, fn. 1 (1945).

31. Ibid. at 539.

32. Franklin D. Roosevelt, "Acceptance Speech for the Renomination for the Presidency," Philadelphia, June 27, 1936, The American Presidency Project, University of California, Santa Barbara.

33. Ibid.

34. See Ry. Emp. Dep't v. Hanson, 351 U.S. 225, 236 (1956); Abood v. Detroit Bd. of Ed., 431 U.S. 209 (1977), overruled by Janus v. Am. Fed'n of State, Cty., & Mun. Emps., Council 31, 138 S. Ct. 2448 (2018).

35. Nat'l Ass'n for Advancement of Colored People v. State of Ala. ex rel. Patterson, 357 U.S. 449 (1958).

36. Ibid. at 460.

37. Bates v. City of Little Rock, 361 U.S. 516 (1960) (holding a municipal ordinance requiring the disclosure of membership lists for public review an unconstitutional measure abridging the right to association).

38. Shelton v. Tucker, 364 U.S. 479 (1960) (ruling that an Arkansas law requiring public school teachers to file affidavits attesting to all organizations they had an affiliation with for five years as violative of the constitutional guarantee of associative freedom).

39. David Plotke, *Building a Democratic Political Order Reshaping American Liberalism in the 1930s and 1940s* (Cambridge: Cambridge University Press, 1996), 157.

40. Eric Rauchway, *Why the New Deal Matters* (New Haven: Yale University Press, 2021).

41. Executive Order 7046, Prescribing Rules and Regulations Relating to Wages, Hours of Work, and Conditions of Employment Under the Emergency Relief Appropriation Act of 1935 (May 10, 1935).

42. Terence Young, "'A Contradiction in Democratic Government': W. J. Trent, Jr., and the Struggle to Desegregate National Park Campgrounds," *Environmental History* 14, no. 4 (January 2009): 673.

43. William E. Leuchtenburg, *The White House Looks South: Franklin D. Roosevelt, Harry S. Truman, Lyndon B. Johnson* (Baton Rouge: Louisiana State University Press, 2005), 62.

44. Notably, some populist Southern Democratic governors like Georgia's Ellis Arnall and Louisiana's Huey Long bucked the trend to some degree by advocating for the repeal of poll taxes. Robinson Woodward-Burns, *Hidden Laws: How State Constitutions Stabilize American Politics* (New Haven: Yale University Press, 2021), 162.

45. Marguerite Cartwright, "The Ives-Quinn Bill: Legislative and Social Background," *Journal of Negro Education* 20 (1951): 115, 117.

46. Executive Order 8802, Reaffirming Policy of Full Participation in the Defense Program by All Persons, Regardless of Race, Creed, Color, or National

Origin, and Directing Certain Action in Furtherance of Said Policy (June 25, 1941).

47. Harry S. Truman, *To Secure These Rights: The Report of the President's Committee on Civil Rights* (Washington, DC: U.S. Government Publishing Office, 1947), 166.

48. Ibid. at 152.

49. Shelley v. Kraemer, 1947 WL 44159 (U.S.), 4 (U.S., 2006).

50. Democratic Party, "1948 Democratic Platform," July 12, 1948, The American Presidency Project, University of California, Santa Barbara.

51. Executive Order 9981, Establishing the President's Committee on Equality of Treatment and Opportunity in the Armed Services (July 25, 1948).

52. Eric Schickler, *Racial Realignment: The Transformation of American Liberalism, 1932–1965* (Princeton: Princeton University Press, 2016), 95.

53. Civil Rights Act of 1964, Pub. L. 88-352, 78 Stat. 241 (1964); Voting Rights Act of 1965, Pub. L. 81-110, 79 Stat. 437 (1965); Fair Housing Act, Pub. L. 90-284, 82 Stat. 73 (1968).

54. David Freeman Engstrom, "The Lost Origins of American Fair Employment Law: Regulatory Choice and the Making of Modern Civil Rights, 1943–1972," *Stanford Law Review* 63 (2011): 1073.

55. N.Y. Exec. Law § 290 (noting a legislative finding that racial discrimination "threatens the rights and proper privileges of its inhabitants but menaces the institutions and foundation of a free democratic state"); N.J. Stat. Ann. § 10:5-3 (West) (same); Wash. Rev. Code Ann. § 49.60.010 (same). Fair Employment Practices Act, California Proposition 11 (1946) (arguing that "A yes vote for Proposition 11 furthers the cause of American Democracy which rests on equality of opportunity.").

56. California Initiative Proposition 11, Equal Employment Opportunity Initiative (November 5, 1946), University of California College of the Law, San Francisco.

57. Chambers v. State of Fla., 309 U.S. 227, 241 (1940).

58. Hirabayashi v. United States, 320 U.S. 81, 100 (1943); Korematsu v. United States, 323 U.S. 214, 216 (1944), abrogated by Trump v. Hawaii, 138 S. Ct. 2392 (2018).

59. Ex parte Endo, 323 U.S. 283, 302 (1944). Eric Muller described the relationship between Korematsu and Endo as the Court navigating between its distaste for racial classifications and the justices' unwillingness to embarrass the president with a major loss: "It didn't want, on the one hand, to approve of racial detentions, or, on the other, to hand President Roosevelt a defeat during wartime." Quoted in Stephanie Buck, "Overlooked No More: Mitsuye Endo, a Name Linked to Justice for Japanese-Americans," *New York Times*, October 9, 2019.

60. Oyama v. California, 332 U.S. 633, 640 (1948) ("In our view of the case, the State has discriminated against Fred Oyama; the discrimination is based solely on his parents' country of origin; and there is absent the compelling justification which would be needed to sustain discrimination of that nature.").

61. Takahashi v. Fish & Game Comm'n, 334 U.S. 410, 420 (1948). Earl Maltz argued that Takahashi "embodied one of the most important themes of post-1937 jurisprudence," namely that it moved away from a "formal concept of

citizenship in favor of a more fluid assessment of the interests involved." Earl M. Maltz, "Citizenship and the Constitution: A History and Critique of the Supreme Court's Alienage Jurisprudence," *Arizona State Law Journal* 28 (1996): 1135, 1163.

62. Randall Kennedy, "Justice Murphy's Concurrence in Oyama v. California: Cussing Out Racism," *Texas Law Review* 74 (1996): 1246. Rose Cuison Villazor argues that notwithstanding the limited application of the Court's ruling, "Oyama represents a triumphant victory against racially discriminatory property laws that coalesced with immigration and nationality law and treated Japanese Americans as second-class citizens." Rose Cuison Villazor, "Rediscovering Oyama v. California: At the Intersection of Property, Race, and Citizenship," *Washington University Law Review* 87 (2010): 991.

63. Takahashi v. Fish & Game Comm'n, 334 U.S. 410, 427 (1948) (Murphy, J., concurring) ("We should not blink at the fact that [the California fishing law] ... is a discriminatory piece of legislation having no relation whatever to any constitutionally cognizable interest of California. It was drawn against a background of racial and economic tension. It is directed in spirit and in effect solely against aliens of Japanese birth.").

64. Sweatt v. Painter, 339 U.S. 629 (1950); McLaughlin v. Oklahoma, 339 U.S. 637 (1950).

65. Brown v. Bd. of Educ. of Topeka, Kan., 347 U.S. 483 (1954), supplemented sub nom. Brown v. Bd. of Educ. of Topeka, Kan., 349 U.S. 294 (1955). The *Brown* decision embraced the position that racial equality, particularly in public education, was a cornerstone of a healthy democracy: "Today, education is perhaps the most important function of state and local governments. Compulsory school attendance laws and the great expenditures for education both demonstrate our recognition of the importance of education to our democratic society. It is required in the performance of our most basic public responsibilities, even service in the armed forces. It is the very foundation of good citizenship." Ibid. at 493.

66. Felix Frankfurter, *The Public and Its Government* (New Haven: Yale University Press, 1930), 2, 123.

67. Franklin D. Roosevelt. "First Inaugural Address of Franklin D. Roosevelt," March 4, 1933, The Avalon Project, Yale Law School.

68. Howard W. Odum, "Orderly Transitional Democracy," *Annals of the American Academy of Political & Social Sciences* 180 (1935): 31.

69. Joseph Patrick Kennedy, *I'm for Roosevelt* (New York: Reynal & Hitchcock, 1936), 102.

70. United States v. Carolene Prod. Co., 304 U.S. 144, 152 (1938).

71. Williamson v. Lee Optical, 348 U.S. 483, 488 (1955).

72. United States v. Carolene Products at fn 4.

73. Nixon v. Herndon, 273 U.S. 536 (1927); Nixon v. Condon, 286 U.S. 73 (1932).

74. Grovey v. Townsend, 295 U.S. 45 (1935), overruled in part by Smith v. Allwright, 321 U.S. 649 (1944).

75. Ibid. at 48.

76. Smith v. Allwright, 321 U.S. 649, 664 (1944).

77. Ibid. at 664.

78. Gomillion v. Lightfoot, 364 U.S. 339, 341 (1960).

79. Harper v. Virginia State Board of Elections, 383 U.S. 663 (1966), overruling Breedlove v. Suttles, 302 U.S. 277 (1937).

80. Gray v. Sanders, 372 U.S. 368, 381 (1963).

81. Reynolds v. Sims, 377 U.S. 533, 577 (1964).

82. Ibid. at 555.

83. Newberry v. United States, 256 U.S. 232, 257 (1921).

84. Ibid. at 257.

85. United States v. Classic, 313 U.S. 299, 316–17 (1941).

86. Smith v. Allwright. See Terry v. Adams, 345 U.S. 461, 463 (1953) (finding that a privately organized anti-Black endorsement process that occurred prior to an official partisan primary election to boost white candidates violated the Fifteenth Amendment despite the lack of state action because the private endorsement process was an "integral part . . . of the elective process that determines who shall rule and govern in the county.").

87. Polly J. Price, "Federalization of the Mosquito: Structural Innovation in the New Deal Administrative State," *Emory Law Journal* 60 (2010): 325, 349.

88. Youngstown Sheet & Tube Co. v. Sawyer, 343 U.S. 579, 588 (1952) ("The President's order does not direct that a congressional policy be executed in a manner prescribed by Congress—it directs that a presidential policy be executed in a manner prescribed by the President.").

89. Ibid. at 651. (Jackson, J., concurring) ("Germany, after the First World War, framed the Weimar Constitution, designed to secure her liberties in the Western tradition. However, the President of the Republic, without concurrence of the Reichstag, was empowered temporarily to suspend any or all individual rights if public safety and order were seriously disturbed or endangered. This proved a temptation to every government, whatever its shade of opinion, and in 13 years suspension of rights was invoked on more than 250 occasions. Finally, Hitler persuaded President Von Hindenberg to suspend all such rights, and they were never restored.").

90. Ibid. at 592–94 (Frankfurter, J., concurring) ("Not so long ago it was fashionable to find our system of checks and balances obstructive to effective government. It was easy to ridicule that system as outmoded—too easy. The experience through which the world has passed in our own day has made vivid the realization that the Framers of our Constitution were not inexperienced doctrinaires. . . . The accretion of dangerous power does not come in a day. It does come, however slowly, from the generative force of unchecked disregard of the restrictions that fence in even the most disinterested assertion of authority.").

91. Shelley v. Kraemer, 334 U.S. 1, 22 (1948).

92. Burton v. Wilmington Parking Auth., 365 U.S. 715, 725 (1961) (finding state action present where a coffeeshop on public property denied service because of customers' race); Reitman v. Mulkey, 387 U.S. 369, 377 (1967) (voiding a California constitutional provision recognizing a right to discriminate in housing on political-process grounds because the "right to discriminate, including the right to discriminate on racial grounds, was . . . embodied in the

State's basic charter, immune from legislative, executive, or judicial regulation at any level of the state government.").

93. Marsh v. State of Ala., 326 U.S. 501, 508–9 (1946).

94. Amalgamated Food Emp. Union Loc. 590 v. Logan Valley Plaza, Inc., 391 U.S. 308, 319 (1968), abrogated by Hudgens v. N.L.R.B., 424 U.S. 507 (1976) ("Here the roadways provided for vehicular movement within the mall and the sidewalks leading from building to building are the functional equivalents of the streets and sidewalks of a normal municipal business district. The shopping center premises are open to the public to the same extent as the commercial center of a normal town.").

CHAPTER 5. THE REAGAN REVOLUTION AND THE NEW RIGHT'S ORDER

1. Kim Phillips-Fein, *Invisible Hands: The Businessmen's Crusade against the New Deal* (New York: W. W. Norton & Company, 2010), 57–58.

2. Heather Cox Richardson, *To Make Men Free: A History of the Republican Party* (New York: Basic Books, 2014), 268.

3. "Text of Goldwater's Speech Formally Opening Presidential Campaign," *New York Times*, September 4, 1965, 12.

4. Ibid.

5. Charles Mohr, "News Analysis: The Extremism Issue; Aides Say Goldwater Sought to Extol Patriotism and Defend His Party Stand," *New York Times*, July 23, 1964, 16.

6. Ibid.

7. Bruce J. Schulman, *The Seventies: The Great Shift in American Culture, Society, and Politics* (New York: The Free Press, 2001), xv.

8. Joshua Zeitz, "Republicans, Beware the Abe Fortas Precedent," *Politico*, February 15, 2016.

9. Ibid.

10. L. A. Powe Jr., "(Re)evaluating the Burger Court," *Tulsa Law Review* 52 (2017): 587, 588.

11. Palmer v. Thompson, 403 U.S. 217, 226 (1971) ("Nothing in the history or the language of the Fourteenth Amendment nor in any of our prior cases persuades us that the closing of the Jackson swimming pools to all its citizens constitutes a denial of 'the equal protection of the laws.'").

12. Swann v. Charlotte-Mecklenburg Bd. of Ed., 402 U.S. 1, 30 (1971) ("The District Court's conclusion that assignment of children to the school nearest their home serving their grade would not produce an effective dismantling of the dual system is supported by the record. . . . We find no basis for holding that the local school authorities may not be required to employ bus transportation as one tool of school desegregation. Desegregation plans cannot be limited to the walk-in school.").

13. San Antonio Indep. Sch. Dist. v. Rodriguez, 411 U.S. 1, 54–55 (1973).

14. Milliken v. Bradley, 418 U.S. 717, 745 (1974).

15. Milliken v. Bradley, 418 U.S. 717, 814–15 (1974) (Marshall, J., dissenting).

16. Griggs v. Duke Power Co., 401 U.S. 424, 429–30 (1971).

17. Washington v. Davis, 426 U.S. 229, 242 (1976) (" . . . we have not held that a law, neutral on its face and serving ends otherwise within the power of government to pursue, is invalid under the Equal Protection Clause simply because it may affect a greater proportion of one race than of another. Disproportionate impact is not irrelevant, but it is not the sole touchstone of an invidious racial discrimination forbidden by the Constitution. Standing alone, it does not trigger the rule that racial classifications are to be subjected to the strictest scrutiny and are justifiable only by the weightiest of considerations.") (internal citations omitted).

18. City of Mobile, Ala. v. Bolden, 446 U.S. 55 (1980) (extending the requirement of intentional discrimination to claims alleging Fifteenth Amendment violations).

19. Regents of University of California v. Bakke, 438 U.S. 265 (1978).

20. Ibid. at 318.

21. Ibid. at 312–13 ("The atmosphere of 'speculation, experiment and creation'—so essential to the quality of higher education—is widely believed to be promoted by a diverse student body. . . . . Universities must be accorded the right to select those students who will contribute the most to the 'robust exchange of ideas' . . . a countervailing constitutional interest, that of the First Amendment.").

22. Ibid. at 301–2.

23. Roe v. Wade, 410 U.S. 113 (1973), holding modified by Planned Parenthood of Se. Pennsylvania v. Casey, 505 U.S. 833 (1992).

24. Ibid. at 163 (" . . . the attending physician, in consultation with his patient, is free to determine, without regulation by the State, that, in his medical judgment, the patient's pregnancy should be terminated. If that decision is reached [prior to a fetus' viability outside the womb], the judgment may be effectuated by an abortion free of interference by the State.") (emphasis added).

25. Notably, some academics contest the claim that the 1980 election was a realignment election because it did not result in Republican control of the House or a durable shift in partisan advantages until 1994. However incomplete the realignment might have been in terms of partisan control by 1980, the Overton window's rightward shift is of greater importance.

26. "Transcript of President Reagan's News Conference," *Washington Post*, August 13, 1986.

27. Republican Party, "Republican Party Platform of 1980," The American Presidency Project, University of California, Santa Barbara.

28. Ronald Reagan, "First Inaugural Address of Ronald Reagan," January 20, 1981, The Avalon Project, Yale Law School.

29. Ronald Reagan, "Ronald Reagan's 1980 Neshoba County Fair Speech," *Neshoba Democrat*, August 3, 1980.

30. Skowronek, *The Politics Presidents Make*, 428.

31. *New York Times*, "Transcript of Reagan's Speech Accepting G.O.P. Nomination," August 24, 1984.

32. Lewis F. Powell Jr., "Memorandum to Eugene B. Sydnor, Jr., Chairman of the Education Committee of the U.S. Chamber of Commerce," August 23,

1971, 26–27, Lewis F. Powell, Jr. Papers, Washington and Lee University School of Law.

33. Robert H. Bork, "Neutral Principles and Some First Amendment Problems," *Indiana Law Journal* 47 (1971): 1.

34. William H. Rehnquist, "The Notion of a Living Constitution," *Texas Law Review* 54 (1976): 695.

35. "About Us," The Federalist Society, n.d., accessed December 13, 2023, https://fedsoc.org/about-us.

36. Edwin Meese III, Speech Before the American Bar Association, July 9, 1985, Washington, DC, United States Department of Justice Digital Archives.

37. Lawrence B. Solum, "Originalism and the Unwritten Constitution," *University of Illinois Law Review* 2013 (2013): 1935, 1941.

38. Republican Party, "Republican Party Platform of 1980."

39. Monica Prasad, *Starving the Beast: Ronald Reagan and the Tax Cut Revolution* (New York: Russell Sage Foundation, 2018), 74.

40. Republican Party, "Republican Party Platform of 1984," The American Presidency Project, University of California, Santa Barbara.

41. Ronald Reagan, "Farewell Address," January 11, 1989, The Ronald Reagan Presidential Library & Museum.

42. Bill Clinton, "1996 State of the Union Address," January 23, 1996, Presidential Libraries—Bill Clinton.

43. David E. Rosenbaum, "Republicans Offer Voters a Deal for Takeover of House," *New York Times*, September 28, 1994.

44. Julian E. Zelizer, "Seizing Power: Conservatives and Congress Since the 1970s," in *New American Polity: Activist Government, the Redefinition of Citizenship, and Conservative Mobilization*, ed. Theda Skocpol and Paul Pierson (Princeton: Princeton University Press, 2007), 116.

45. Philip Shabecoff, "Reagan and Environment: To Many, a Stalemate," *New York Times*, January 2, 1989, 1.

46. U.S. v. Lopez, 1994 WL 242541 (U.S.), 22 (U.S.Pet.Brief, 1994).

47. United States v. Lopez, 514 U.S. 549, 560 (1995).

48. U.S. v. Morrison, 1999 WL 1032805 (U.S.), 13 (U.S.Amicus.Brief, 1999).

49. U.S. v. Morrison, 1999 WL 1037259 (U.S.), 17 (U.S.Pet.Brief, 1999).

50. United States v. Morrison, 529 U.S. 598, 612 (2000).

51. Nat'l Fed'n of Indep. Bus. v. Sebelius, 567 U.S. 519 (2012).

52. Ibid. at 555.

53. Morrison at 622.

54. City of Boerne v. Flores, 521 U.S. 507, 519 (1997).

55. United States v. Butler, 297 U.S. 1, 66 (1936) ("the power of Congress to authorize expenditure of public moneys for public purposes is not limited by the direct grants of legislative power found in the Constitution.").

56. Oklahoma v. U.S. Civ. Serv. Comm'n, 330 U.S. 127, 143 (1947).

57. South Dakota v. Dole, 483 U.S. 203, 211 (1987) ("Our decisions have recognized that in some circumstances the financial inducement offered by Congress might be so coercive as to pass the point at which "pressure turns into compulsion.").

58. Nat'l Fed'n of Indep. Bus. v. Sebelius, 567 U.S. 519, 523 (2012).

59. Ronald Reagan, "A Time for Choosing," October 27, 1964, The American Presidency Project, University of California, Santa Barbara.

60. Ronald Reagan, "Address Before a Joint Session of the Congress on the Program for Economic Recovery," February 18, 1981, The American Presidency Project, University of California, Santa Barbara.

61. Samuel A. Alito, "Memorandum to Litigation Strategy Group," February 5, 1986, National Archives.

62. Free Enter. Fund v. Pub. Co. Acct. Oversight Bd., 561 U.S. 477 (2010); Seila L. LLC v. Consumer Fin. Prot. Bureau, 140 S. Ct. 2183 (2020).

63. Chevron U.S.A., Inc. v. Natural Resources Defense Council, Inc., 467 U.S. 837 (1984).

64. Util. Air Regul. Grp. (UARG) v. EPA, 573 U.S. 302, 324 (2014).

65. MCI Telecomms. Corp. v. AT&T Co., 512 U.S. 218 (1994).

66. FDA v. Brown & Williamson Tobacco Corp., 529 U.S. 120 (2000).

67. Whitman v. American Trucking Ass'ns, Inc., 531 U.S. 457 (2001).

68. Gonzales v. Oregon, 546 U.S. 243 (2006).

69. Util. Air Regul. Grp. (UARG) v. EPA (2014).

70. Alabama Association of Realtors v. HHS, 141 S. Ct. 2485 (2021) (per curiam).

71. National Federation of Independent Business v. OSHA, 142 S. Ct. 661 (2022) (per curiam).

72. West Virginia v. Environmental Protection Agency, 597 U.S. ___ (2022).

73. Editorializing by Broadcast Licensees, 13 F.C.C. 1246 (1949).

74. Fairness Report Regarding Handling of Public Issues, 39 Fed. Reg. 26,372, 26,374 (July 18, 1974).

75. Red Lion Broad. Co. v. F.C.C., 395 U.S. 367, 389 (1969).

76. In re Complaint of Syracuse Peach Council against Television Station WTVH Syracuse, New York, 2 FCC Rcd 5043 (1987).

77. Veto of the Fairness in Broadcasting Act of 1987, 23 Weekly Comp. Pres. Documents (June 19, 1987), 715, 716.

78. Linda Greenhouse and Reva B. Siegel, "Before (and After) Roe v. Wade: New Questions about Backlash," *Yale Law Journal* 120 (2011): 2028, 2079.

79. "Reagan Affirms Anti-abortion Stand," *New York Times*, February 8, 1976.

80. Republican Party, "1976 Republican Party Platform," The American Presidency Project, University of California, Santa Barbara.

81. Republican Party, "Republican Party Platform of 1980."

82. Republican Party, "Republican Party Platform of 1984."

83. Harris v. McRae, 448 U.S. 297 (1980).

84. Dobbs v. Jackson Women's Health Org., 142 S. Ct. 2228, 2242 (2022) (internal citations omitted).

85. Cruzan by Cruzan v. Dir., Missouri Dep't of Health, 497 U.S. 261, 280 (1990).

86. Washington v. Glucksberg, 521 U.S. 702, 728 (1997).

87. Joseph Patrick Buchanan, "Culture War Speech," Republican National Convention of 1992, August 17, 1992, The Avalon Project, Yale Law School.

88. Republican Party, "Republican Party Platform of 1992," The American Presidency Project, University of California, Santa Barbara.

89. Bowers v. Hardwick, 478 U.S. 186, 196 (1986), overruled by Lawrence v. Texas, 539 U.S. 558, 508 (2003).

90. 1993 Nev. Stat. Ch. 236 (repealing Nev. Rev. Stat. § 201.193); Jegley, 80 S.W.3d 332 (Ark.); Wasson, 842 S.W.2d 487 (Ky.); Gryczan, 942 P.2d 112 (Mont.); Campbell, 926 S.W.2d 250 (Tenn.). Repeal or invalidation of facially evenhanded sodomy laws since Bowers: 2001 Ariz. Legis. Serv. 382 (West) (repealing Ariz. Rev. Stat. §§ 13-1411, 13-1412); 1993 D.C. Laws 10–14 (amending D.C. Stat. § 22-3502 to exclude private consensual adult conduct); 1998 R.I. Pub. Laws 24 (amending R.I. Gen. Laws § 11-10-1 to exclude conduct with other persons); Powell v. State, 510 S.E.2d 18 (Ga. 1998); Williams v. State, No. 98036031/CL-1059, 1998 Extra LEXIS 260 (Md. Cir. Ct. Balt. City Oct. 15, 1998); Michigan Org. for Human Rights v. Kelley, No. 88-815820 CZ (Mich. Cir. Ct. Wayne County July 9, 1990); Doe v. Ventura, No. MC 01-489, 2001 WL 543734 (Minn. Dist. Ct. May 15, 2001). Maryland, Michigan, and Minnesota declined to appeal the trial court rulings.

91. Dean v. District of Columbia, No. CIV.A. 90-13892, 1992 WL 685364, at *1 (D.C. Super. Ct. June 2, 1992) (affirming the decision that "same-sex marriages are not authorized under the District of Columbia Marriage and Divorce Act."), aff'd, 653 A.2d 307 (D.C. Cir. 1995).

92. Baehr v. Lewin, 852 P.2d 44, 48 (Haw. 1993) (holding that there is no fundamental right for same-sex couples to marry, but that strict scrutiny must be applied to statutes limiting marriage based on sex), abrogated by Obergefell v. Hodges, 135 S. Ct. 2584 (2015).

93. Alaska Constitution Article I, § 25 (1998) ("To be valid or recognized in this State, a marriage may exist only between one man and one woman."), invalidated by Hamby v. Parnell, 56 F. Supp. 3d 1056 (2014); Hawaii Constitution Article I, § 23 (1998) ("The legislature shall have the power to reserve marriage to opposite-sex couples.").

94. Baker v. State, 744 A.2d 864 (Vt. 1999); Goodridge v. Department of Public Health 798 N.E.2d 941 (2003).

95. Anthony Michael Kreis, "Stages of Constitutional Grief: Democratic Constitutionalism and the Marriage Revolution," *University of Pennsylvania Journal of Constitutional Law* 20 (2018): 871, 874–75.

96. Obergefell v. Hodges, 576 U.S. 644, 668 (2015) ("Without the recognition, stability, and predictability marriage offers, their children suffer the stigma of knowing their families are somehow lesser.").

97. Ibid. at 681.

98. Allison Anna Tait, "The Return of Coverture," *Michigan Law Review Online* 114 (2016): 99, 108.

99. Roberts v. United States Jaycees, 468 U.S. 609 (1984).

100. Dale v. Boy Scouts of Am., 160 N.J. 562, 608–9 (1999), rev'd and remanded, 530 U.S. 640 (2000).

101. Boy Scouts of Am. v. Dale, 530 U.S. 640, 659 (2000).

102. Masterpiece Cakeshop, Ltd. v. Colorado C.R. Comm'n, 138 S. Ct. 1719 (2018).

103. Fulton v. City of Philadelphia, Pennsylvania, 210 L. Ed. 2d 137, 141 S. Ct. 1868, 1882 (2021).

104. Hosanna-Tabor Evangelical Lutheran Church and School v. Equal Employment Opportunity Commission, 565 U.S. 171 (2012); Our Lady of Guadalupe School v. Morrissey-Berru, 140 S.Ct. 2049 (2020).

105. Marsh v. Chambers, 463 U.S. 783 (1983); Lynch v. Donnelly, 465 U.S. 668 (1984); County of Allegheny v. American Civil Liberties Union, 492 U.S. 573 (1989); Van Orden v. Perry, 545 U.S. 677 (2005); Town of Greece v. Galloway, 572 U.S. 565 (2014); American Legion v. American Humanist Association, 588 U.S. ___ (2019). In the public school context, see Lee v. Weisman, 505 U.S. 577 (1992); Santa Fe Independent School Dist. v. Doe, 530 U.S. 290 (2000).

106. James M. Oleske Jr., "The Born-Again Champion of Conscience, Conscience and Its Enemies," *Harvard Law Review* 128 (2015): 75–90; Robert P. George, *Confronting the Dogmas of Liberal Secularism* (Wilmington: ISI Books, 2016), 290; Stephen Pepper, "Taking the Free Exercise Clause Seriously," *Brigham Young University Law Review* 1986 (1986): 299, 329.

107. Jensen v. Quaring, 472 U.S. 478 (1985); Bowen v. Roy, 476 U.S. 693; Goldman v. Weinberger, 475 U.S. 503, 509 (1986).

108. Douglas Laycock, "A Survey of Religious Liberty in the United States," *Ohio State Law Journal* 47 (1986): 409, 431.

109. Emp. Div., Dep't of Hum. Res. of Oregon v. Smith, 494 U.S. 872, 888 (1990).

110. Ibid. at 890.

111. Burwell v. Hobby Lobby Stores, Inc., 573 U.S. 682 (2014) (holding that the federal government's mandate that a for-profit company provide health care insurance that covers contraception was a substantial burden on the religious practice of the owners who believed that multiple forms of contraception were abortifacients and therefore was not justified).

112. Tandon v. Newsom, 209 L. Ed. 2d 355, 141 S. Ct. 1294, 1297 (2021) (per curiam) (California "treats some comparable secular activities more favorably than at-home religious exercise, permitting hair salons, retail stores, personal care services, movie theaters, private suites at sporting events and concerts, and indoor restaurants to bring together more than three households at a time.").

113. Shaw v. Reno, 509 U.S. 630, 647 (1993).

114. Ibid at 679 (Stevens, J., dissenting).

115. Miller v. Johnson, 515 U.S. 900 (1995); Bush v. Vera, 517 U.S. 952 (1996).

116. Nw. Austin Mun. Util. Dist. No. One v. Holder, 557 U.S. 193, 202 (2009).

117. Shelby Cnty., Ala. v. Holder, 570 U.S. 529, 544–45 (2013).

118. Laurence I. Barrett, *Gambling with History: Ronald Regan in the White House* (New York: Doubleday, 1983), 426.

119. "President Seeks Assessment of Voting Rights Act," *New York Times*, June 16, 1981.

120. Transcript of Oral Argument at 47, Shelby Cty. v. Holder, 570 U.S 529 (2013) (No. 12-96).

121. Ricci v. DeStefano, 557 U.S. 557 (2009).

122. The 1984 Republican Party platform made considerable hay over this point: "Just as we must guarantee opportunity, we oppose attempts to dictate results. We will resist efforts to replace equal rights with discriminatory quota systems and preferential treatment. Quotas are the most insidious form of discrimination: reverse discrimination against the innocent. We must always remember that, in a free society, different individual goals will yield different results."

123. Matthew D. Lassiter, *The Silent Majority Suburban Politics in the Sunbelt South* (Princeton: Princeton University Press, 2013), 122.

124. Wygant v. Jackson Bd. of Educ., 476 U.S. 267, 276 (1986).

125. City of Richmond v. J. A. Croson Co., 488 U.S. 469 (1989).

126. Adarand Constructors, Inc. v. Peña, 515 U.S. 200 (1995).

127. Adarand Constructors, Inc. v. Pena, 515 U.S. 200, 239 (Scalia, J., concurring); Ibid. at 240 (Thomas, J., concurring).

128. Gratz v. Bollinger, 539 U.S. 244 (striking down the Michigan undergraduate admissions system); Grutter v. Bollinger, 539 U.S. 306 (upholding the University of Michigan School of Law admissions program).

129. Grutter at 343 ("It has been 25 years since Justice Powell first approved the use of race to further an interest in student body diversity in the context of public higher education. Since that time, the number of minority applicants with high grades and test scores has indeed increased. We expect that 25 years from now, the use of racial preferences will no longer be necessary to further the interest approved today.").

130. Parents Involved in Cmty. Sch. v. Seattle Sch. Dist. No. 1, 551 U.S. 701, 748 (2007) (plurality).

131. Students for Fair Admissions, Inc. v. President & Fellows of Harvard Coll., 143 S. Ct. 2141, 2147 (2023).

CHAPTER 6. OF WAX AND TIME

1. Alexander M. Bickel, *The Least Dangerous Branch: The Supreme Court at the Bar of Politics* (New Haven: Yale University Press, 1986), 18.

2. Ibid. at 16–17.

3. Ibid. at 33.

Bibliography

Ackerman, Bruce A. *We the People: Transformations.* Cambridge, MA: Belknap Press, 1998.

Ackerman, Bruce, and Jennifer Nou. "Canonizing the Civil Rights Revolution: The People and the Poll Tax." *Northwestern University Law Review* 103 (2009): 63–148.

Adler, William D. "Whose President? Donald Trump and the Reagan Regime." In *American Political Development and the Trump Presidency*, edited by Zachary Callen and Philip Rocco. Philadelphia: University of Pennsylvania Press, 2020.

Alito, Samuel A. "Memorandum to Litigation Strategy Group." February 5, 1986. National Archives.

Allen, Austin. *Origins of the Dred Scott Case: Jacksonian Jurisprudence and the Supreme Court, 1837–1857.* Athens: University of Georgia Press, 2006.

Amar, Akhil Reed. *America's Constitution: A Biography.* New York: Random House, 2012.

Anemona, Hartocollis. "Justice Dept. Sues Yale, Citing Illegal Race Discrimination." *New York Times*, October 8, 2020.

Applebone, Peter. "Subtly and Not, Race Bubbles Up as Issue in North Carolina Contest." *New York Times*, November 2, 1990.

The Atlantic. "The Result in South Carolina." January 1878.

Azari, Julia R. "The Scrambled Cycle." In *American Political Development and the Trump Presidency*, edited by Zachary Callen and Philip Rocco. Philadelphia: University of Pennsylvania Press, 2020.

Baker, Jean H. *James Buchanan: The American President Series.* New York: Macmillan, 2004.

Balkin, Jack M. "The Reconstruction Power." *New York University Law Review* 85 (2010): 1801–61.

———. *The Cycles of Constitutional Time*: New Haven: Yale University Press, 2020.

Balmer, Randall. "The Real Origins of the Religious Right." *Politico*, May 27, 2014.

———. *Bad Faith Race and the Rise of the Religious Right*. Grand Rapids: William B. Eerdmans, 2021.

Barrett, Laurence I. *Gambling with History: Ronald Regan in the White House.* New York: Doubleday, 1983.

Bateman, David A. "Transatlantic Anxieties: Democracy and Diversity in Nineteenth-Century Discourse." *Studies in American Political Development* 33, no. 2 (2019): 139–77.

Beachler, Donald. "Racial Gerrymandering and Republican Gains in Southern House Elections." *Journal of Political Science* 23, no. 1, article 4 (1995): 65–86.

Bedford Inquirer and Chronicle. "Majority Report of the Select Committee of the Senate of Pennsylvania, upon the decision in the case of Dred Scott vs. John F. A. Sanford." May 15, 1857.

Bellegarde, Aderson. "The Brand of Inferiority: The Civil Rights Act of 1875, White Supremacy, and Affirmative Action." *Howard Law Journal* 57 (2014): 573–99.

Benedict, Michael Les. "Salmon P. Chase and Constitutional Politics." *Law & Social Inquiry* 22, no. 2 (1997): 459–500.

Benson, Lee. *The Concept of Jacksonian Democracy: New York as a Test Case.* Princeton: Princeton University Press, 1961.

Berger, Bethany R. "Power over This Unfortunate Race: Race, Politics and Indian Law in United States v. Roger." *William & Mary Law Review* 45 (2004): 1957–2052.

Bickel, Alexander M. *The Least Dangerous Branch*. New Haven: Yale University Press, 1986.

Blackhawk, Maggie. "Federal Indian Law as Paradigm within Public Law." *Harvard Law Review* 132 (2019): 1787–877.

Bloch, Susan Low. "The Marbury Mystery: Why Did William Marbury Sue in the Supreme Court?" *Constitutional Commentary* 18 (2001): 607–27.

Bluestein, Greg. "Nathan Deal Vetoes Georgia's 'Religious Liberty' Bill." *Atlanta Journal-Constitution*, March 28, 2016.

Boddie, Elise C. "Adaptive Discrimination." *North Carolina Law Review* 94 (2016): 1235–313.

Bork, Robert H. "Neutral Principles and Some First Amendment Problems." *Indiana Law Journal* 47 (1971): 1–35.

———. *The Tempting of America: The Political Seduction of the Law.* New York: Simon and Schuster, 1990.

Bradley, Joseph P. "Letter from Joseph P. Bradley to Carry Bradley." April 30, 1867. MG 26, box 3, Joseph P. Bradley Papers, New Jersey Historical Society, Newark.

Brandwein, Pamela. *Rethinking the Judicial Settlement of Reconstruction.* Cambridge: Cambridge University Press, 2014.

Brattain, Michelle. *The Politics of Whiteness: Race, Workers, and Culture in the Modern South*. Athens: University of Georgia Press, 2001.

Braver, Joshua. "Court-Packing: An American Tradition?" *Boston College Law Review* 61 (2020): 2747–807.

Breyer, Stephen G. *Making Our Democracy Work: A Judge's View.* New York: Knopf Doubleday, 2011.

Buchanan, James. "Fourth Annual Message to Congress on the State of the Union." December 3, 1860. University of Virginia Miller Center.

———. "Inaugural Address." United States Capitol, Washington, DC, March 4, 1875. University of Virginia Miller Center.

———. "Message to Congress Transmitting the Constitution of Kansas." February 2, 1858. University of Virginia Miller Center.

Buchanan, Joseph Patrick. "Culture War Speech." Republican National Convention of 1992. August 17, 1992. The Avalon Project, Yale Law School.

Buck, Solon Justus. *The Granger Movement: A Study of Agricultural Organization and Its Political and Economic Manifestations, 1870–1880.* Lincoln: University of Nebraska Press, 1913.

Buck, Stephanie. "Overlooked No More: Mitsuye Endo, a Name Linked to Justice for Japanese-Americans." *New York Times,* October 9, 2019.

Buckley, William F., Jr. "Why the South Must Prevail." *National Review,* August 24, 1957.

Burgess, John William. *The Middle Period.* New York: Scribner's, 1897.

Burns, Anthony. *Boston Slave Riot, and Trial of Anthony Burns.* Boston: Fetridge, 1854.

Caldwell, Earl. "Martin Luther King Is Slain in Memphis; A White Is Suspected; Johnson Urges Calm." *New York Times,* April 4, 1968.

Cameron, Charles, David Epstein, and Sharyn O'Halloran. "Do Majority-Minority Districts Maximize Substantive Black Representation in Congress?" *American Political Science Review* 90, no. 4 (1996): 794–812.

Carpenter, Daniel, and Benjamin Schneer. "Party Formation through Petitions: The Whigs and the Bank War of 1832–1834." *Studies in American Political Development* 29, no. 2 (2015): 213–34.

Carter, Edward L., and Edward E. Adams. "Justice Owen J. Roberts on 1937." *Green Bag* 15 (2012): 375–88.

Cartwright, Marguerite. "The Ives-Quinn Bill: Legislative and Social Background." *Journal of Negro Education* 20 (1951): 115–18.

Carson, Jamie L., and Joel Sievert. *Electoral Incentives in Congress.* Ann Arbor: University of Michigan Press, 2019.

Chafetz, Josh. "Impeachment and Assassination." *Minnesota Law Review* 95 (2010): 347–423.

———. "Unprecedented? Judicial Confirmation Battles and the Search for a Usable Past." *Harvard Law Review* 131, no. 1 (2017): 96–132.

Charleston Daily Courier. "The Legislature." August 17, 1868.

Charleston Daily News. "The Negro Declaration of War!" November 7, 1870.

Charleston News & Courier. "Slavery in Colleton." May 29, 1876.

———. "The Hawaiian Treaty Bill." August 16, 1876.

———. "The Rice Laborers' Strike." May 26, 1876.

———. "The Strike along the Combahee." May 23, 1876.

———. "Suffering in the Low Country." May 17, 1876.

Chatfield, Sara. "Married Women's Economic Rights Reform in State Legislatures and Courts, 1839–1920." *Studies in American Political Development* 32, no. 2 (2018): 236–56.

Chen, Anthony S. "The Party of Lincoln and the Politics of State Fair Employment Practices Legislation in the North, 1945–1964." *American Journal of Sociology* 112, no. 6 (2007): 1713–74.

Chicago Tribune. "The Civil-Wrongs Bill." May 31, 1874.

———. "A New Federal Constitution." March 13, 1857.

Clinton, Bill. "1996 State of the Union Address." January 23, 1996. Presidential Libraries—Bill Clinton.

Coenen, Dan T. "Quiet-Revolution Rulings in Constitutional Law." *Boston University Law Review* 99 (2019): 2061–138.

Congressional Globe. 21st Congress, 1st Session (Apr. 28, 1830). Library of Congress.

———. 31st Congress, 1st Session (Mar. 4, 1850). Library of Congress.

———. 37th Congress, 2nd Session (Feb. 28, 1862). Library of Congress.

———. 39th Congress, 2nd Session (Dec. 5, 1866). Library of Congress.

———. 42nd Congress, 2nd Session (May 18, 1872). Library of Congress.

Crowe, Justin. *Building the Judiciary: Law, Courts, and the Politics of Institutional Development.* Princeton: Princeton University Press, 2012.

———. "Westward Expansion, Preappointment Politics, and the Making of the Southern Slaveholding Supreme Court." *Studies in American Political Development* 24, no. 1 (2010): 90–120.

Currie, David P. "The Civil War Congress." *University of Chicago Law Review* 73 (2006): 1131–226.

Cushman, Barry. *Rethinking the New Deal Court: The Structure of a Constitutional Revolution.* New York: Oxford University Press, 1998.

Dahl, Robert A. "Decision-Making in a Democracy: The Supreme Court as a National Policymaker." *Journal of Public Law* 6 (1957): 279–95.

Daily Memphis Avalanche. March 30, 1875.

The Daily Phoenix. "The Labor Convention—Third Day." November 27, 1869.

Davey, Monica, and Laurie Goodstein. "Religion Laws Quickly Fall into Retreat in Indiana and Arkansas." *New York Times*, April 2, 2015.

Davis, David Brion. *The Slave Power Conspiracy and the Paranoid Style.* Baton Rouge: Louisiana State University Press, 1970.

Davis, John P. "A Black Inventory of the New Deal." *The Crisis*, May 1935.

Decker, Jefferson. *The Other Rights Revolution.* New York: Oxford University Press, 2016.

Democratic Party. "1844 Democratic Party Platform." May 27, 1844. The American Presidency Project, University of California, Santa Barbara.

———. "1848 Democratic Party Platform." May 22, 1848. The American Presidency Project, University of California, Santa Barbara.

———. "1856 Democratic Party Platform." June 2, 1856. The American Presidency Project, University of California, Santa Barbara.

———. "1948 Democratic Platform." July 12, 1948. The American Presidency Project, University of California, Santa Barbara.

The Democrat (Penn.). "The Decision of the Supreme Court Reversed." March 26, 1857.

Denny, Harold. "Russia Rounds Up Religious People Archbishop Held." *New York Times*, April 25, 1938.

———. "Stalin, Supreme in Soviet, Seeks National Approval." *New York Times*, April 23, 1938.

Detroit Free Press. "Law and Partisanship." March 25, 1875.

Devins, Neal. "Reagan Redux: Civil Rights Under Bush." *North Dakota Law Review* 68 (1993): 955–1001.

———. "Social Meaning and School Vouchers." *William & Mary Law Review* 42 (2001): 919–62.

DeWitt, Larry. "The Decision to Exclude Agricultural and Domestic Workers from the 1935 Social Security Act." *Social Security Bulletin* 70 (2010).

Dodd, Lynda G. "Presidential Leadership and Civil Rights Lawyering in the Era before Brown." *Indiana Law Journal* 85 (2010): 1599–657.

Donald, David Herbert. *Charles Sumner and the Rights of Man*. New York: Knopf, 1970.

Douglas, Stephen A. "The Lincoln-Douglas Debates: Third Debate." Jonesboro, Illinois, September 15, 1858. Northern Illinois University Library.

———. "The Lincoln-Douglas Debates: Sixth Debate." Quincy, Illinois, October 13, 1858. Northern Illinois University Library.

Douglass, Frederick. *Two Speeches*. New York: C. P. Dewey, 1857.

Driver, Justin. "Supremacies and the Southern Manifesto." *Texas Law Review* 92 (2014): 1053–135.

Du Bois, W. E. B. *Black Reconstruction in America: Toward a History of the Part Which Black Folk Played in the Attempt to Reconstruct Democracy in America, 1860–1880*. San Diego: Harcourt, Brace, and Company, 1935.

Dudziak, Mary L. *Cold War Civil Rights: Race and the Image of American Democracy*. Princeton: Princeton University Press, 2001.

Dunn, Susan. *Roosevelt's Purge: How FDR Fought to Change the Democratic Party*. Cambridge, MA: Harvard University Press, 2012.

Dworkin, Ronald. *Taking Rights Seriously*. New York: Bloomsbury, 1977.

Elinson, Gregory. "Judicial Partisanship and the Slaughterhouse Cases: Investigating the Relationship between Courts and Parties." *Studies in American Political Development* 31, no. 1 (2017): 24–46.

Emerson, Ralph Waldo. *Emerson in His Journals*. Edited by Joel Porte. Cambridge, MA: Harvard University Press, 1982.

Engerman, Stanley L., and Kenneth L. Sokoloff. "The Evolution of Suffrage Institutions in the New World." *Journal of Economic History* 65 (2005): 891–921.

Engstrom, David Freeman. "The Lost Origins of American Fair Employment Law: Regulatory Choice and the Making of Modern Civil Rights, 1943–1972." *Stanford Law Review* 63 (2011): 1071–143.

Epps, Garrett. "The Antebellum Political Background of the Fourteenth Amendment." *Law and Contemporary Problems* 67 (2004): 175–212.

Epstein, David L., and Sharyn O'Halloran. "Trends in Minority Representation, 1974 to 2000." In *The Future of the Voting Rights*, edited by David

Epstein, Richard H. Pildes, Rodolfo O. de la Garza, and Sharyn O'Halloran. New York: Russell Sage Foundation, 2006.

Epstein, Lee, and Jeffrey A. Segal. *Advice and Consent: The Politics of Judicial Appointments.* New York: Oxford University Press, 2005.

Everett, Edward. "Speech on the Bill for Removing the Indians from the East to the West Side of the Mississippi, Delivered in the House of Representatives." Washington, DC, May 19, 1830. Library of Congress.

Fairman, Charles. *The History of the Supreme Court of the United States: Reconstruction and Reunion, 1864–1868.* Part 1, edited by Paul A. Freund. New York: Macmillan, 1971.

Farber, Daniel A. *Lincoln's Constitution.* Chicago: University of Chicago Press, 2011.

Farhang, Sean, and Ira Katznelson. "The Southern Imposition: Congress and Labor in the New Deal and Fair Deal." *Studies in American Political Development* 19, no. 1 (2005): 1–30.

Fehrenbacher, Don E. *The Dred Scott Case in Historical Perspective.* New York: Oxford University Press, 1981.

Feld, Barry C. "Race, Politics, and Juvenile Justice: The Warren Court and the Conservative "Backlash." *Minnesota Law Review* 87 (2003): 1447–578.

Fishkin, Joseph, and William E. Forbath. *The Anti-oligarchy Constitution: Reconstructing the Economic Foundations of American Democracy.* Cambridge, MA: Harvard University Press, 2022.

Fisk, Catherine L. "The Once and Future Countervailing Power of Labor." *Yale Law Journal Forum* 130 (2021): 685–707.

Fisk, Catherine L., and Erwin Chemerinsky. "Political Speech and Association Rights after Knox v. Seiu, Local 1000." *Cornell Law Review* 98 (2013): 1023–91.

Flamm, Michael W. *Law and Order Street Crime, Civil Unrest, and the Crisis of Liberalism in the 1960s.* New York: Columbia University Press, 2007.

Foner, Eric. *The Fiery Trial: Abraham Lincoln and American Slavery.* New York: W. W. Norton & Company, 2011.

———. *Free Soil, Free Labor, Free Men: The Ideology of the Republican Party before the Civil War.* Oxford: Oxford University Press, 1995.

———. *Nothing but Freedom: Emancipation and Its Legacy.* Baton Rouge: Louisiana State University Press, 1983.

———. *Reconstruction: America's Unfinished Revolution, 1863–1877.* New York: Harper & Row, 1988.

———. *The Second Founding: How the Civil War and Reconstruction Remade the Constitution.* New York: W. W. Norton & Company, 2020.

Forbath, William E. "Caste, Class, and Equal Citizenship." *Michigan Law Review* 98, no. 1 (1999): 1–91.

Formisano, Ronald P. "The 'Party Period' Revisited." *Journal of American History* 86, no. 1 (1999): 93–120.

Frankfurter, Felix. *The Public and Its Government.* New Haven: Yale University Press, 1930.

Franklin, John Hope. "The Enforcement of the Civil Rights Act of 1875." *Prologue Magazine,* Winter 1974.

———. *Reconstruction after the Civil War*. Chicago: University of Chicago Press, 2013.

Fraser, Steve, and Gary Gerstle, eds. *The Rise and Fall of the New Deal Order, 1930–1980*. Princeton: Princeton University Press, 1989.

Freehling, William W. *The Road to Disunion: Secessionists at Bay, 1776–1854*. New York: Oxford University Press, 1991.

———. *The Road to Disunion: Secessionists Triumphant, 1854–1861*. New York: Oxford University Press, 2007.

Free Soil Party. "Free Soil Party Platform of 1848." June 22, 1848. The American Presidency Project, University of California, Santa Barbara.

Friedman, Barry. "The Birth of an Academic Obsession: The History of the Countermajoritarian Difficulty, Part Five." *Yale Law Journal* 112 (2002): 153–259.

———. "The History of the Countermajoritarian Difficulty, Part Four: Law's Politics." *University of Pennsylvania Law Review* 148, no. 4 (2000): 974–1061.

———. *The Will of the People: How Public Opinion Has Influenced the Supreme Court and Shaped the Meaning of the Constitution*. New York: Farrar, Straus and Giroux, 2010.

Friedman, Lawrence M. *A History of American Law*. 3rd ed. New York: Oxford University Press, 2019.

Friedman, Richard D. "Switching Time and Other Thought Experiments: The Hughes Court and Constitutional Transformation." *University of Pennsylvania Law Review* 142, no. 6 (1994): 1891–1984.

Gales, Joseph, and William Winston Seaton. Register of Debates in Congress, 21st Congress, 1st session, pt. 1. Dec. 7, 1829 to Mar. 24, 1830.

Gaynes, J. L. "Letter from J. L. Gaynes, Colonel First Texas Calvary to Captain B. F. Morey, Assistant Adjutant General." July 8, 1865. Smithsonian Institute.

Gedye, G. E. R. "Austrian Jews Set Adrift on Borders." *New York Times*, April 20, 1938.

———. "Nazi Terrorism in Austria Bared, Vienna Arrests Are Put at 34,000." *New York Times*, April 3, 1938.

George, Robert P. *Confronting the Dogmas of Liberal Secularism*. Wilmington: ISI Books, 2016.

Gerhardt, Michael J. *Forgotten Presidents: Their Untold Constitutional Legacy*. New York: Oxford University Press, 2013.

Gerring, John. *Party Ideologies in America, 1828–1996*. Cambridge: Cambridge University Press, 2001.

Gewirtz, Paul. "Remedies and Resistance." *Yale Law Journal* 92 (1983): 585–681.

Gienapp, William E. *The Origins of the Republican Party, 1852–1856*. New York: Oxford University Press, 1987.

Ginsburg, Ruth Bader. "Some Thoughts on Autonomy and Equality in Relation to Roe v. Wade." *North Carolina Law Review* 63 (1985): 375–86.

Glenn, Brian J. "Conservatives and American Political Development." *Political Science Quarterly* 125, no. 4 (2010): 611–38.

Glymph, Thavolia. "'I Could Not Come in Unless Over Their Dead Bodies': Dignitary Offenses." *Law and History Review* 38, no. 3 (2020): 585–98.

Goldberg, Michael J. "Cleaning Labor's House: Institutional Reform Litigation in the Labor Movement." *Duke Law Journal* 1989, no. 4 (1989): 903–1011.

Goluboff, Risa Lauren. *Vagrant Nation: Police Power, Constitutional Change, and the Making of the 1960s.* New York: Oxford University Press, 2016.

Graber, Mark A. *Dred Scott and the Problem of Constitutional Evil.* Cambridge: Cambridge University Press, 2006.

———. "Federalist or Friends of Adams: The Marshall Court and Party Politics." *Studies in American Political Development* 12, no.2 (1998): 229–66.

Graham, Fred. P. "Fortas Quits the Supreme Court, Defends Dealings With Wolfson." *New York Times,* May 16, 1969.

Graham, Howard Jay. "Justice Field and the Fourteenth Amendment." *Yale Law Journal* 52, no. 4 (1943): 851–89.

Grant, Keneshia Nicole. *The Great Migration and the Democratic Party: Black Voters and the Realignment of American Politics in the 20th Century.* Philadelphia: Temple University Press, 2020.

Green, Erica L., Matt Apuzzo, and Katie Benner. "Trump Officials Reverse Obama's Policy on Affirmative Action in Schools." *New York Times,* July 8, 2018.

Greenhouse, Linda, and Reva B. Siegel. "Before (and after) Roe v. Wade: New Questions about Backlash." *Yale Law Journal* 120 (2011): 2028–87.

Groppe, Maureen. "National Uproar over Indiana's RFRA Brings Mixed Results in Other States." *Indianapolis Star,* March 31, 2015.

Gudridge, Patrick O. "Remember 'Endo'?" *Harvard Law Review* 116, no. 7 (2003): 1933–70.

Guzda, Henry P. "Frances Perkins' Interest in a New Deal for Blacks." *Monthly Labor Review* 4 (1980): 31–35.

Hacker, Jacob S., and Paul Pierson, *Let Them Eat Tweets: How the Right Rules in an Age of Extreme Inequality.* New York: Liveright, 2020.

Halliwell, Martin, and Nick Witham. *Reframing 1968: American Politics, Protest and Identity.* Edinburgh: Edinburgh University Press, 2018.

Harrison, John. "Reconstructing the Privileges or Immunities Clause." *Yale Law Journal* 101, no. 7 (1992): 1385–474.

Harvard Law Review. "The Decisions of the National Labor Relations Board." Vol. 48, no. 4 (1935): 630–59.

———. "The Evolution of the State Action Doctrine and the Current Debate." Vol. 123 (2010): 1255.

Hasbrouck, Brandon. "The Just Prosecutor." *Washington University Law Review* 99 (2021): 627–93.

Hasen, Richard L. "Identifying and Minimizing the Risk of Election Subversion and Stolen Elections in the Contemporary United States." *Harvard Law Review* 135 (2022): 265–301.

Healy, Patrick. "Hopefuls Differ as They Reject Gay Marriage." *New York Times,* October 31, 2008.

Hechinger, Fred M. "The Reagan Effect; The Department That Would Not Die." *New York Times,* November 14, 1982.

Heersink, Boris, and Jeffery A. Jenkins. *Republican Party Politics and the American South, 1865–1968.* Cambridge: Cambridge University Press, 2020.

Hernandez, Joe. "You Can Now Carry a Handgun in Texas without a License, Training or Background Check." *NPR*, September 2, 2021.

Ho, Daniel E., and Kevin M. Quinn. "Did a Switch in Time Save Nine?" *Journal of Legal Analysis* 2, no. 1 (2010): 69–113.

Hofstadter, Richard. *The American Political Tradition and the Men Who Made It*. New York: Knopf, 1948.

Hollis-Brusky, Amanda. *Ideas with Consequences: The Federalist Society and the Conservative Counterrevolution*. New York: Oxford University Press, 2015.

Hollis-Brusky, Amanda, and Joshua C. Wilson. *Separate but Faithful: The Christian Right's Radical Struggle to Transform Law and Legal Culture*. New York: Oxford University Press, 2020.

Holt, Michael F. *The Rise and Fall of the American Whig Party Jacksonian Politics and the Onset of the Civil War*. New York: Oxford University Press, 2003.

Horton, R. G. *The Life and Public Services of James Buchanan*. New York: Derby & Jackson, 1856.

HoSang, Daniel Martinez. *Racial Propositions: Ballot Initiatives and the Making of Postwar California*. Berkeley: University of California Press, 2010.

Howard, A. E. Dick. "The Changing Face of the Supreme Court." *Virginia Law Review* 101, no. 2 (2015): 231–316.

Howe, Daniel Walker. *What Hath God Wrought: The Transformation of America, 1815–1848*. New York: Oxford University Press, 2007.

Jackson, Andrew. "Bank Veto Message." July 10, 1832. National Constitution Center.

———. "Farewell Address." March 4, 1837. University of Virginia Miller Center.

———. "First Annual Message to Congress." December 8, 1829. University of Virginia Miller Center.

———. "Letter from Andrew Jackson to Amos Kendall." August 9, 1835. Library of Congress.

———. "Letter from Andrew Jackson to James Hamilton Jr." June 29, 1828. Library of Congress.

———. "Letter from Andrew Jackson to John Freeman Schermerhorn." June 12, 1832. Library of Congress.

———. "Maysville Road Veto Message." May 27, 1830. University of Virginia Miller Center.

———. "Second Annual Message to Congress." December 6, 1830. University of Virginia Miller Center.

Jacobs, Meg. "State Building from the Bottom Up: The New Deal and Beyond." In *Beyond the New Deal Order: U.S. Politics from the Great Depression to the Great Recession*, edited by Gary Gerstle, Nelson Lichtenstein, and Alice O'Connor. Philadelphia: University of Pennsylvania Press, 2019.

Jardina, Ashley. *White Identity Politics*. Cambridge: Cambridge University Press, 2019.

Jefferson, Thomas. "Letter from Thomas Jefferson to Spencer Roane." September 6, 1819.

Jones, Henry. *An Abridgment of the Debates of Congress*. New York: Henry Holt and Company, 1875.

Kahn, Paul W. *The Reign of Law: Marbury v. Madison and the Construction of America*. New Haven: Yale University Press, 2002.

Kahn, Ronald. "Institutional Norms and the Historical Development of Supreme Court Politics: Changing 'Social Facts' and Doctrinal Development." In *The Supreme Court in American Politics: New Institutionalist Interpretations*, edited by Howard Gillman and Cornell Clayton. Lawrence: University Press of Kansas, 1999.

Kalman, Laura. "Law, Politics, and the New Deal(s)." *Yale Law Journal* 108, no. 8 (1999): 2165–213.

———. *The Strange Career of Legal Liberalism*. New Haven: Yale University Press, 1998.

Karlan, Pamela S. "The New Countermajoritarian Difficulty." *California Law Review* 109, no. 6 (2021): 2323–55.

Karsten, Peter. "Supervising the 'Spoiled Children of Legislation': Judicial Judgments Involving Quasi-Public Corporations in the Nineteenth Century U.S." *American Journal of Legal History* 41, no. 3 (1997): 315–67.

Katz, Philip M. *From Appomattox to Montmartre: Americans and the Paris Commune*. Cambridge, MA: Harvard University Press, 1998.

Katznelson, Ira. *Fear Itself: The New Deal and the Origins of Our Time*. New York: W. W. Norton & Company, 2013.

———. *When Affirmative Action Was White*. New York: W. W. Norton & Company, 2005.

Kelly, Brian. "Black Laborers, the Republican Party, and the Crisis of Reconstruction in Lowcountry South Carolina." *International Review of Social History* 51, no. 3 (2006): 375–414.

Kennedy, Joseph Patrick. *I'm for Roosevelt*. New York: Reynal & Hitchcock, 1936.

Kennedy, Randall. *For Discrimination Race, Affirmative Action, and the Law*. New York: Vintage Books, 2015.

———. "Justice Murphy's Concurrence in Oyama v. California: Cussing Out Racism." *Texas Law Review* 74 (1996): 1245–46.

Kersch, Kenneth Ira. *Conservatives and the Constitution: Imagining Constitutional Restoration in the Heyday of American Liberalism*. Cambridge: Cambridge University Press, 2019.

Keyssar, Alexander. *The Right to Vote: The Contested History of Democracy in the United States*. New York: Basic Books, 2009.

King, Desmond S. *Still a House Divided: Race and Politics in Obama's America*. Princeton: Princeton University Press, 2014.

King, Desmond S., and Rogers M. Smith. "Racial Orders in American Political Development." *American Political Science Review* 99, no. 1 (2005): 75–92.

Klarman, Michael J. "Foreword: The Degradation of American Democracy—and the Court." *Harvard Law Review* 134 (2020): 4–264.

———. *From Jim Crow to Civil Rights*. New York: Oxford University Press, 2006.

———. "Rethinking the Civil Rights and Civil Liberties Revolutions." *Virginia Law Review* 82 (February 1996): 1–67.

Kovacs, Kathryn E. "Avoiding Authoritarianism in the Administrative Procedure Act." *George Mason Law Review* 28 (2021): 573–607.

Kreis, Anthony Michael. "The New Redeemers." *Georgia Law Review* 55 (2020): 1483–528.

———. "Stages of Constitutional Grief: Democratic Constitutionalism and the Marriage Revolution." *University of Pennsylvania Journal of Constitutional Law* 20 (2018): 871–982.

Kruman, Marc W. "Quotas for Blacks: The Public Works Administration and the Black Construction Worker." *Labor History* 16, no. 1 (1975): 37–51.

Kruse, Kevin M., and Julian E. Zelizer, *Fault Lines: A History of the United States since 1974*. New York: W. W. Norton & Company, 2019.

LaFeber, Walter. *The New Empire: An Interpretation of American Expansion, 1860–1898*. Ithaca: Cornell University, 1998.

Lassiter, Matthew D. *The Silent Majority Suburban Politics in the Sunbelt South*. Princeton: Princeton University Press, 2013.

Laycock, Douglas. "A Survey of Religious Liberty in the United States." *Ohio State Law Journal* 47 (1986): 409-52.

Lehr, Dick. "The Racist Legacy of Woodrow Wilson." *The Atlantic,* November 27, 2015.

Lepore, Jill. "The Last Time Democracy Almost Died." *The New Yorker*, February 3, 2020.

Leuchtenburg, William E. *Franklin D. Roosevelt and the New Deal, 1932–1940*. New York: Harper Perennial, 2009.

———. *The Supreme Court Reborn: The Constitutional Revolution in the Age of Roosevelt*. New York: Oxford University Press, 1995.

———. *The White House Looks South: Franklin D. Roosevelt, Harry S. Truman, Lyndon B. Johnson*. Baton Rouge: Louisiana State University Press, 2005.

Lewis, Neil A. "Bush Opposes University of Michigan on Race." *New York Times*, January 15, 2003.

The Liberator. "The Meeting at Framingham." July 7, 1854.

Lincoln, Abraham. *The Collected Works of Abraham Lincoln: The Abraham Lincoln Association, Springfield, Illinois*. Edited by Roy P. Basler. Vol. 3. New Brunswick: Rutgers University Press, 1953 [Ann Arbor: University of Michigan Digital Library Production Services, 2001].

———. *Abraham Lincoln: Speeches and Writings: 1859–1865*. Vol. 2. New York: Library of America, 2012.

Liu, Goodwin, Pamela S. Karlan, and Christopher H. Schroeder, *Keeping Faith with the Constitution*. New York: Oxford University Press, 2010.

Lowndes, Joseph E. *From the New Deal to the New Right Race and the Southern Origins of Modern Conservatism*. New Haven: Yale University Press, 2009.

Magliocca, Gerard N. *Andrew Jackson and the Constitution: The Rise and Fall of Generational Regimes*. Lawrence: University Press of Kansas, 2007.

Maltese, John Anthony. *The Selling of Supreme Court Nominees*. Baltimore: Johns Hopkins University Press, 1998.

Maltz, Earl M. "Citizenship and the Constitution: A History and Critique of the Supreme Court's Alienage Jurisprudence." *Arizona State Law Journal* 28 (1996): 1135–91.

Mason, Robert. *The Republican Party and American Politics from Hoover to Reagan.* Cambridge: Cambridge University Press, 2011.

Massey, Douglas S., and Nancy A. Denton. *American Apartheid: Segregation and the Making of the Underclass.* Cambridge, MA: Harvard University Press, 1993.

Maxwell, Angie, and Wayne Parent. "The Obama Trigger: Presidential Approval and Tea Party Membership." *Social Science Quarterly* 93, no. 5 (2012): 1384–401.

Maxwell, Angie, and Todd Shields. *The Long Southern Strategy: How Chasing White Voters in the South Change American Politics.* New York: Oxford University Press, 2019.

Mayer, William G. "The Cycles of Constitutional Time: Some Skeptical Questions." *Northeastern University Law Review* 13 (2021): 655–73.

Mayhew, David R. *Electoral Realignments: A Critique of an American Genre.* New Haven: Yale University Press, 2002.

McCarthy, Justin. "Americans' Support for Gay Marriage Remains High, at 61%." Gallup.com, May 19, 2016.

McCloskey, Robert G., and Sanford Levinson. *The American Supreme Court,* 6th ed. Chicago: University of Chicago Press, 2016.

McPherson, James M. "Abolitionists and the Civil Rights Act of 1875." *Journal of American History* 52, no. 3 (1965): 493–510.

Meese, Edwin, III. Speech Before the American Bar Association, July 9, 1985. Washington, DC: United States Department of Justice Digital Archives.

Memphis Appeal. "The Decision of Judge Emmons." March 24, 1875.

Merida, Kevin. "Dole Aims at Affirmative Action." *Washington Post,* July 28, 1995.

Mickey, Robert. *Paths out of Dixie: The Democratization of Authoritarian Enclaves in America's Deep South.* Princeton: Princeton University Press, 2015.

Milkis, Sidney M., and Daniel J. Tichenor, *Rivalry and Reform: Presidents, Social Movements and the Transformation of American Politics.* Chicago: University of Chicago Press, 2019.

Milligan, Joy. "Plessy Preserved: Agencies and the Effective Constitution." *Yale Law Journal* 129 (2020): 924–1018.

Mohr, Charles. "News Analysis: The Extremism Issue; Aides Say Goldwater Sought to Extol Patriotism and Defend His Party Stand." *New York Times,* July 23, 1964.

Moore, Homer H. *An Anatomy of Atheism: As Demonstrated in the Light of the Constitution and Laws of Nature.* Cincinnati: Cranston and Stowe, 1890.

Nackenoff, Carol. "Is There a Political Tilt to 'Juristocracy'?" *Maryland Law Review* 65 (2006): 139–51.

Nelson, William E. "Brown v. Board of Education and the Jurisprudence of Legal Realism." *St. Louis University Law Journal* 48 (2004): 795–838.

New England Farmer. "Arrest of a Fugitive Slave in Boston!" May 27, 1854.

Newmyer, R. Kent. *John Marshall and the Heroic Age of the Supreme Court.* Baton Rouge: Louisiana State University Press, 2007.

New Orleans Crescent. "Governor Warmoth's Veto." September 29, 1868.

New Orleans Crescent Sun. September 27, 1868.

New York Daily Herald. "The Woes of South Carolina." May 10, 1871.

New York Times. "A New Democratic Grievance." March 28, 1871.

———. "Anti-Semetic Feeling in Greece Is Rising." April 16, 1938.

———. "The Dred Scott Decision in the Ohio Legislature." April 11, 1857.

———. "The Dred Scott Decision in the Pennsylvania Legislature." April 27, 1857.

———. "Nazis to Purge Vienna Library; 'Non-Aryan' Works to Be Burned." April 24, 1938.

———. "Negro Co-operation." August 17, 1873.

———. "Negro Rule in South Carolina." February 17, 1874.

———. "North Carolina Politics." June 1, 1874.

———. "Oath to Obey Hitler Is Imposed on Pastors; Reich Protestants Who Balk Will Be Dropped." April 20, 1938.

———. "President Seeks Assessment of Voting Rights Act." June 16, 1981.

———. "Reagan Affirms Anti-abortion Stand." February 8, 1976.

———. "Reich Aims New Blow at Jews in Austria; Concealed Ownership or Legal Help Punished." April 25, 1938.

———. "The Rulers of the South." March 8, 1875.

———. "Rumania Arrests 100 Iron Guard Members as Government Moves to Halt Terrorists." April 18, 1938.

———. "South Carolina Afflictions." June 1, 1876.

———. "South Carolina." June 8, 1874.

———. "Text of Goldwater's Speech Formally Opening Presidential Campaign." September 4, 1965.

———. "Text of Governor Roosevelt's Speech at Commonwealth Club, San Francisco." September 24, 1932.

———. "Transcript of Reagan's Speech Accepting G.O.P. Nomination." August 24, 1984.

———. "What Has Become of the Southern Negro?" March 7, 1871.

New York Tribune. Editorial. March 12, 1857.

———. "The Political Judges and their Belongings." March 21, 1857.

———. "Through the South." June 21, 1871.

Nicoletti, Cynthia. *Secession on Trial: The Treason Prosecution of Jefferson Davis.* New York: Cambridge University Press, 2017.

O'Brian, Neil A. "Before Reagan: The Development of Abortion's Partisan Divide." *Perspectives on Politics* 18, no. 4 (2020): 1031–47.

Odum, Howard W. "Orderly Transitional Democracy." *Annals of the American Academy of Political & Social Sciences* 180 (1935): 31–39.

Oleske, James M., Jr. "The Born-Again Champion of Conscience, Conscience and Its Enemies." *Harvard Law Review* 128 (2015): 75–90.

Olson, James Stuart. *Saving Capitalism: The Reconstruction Finance Corporation and the New Deal, 1933–1940.* Princeton: Princeton University Press, 2017.

Osterhaus, Peter Joseph. "Statement from Peter Joseph Osterhaus, Major General United States Volunteers to Carl Schurz." August 27, 1865. In *Report of Carl Schurz on the States of South Carolina, Georgia, Alabama, Mississippi, and Louisiana. Executive Documents of the Senate of the United States for the First Session Thirty-Ninth Congress, 1865–1866* 1, no. 2 (1866).

Parton, James. *General Butler in New Orleans: History of the Administration of the Department of the Gulf in the Year 1862.* New York: Mason Brothers, 1864.

Paul, Joel Richard. *Without Precedent: Chief Justice Marshall and His Times.* New York: Riverhead Books, 2019.

Paulsen, Michael Stokes "Originalism: A Logical Necessity." *National Review,* June 20, 2022.

Pear, Robert. "Reagan Aides Map Repeal of Rules on Bias in Hiring." *New York Times,* August 15, 1985.

Pepper, Stephen. "Taking the Free Exercise Clause Seriously." *Brigham Young University Law Review* (1986): 299–336.

Perea, Juan F. "The Echoes of Slavery: Recognizing the Racist Origins of the Agricultural and Domestic Worker Exclusion from the National Labor Relations Act." *Ohio State Law Journal* 72 (2011): 95–138.

Perkins, Emily, and John Magill. "In the Late 1800s, Devastating Yellow Fever Epidemics Forced New Orleans to Confront Its Sanitation Problem." The Historic New Orleans Collection, May 12, 2020.

Phillips, Kimberley L. "Did the Battlefield Kill Jim Crow? The Cold War Military, Civil Rights, and Black Freedom Struggles." In *Fog of War: The Second World War and the Civil Rights Movement,* edited by Kevin M. Kruse and Stephen Tuck. New York: Oxford University Press, 2012.

Phillips-Fein, Kim. *Invisible Hands: The Businessmen's Crusade against the New Deal.* New York: W. W. Norton & Company, 2010.

Pianin, Eric. "Switching Parties Has Been No Picnic for Some GOP Lawmakers." *Washington Post,* September 5, 1996.

Pierson, Paul. "When Effect Becomes Cause: Policy Feedback and Political Change." *World Politics* 45 (1993): 595–628.

Pierson, Paul, and Theda Skocpol. "American Politics in the Long Run." In *The Transformation of American Politics: Activist Government and the Rise of Conservatism,* edited by Paul Pierson and Theda Skocpol. Princeton: Princeton University Press, 2007.

———. "Political Development and Contemporary American Politics." In *The Transformation of American Politics: Activist Government and the Rise of Conservatism,* edited by Paul Pierson and Theda Skocpol. Princeton: Princeton University Press, 2007.

Plotke, David. *Building a Democratic Political Order: Reshaping American Liberalism in the 1930s and 1940s.* Cambridge: Cambridge University Press, 1996.

Polsky, Andrew J. "Partisan Regimes in American Politics." *Polity* 44 (2011).

Pope, James Gray. "Snubbed Landmark: Why United States v. Cruikshank (1876) Belongs at the Heart of the American Constitutional Canon." *Harvard Civil Rights—Civil Liberties Law Review* 49 (2014): 385–447.

Powe, L. A., Jr. "(Re)evaluating the Burger Court." *Tulsa Law Review* 52 (2017): 587–98.

Powell, Catherine, and Camille Gear Rich. "The 'Welfare Queen' Goes to the Polls: Race-Based Fractures in Gender Politics and Opportunities for Intersectional Coalitions." *Georgetown Law Journal* 108 (2020): 105–65.

Powell, Lawrence. "Centralization and Its Discontents in Reconstruction Louisiana." *Studies in American Political Development* 20, no. 2 (2006): 105–31.

Powell, Lewis F., Jr. "Memorandum to Eugene B. Sydnor, Jr., Chairman of the Education Committee of the U.S. Chamber of Commerce." August 23, 1971. Lewis F. Powell, Jr. Papers, Washington and Lee University School of Law.

Prasad, Monica. *Starving the Beast: Ronald Reagan and the Tax Cut Revolution.* New York: Russell Sage Foundation, 2018.

Price, Polly J. "Federalization of the Mosquito: Structural Innovation in the New Deal Administrative State." *Emory Law Journal* 60 (2010): 325–76.

Pritchett, Wendell E. "Where Shall We Live? Class and the Limitations of Fair Housing Law." *Urban Lawyer* 35 (2003): 399–470.

Proceedings of the Constitutional Convention of South Carolina. Charleston: South Carolina Constitutional Convention, 1868.

Proceedings of the Tax-Payers' Convention of South Carolina. Charleston: Tax-Payers' Convention of South Carolina, 1871.

Proceedings of the Tax-Payers' Convention of South Carolina. Charleston: Tax-Payers' Convention of South Carolina, 1874.

Pruitt, Lisa R. "Welfare Queens and White Trash." *Southern California Interdisciplinary Law Journal* 25 (2016): 289–312.

Quanchita Telegraph. "Debate on Social Equality." October 7, 1868.

Rahim, Asad. "Diversity to Deradicalize." *California Law Review* 108 (2020): 1423–86.

Rauchway, Eric. *Why the New Deal Matters.* New Haven: Yale University Press, 2021.

Ravitch, Diane. *The Great School Wars: A History of the New York City Public Schools.* Baltimore: Johns Hopkins University Press, 2000.

Raymond, Margaret. "Rejecting Totalitarianism: Translating the Guarantees of Constitutional Criminal Procedure." *North Carolina Law Review* 76 (1998): 1193–263.

Read, John M. "Speech of Honorable John. M. Read on the Power of Congress Over the Territories." September 30, 1856.

Reagan, Ronald. "Address Before a Joint Session of the Congress on the Program for Economic Recovery." February 18, 1981. The American Presidency Project, University of California, Santa Barbara.

———. "A Time for Choosing." October 27, 1964. The American Presidency Project, University of California, Santa Barbara.

———. "Farewell Address." January 11, 1989. The Ronald Reagan Presidential Library & Museum.

———. "First Inaugural Address of Ronald Reagan." January 20, 1981. The Avalon Project, Yale Law School.

———. "Ronald Reagan's 1980 Neshoba County Fair Speech." *Neshoba Democrat*, August 3, 1980.

Reed, Adolph, Jr. "The New Deal Wasn't Intrinsically Racist." *The New Republic*, Nov. 26, 2019.

Rehnquist, William H. "The Notion of a Living Constitution." *Texas Law Review* 54 (1976): 693–706.

Reinstein, Robert J., and Mark C. Radhert. "Reconstructing Marbury." *Arkansas Law Review* 57 (2005): 729–833.

Republican Banner. "Civil Rights." March 23, 1875.

———. "Its Effect in the South." March 26, 1875.

Republican Party. "1976 Republican Party Platform." The American Presidency Project, University of California, Santa Barbara.

———. "Republican Party Platform of 1980." The American Presidency Project, University of California, Santa Barbara.

———. "Republican Party Platform of 1984." The American Presidency Project, University of California, Santa Barbara.

———. "Republican Party Platform of 1992." The American Presidency Project, University of California, Santa Barbara.

Richardson, Heather Cox. *The Death of Reconstruction: Race, Labor, and Politics in the Post–Civil War North, 1865–1901.* Cambridge, MA: Harvard University Press, 2004.

———. *How the South Won the Civil War: Oligarchy, Democracy, and the Continuing Fight for the Soul of America.* New York: Oxford University Press, 2020.

———. *To Make Men Free: A History of the Republican Party.* New York: Basic Books, 2014.

Rodell, Fred. *Nine Men: A Political History of the Supreme Court from 1790 to 1955.* New York: Vintage Books, 1955.

Rogers, Brishen. "Three Concepts of Workplace Freedom of Association." *Berkeley Journal of Employment and Labor Law* 37 (2016): 177–222.

Roosevelt, Franklin D. "Acceptance Speech for the Renomination for the Presidency." Philadelphia, June 27, 1936. The American Presidency Project, University of California, Santa Barbara.

———. "Address Accepting the Presidential Nomination." Democratic National Convention, Chicago, July 2, 1932. The American Presidency Project, University of California, Santa Barbara.

———. "First Inaugural Address of Franklin D. Roosevelt." March 4, 1933. The Avalon Project, Yale Law School.

———. "Message to Congress on Curbing Monopolies." April 29, 1938. The American Presidency Project, University of California, Santa Barbara.

Roosevelt, Kermit. "Bait and Switch: Why United States v. Morrison Is Wrong about Section." *Cornell Law Review* 100 (2015): 603–54.

Rosen, Jeffrey. *The Most Democratic Branch: How the Courts Serve America.* Oxford: Oxford University Press, 2006.

Rosenbaum, David E. "Republicans Offer Voters a Deal for Takeover of House." *New York Times*, September 28, 1994.

———. "Social Security a Major Issue in Florida as Primary Day Nears." *New York Times*, March 5, 1976.

Rosenberg, Gerald N. *The Hollow Hope: Can Courts Bring About Social Change?* 2nd ed. Chicago: University of Chicago Press, 2008.

Rosenblum, Noah A. "The Antifascist Roots of Presidential Administration." *Columbia Law Review* 122, no. 1 (2022): 1–86.

Ross, Michael A. "Justice Miller's Reconstruction: The Slaughter-House Cases, Health Codes, and Civil Rights in New Orleans, 1861–1873." *Journal of Southern History* 64, no. 4 (1998): 649–76.

———. *Justice of Shattered Dreams: Samuel Freeman Miller and the Supreme Court during the Civil War Era.* Baton Rouge: Louisiana State University Press, 2003.

Rothstein, Richard. *The Color of Law: A Forgotten History of How Our Government Segregated America.* New York: Liveright, 2017.

Rutherglen, George. "The Improbable History of Section 1981: Clio Still Bemused and Confused." *Supreme Court Review* 55 (2003): 303–55.

Sack, Kevin. "Protester Thrusts Fetus at a Surprised Clinton." *New York Times,* July 15, 1992.

Sandoval-Strausz, A. K. "Travelers, Strangers, and Jim Crow: Law, Public Accommodations, and Civil Rights in America." *Law and History Review* 23, no. 1 (2005): 53–94.

Savage, Charlie. "Justice Dept. to Take On Affirmative Action in College Admissions." *New York Times,* August 1, 2017.

Sawyer, Logan. "Originalism from the Soft Southern Strategy to the New Right: The Constitutional Politics of Sam Ervin Jr." *Journal of Policy History* 33, no. 1 (2021): 32–59.

Schickler, Eric. *Racial Realignment: The Transformation of American Liberalism, 1932–1965.* Princeton: Princeton University Press, 2016.

Schlesinger, Arthur M. *The Age of Jackson.* Boston: Little, Brown, and Company, 1945.

Schmidt, Christopher W. "On Doctrinal Confusion: The Case of the State Action Doctrine." *Brigham Young University Law Review* 2016 (2016): 575–628.

Schulman, Bruce J. *The Seventies: The Great Shift in American Culture, Society, and Politics.* New York: The Free Press, 2001.

Schurz, Carl. "Letter from Carl Schurz to Andrew Johnson." August 13, 1865. In *Advice after Appomattox: Letters to Andrew Johnson, 1865–1866,* edited by Brooks D. Simpson, LeRoy P. Graf, and John Muldowny. Knoxville: University of Tennessee Press, 1987.

———. *Report of Carl Schurz on the States of South Carolina, Georgia, Alabama, Mississippi, and Louisiana. Executive Documents of the Senate of the United States for the First Session Thirty-Ninth Congress, 1865–1866* 1, no. 2 (1866).

———. *Report on the Condition of the South: Views Expressed by Major General Steedman in Conversation with Carl Schurz.* Washington, DC: US Congress, Senate, 1865.

Shabecoff, Philip. "Reagan and Environment: To Many, a Stalemate." *New York Times,* January 2, 1989.

Shah, Bijal. "Executive (Agency) Administration." *Stanford Law Review* 72 (2020): 641–746.

Shepherd, George B. "Fierce Compromise: The Administrative Procedure Act Emerges from New Deal Politics." *Northwestern University Law Review* 90 (1996): 1557–683.

Shugerman, Jed Handelsman. "The Creation of the Department of Justice." *Stanford Law Review* 22 (2014): 121–72.

Sides, John, Michael Tesler, and Lynn Vavreck. *Identity Crisis: The 2016 Presidential Campaign and the Battle for the Meaning of America.* Princeton: Princeton University Press, 2019.

Silbey, Joel H. *American Political Nation, 1838–1893.* Stanford: Stanford University Press, 1994.

———. "The Political World of Antebellum Presidents." In *A Companion to the Antebellum Presidents, 1837–1861,* edited by Joel H. Silbey. Chichester: John Wiley & Sons, 2014.

Skowronek, Stephen. *The Politics Presidents Make: Leadership from John Adams to George Bush.* Cambridge, MA: Belknap Press, 1997.

Slap, Andrew L. *The Doom of Reconstruction: The Liberal Republicans in the Civil War Era.* New York: Fordham University Press, 2010.

Smith, Rogers M. *Civic Ideals.* New Haven: Yale University Press, 1997.

Solum, Lawrence B. "Originalism and the Unwritten Constitution." *University of Illinois Law Review* 2013 (2013): 1935–84.

Somers, Robert. *The Southern States Since the War, 1870–7zzzzzz1.* London: Macmillan, 1871.

Stampp, Kenneth M. *America in 1857: A Nation on the Brink.* Rev. ed. New York: Oxford University Press, 1990.

Statement on Signing the Independent Counsel Reauthorization Act of 1987, Dec. 15, 1987.

Statement on Signing the United States Commission on Civil Rights Act of 1983, Nov. 30, 1983.

Stout, David. "Bush Backs Ban in Constitution on Gay Marriage." *New York Times,* February 24, 2004.

Sumner, Charles, and George Frisbie Hoar, *Charles Sumner: His Complete Works.* Norwood: Norwood Press, 1900.

Tait, Allison Anna. "The Return of Coverture." *Michigan Law Review* 114 (2016): 99–110.

Teles, Steven M. *The Rise of the Conservative Legal Movement: The Battle for Control of the Law.* New Jersey: Princeton University Press, 2012.

———. "Transformative Bureaucracy: Reagan's Lawyers and the Dynamics of Political Investment." *Studies in American Political Development* 23 (2009): 61–83.

Tolchin, Martin. "Reagan Buoyed by National Swing to the Right; Position Bolstered by G.O.P. Senate Control." *New York Times,* November 6, 1980.

Tolson, Franita. "Countering the Real Countermajoritarian Difficulty." *California Law Review* 109 (2021): 2381–405.

"Transportation of the Mail on the Sabbath." January 19, 1829. Library of Congress.

Treanor, William Michael. "Judicial Review before Marbury." *Stanford Law Review* 58 (2005): 455–562.

Truman, Harry S. "June 29, 1947: Address before the NAACP." Presidential Speeches, University of Virginia Miller Center.

———. *To Secure These Rights: The Report of the President's Committee on Civil Rights*. Washington, DC: US Government Publishing Office, 1947.

Tsai, Robert L. "The Troubling Sheriffs' Movement That Joe Arpaio Supports." *Politico*, September 1, 2017.

Tsesis, Alexander. "Furthering American Freedom: Civil Rights and the Thirteenth Amendment." *Boston College Law Review* 45 (2004): 307–93.

———. *The Promises of Liberty: The History and Contemporary Relevance of the Thirteenth Amendment*. New York: Columbia University Press, 2010.

Turner, Ronald. "On Brown v. Board of Education and Discretionary Originalism." *Utah Law Review* no. 5, article 4 (2015): 1143–99.

Tushnet, Mark. "Policy Distortion and Democratic Debilitation: Comparative Illumination of the Countermajoritarian Difficulty." *Michigan Law Review* 94 (1995): 245–301.

———. "The Politics of Equality in Constitutional Law: The Equal Protection Clause, Dr. Du Bois, and Charles Hamilton Houston." *Journal of American History* 74, no. 3 (1987): 884–903.

US Bureau of the Census. "Component of Population Change, 1950 to 1960, for Counties, Standard Metropolitan Statistical Areas, State Economic Areas, and Economic Subregions." *Current Population Reports*, § P-23, no. 7 (1962).

US House of Representatives. "Party Divisions of the House of Representatives, 1789 to Present." https://history.house.gov/Institution/Party-Divisions/Party-Divisions.

US Senate. *Hearings Before a Subcommittee of the Committee on Education and Labor*. Statement of Robert C. Weaver, Representing Mayor Kelly's Committee on Race Relations, Chicago, IL, Fair Employment Practices, 1944.

Ura, Joseph Daniel. "Backlash and Legitimation: Macro Political Responses to Supreme Court Decisions." *American Journal of Political Science* 58 (2014): 110–26.

Verhoeven, Tim. "The Case for Sunday Mails: Sabbath Laws and the Separation of Church and State in Jacksonian America." *Journal of Church and State* 55, no. 1 (2013): 71–91.

Villazor, Rose Cuison. "Rediscovering Oyama v. California: At the Intersection of Property, Race, and Citizenship." *Washington University Law Review* 87 (2010): 979–1042.

Vladeck, Stephen I. "F.D.R.'s Court-Packing Plan Had Two Parts: We Need to Bring Back the Second." *New York Times*, January 7, 2022.

Ward, Artemus. *Deciding to Leave the Politics of Retirement from the United States Supreme Court*. Albany: State University of New York Press, 2012.

Warren, Charles. *The Supreme Court in United States History*. Boston: Little, Brown, and Company, 1926.

Washington Post. "Transcript of President Reagan's News Conference." August 13, 1986.

Wasow, Omar. "Agenda Seeding: How 1960s Black Protests Moved Elites, Public Opinion and Voting." *American Political Science Review* 114 (2020): 638–59.

Watson, Harry L. *Liberty and Power: The Politics of Jacksonian America.* New York: Hill and Wang, 1990.

The Weekly Mississippi Pilot. August 20, 1870.

Weisman, Steven R. "Reagan Blames 'Great Society' For Economic Woes." *New York Times,* May 10, 1983.

Wells, J. Madison. "Letter from J. Madison Wells, Governor of Louisiana, to Andrew Johnson, President of the United States." July 29, 1865. Reprinted in *The Papers of Andrew Johnson,* edited by Paul H. Bergeron. Knoxville: University of Tennessee Press, 1989.

West, Robin. "Constitutional Skepticism." *Boston University Law Review* 72 (1992): 765–99.

———. *Progressive Constitutionalism: Reconstructing the Fourteenth Amendment.* Durham: Duke University Press, 1994.

White, G. Edward. *The Constitution and the New Deal.* Cambridge, MA: Harvard University Press, 2000.

———. *Law in American History: From Reconstruction through the 1920s.* New York: Oxford University Press, 2012.

Whittington, Keith E. *Political Foundations of Judicial Supremacy: The Presidency, the Supreme Court, and Constitutional Leadership in U.S. History.* Princeton: Princeton University Press, 2007.

Wilentz, Sean. *The Rise of American Democracy: Jefferson to Lincoln.* New York: W.W. Norton & Company, 2006.

Williamson, Vanessa, and Theda Skocpol. *The Tea Party and the Remaking of Republican Conservatism.* New York: Oxford University Press, 2013.

Woodward, C. Vann. *Origins of the New South, 1877–1913: A History of the South.* Baton Rouge: Louisiana State University Press, 1995),

———. *Reunion and Reaction: The Compromise of 1877 and the End of Reconstruction.* New York: Oxford University Press, 1991.

Woodward-Burns, Robinson. *Hidden Laws: How State Constitutions Stabilize American Politics.* New Haven: Yale University Press, 2021.

Wyatt-Brown, Bertram. "The Abolitionists' Postal Campaign of 1835." *Journal of Negro History* 50, no. 4 (1965): 227–38.

———. "Prelude to Abolitionism: Sabbatarian Politics and the Rise of the Second Party System." *Journal of American History* 58, no. 2 (1971): 316–41.

Yellin, Eric Steven. *Racism in the Nation's Service: Government Workers and the Color Line in Woodrow Wilson's America.* Chapel Hill: University of North Carolina, 2013.

Yoo, Christopher S., Steven G. Calabresi, and Laurence D. Nee. "The Unitary Executive During the Third Half-Century, 1889–1945." *Notre Dame Law Review* 80 (2005): 1–109.

Young, Terence. "'A Contradiction in Democratic Government': W.J. Trent, Jr., and the Struggle to Desegregate National Park Campgrounds." *Environmental History* 14, no. 4 (2009): 651–82.

Zackin, Emily. "'To Change the Fundamental Law of the State': Protective Labor Provisions in U.S. Constitutions." *Studies in American Political Development* 24, no. 1 (2010): 1–23.

Zeitz, Joshua. *Building the Great Society Inside Lyndon Johnson's White House*. New York: Penguin Books, 2019.

———. "Republicans, Beware the Abe Fortas Precedent." *Politico*, February 15, 2016.

Zelizer, Julian E. "Seizing Power: Conservatives and Congress Since the 1970s." In *The New American Polity: Activist Government, the Redefinition of Citizenship, and Conservative Mobilization*, edited by Theda Skocpol and Paul Pierson. Princeton: Princeton University Press, 2007.

Ziegler, Mary. "Grassroots Originalism: Rethinking the Politics of Judicial Philosophy." *University of Louisville Law Review* 51 (2012): 201–38.

Zietlow, Rebecca E. *Enforcing Equality: Congress, the Constitution, and the Protection of Individual Rights*. New York: New York University Press, 2006.

Index

abortion rights, 111, 125–27
"activist judging," 133
Adams, John, 1
Adams, John Quincy, 15
administrative-law rules: inception of, and
    New Deal, 101; New Right's order on,
    123
affirmative action, 138–42, 173n122
Affordable Care Act (ACA), 119, 120
agriculture: Agricultural Adjustment Act,
    84; Black cooperatives (plantations), 67;
    grain storage warehouses, 78; Granger
    Movement, 74; and Social Security Act
    (1935), 91–92; and South Carolina rice
    strikes (1876), 68. *See also* slavery
Air Force dress codes, 133–34
Alabama, Black Codes of, 47–48
A. L. A. Schechter Poultry Corporation v.
    United States (1935), 85
Alito, Samuel, 122, 141, 142
Allgeyer v. Louisiana (1897), 78
Amalgamated Food Employees Union v.
    Logan Valley Plaza (1968), 102, 167n94
American Political Development (APD), 3–7
The American Supreme Court
    (McCloskey), 9
American System, 19
Amnesty Act (1872), 65–66
anti-lynching legislation, 90, 94
Arkansas, on education (Reconstruction
    era), 59

The Atlantic, on Republicanism, 70
authoritarianism, fears of (World War II),
    97–102

Bailey v. Drexel Furniture Co. (1922),
    162n23
Baldwin, Henry, 20
Balkin, Jack, 6
Barbour, Philip, 20
Barrett, Amy Coney, 135
Barron v. Baltimore (1833), 153n21
Bates v. City of Little Rock (1960), 90,
    163n37
Berger, Bethany, 27
Berger, Raoul, 114
Bickel, Alexander, 9, 146
Biden, Joe, 127, 136
"big government": government intervention
    by New Deal, 83–87; Reagan revolution
    and New Right's order on, 112–13,
    115–21; Republican Party's precautions
    about, Reconstruction era, 52
Black, Hugo, 96, 109
Black Codes, 47–48, 50
Black cooperatives, 67
Blackhawk, Maggie, 26–27
Blackmun, Harry, 109, 111
Bork, Robert, 114
Bowers v. Hardwick (1986), 128–29
Boy Scouts of America, 131–32
Bradley, Joseph, 54, 67, 76

Founded in 1893,
UNIVERSITY OF CALIFORNIA PRESS
publishes bold, progressive books and journals
on topics in the arts, humanities, social sciences,
and natural sciences—with a focus on social
justice issues—that inspire thought and action
among readers worldwide.

The UC PRESS FOUNDATION
raises funds to uphold the press's vital role
as an independent, nonprofit publisher, and
receives philanthropic support from a wide
range of individuals and institutions—and from
committed readers like you. To learn more, visit
ucpress.edu/supportus.